PORTUGUESE STUDIES

VOLUME 29 NUMBER 2
2013

International Dimensions of Portuguese Late Colonialism and Decolonization

Founding Editor
HELDER MACEDO

Guest Editors
MIGUEL BANDEIRA JERÓNIMO
ANTÓNIO COSTA PINTO

Editors
FRANCISCO BETHENCOURT
JULIET PERKINS
LÚCIA SÁ
DAVID TREECE
ABDOOLKARIM VAKIL

Editorial Assistant
RICHARD CORRELL

Production Editor
GRAHAM NELSON

MODERN HUMANITIES RESEARCH ASSOCIATION

PORTUGUESE STUDIES

A peer-reviewed biannual multi-disciplinary journal devoted to research on the cultures, societies, and history of the Lusophone world

International Advisory Board

Articles to be considered for publication may be on any subject within the field but should not exceed 7,500 words and should be written in English. The Editorial Assistant is willing to undertake translations of texts from Portuguese if required; there will be a charge for this service. Contributions should be submitted in a form ready for publication in English and sent as an email attachment to the Editorial Assistant at richard.correll@kcl.ac.uk. The text should conform precisely to the conventions of the *MHRA Style Guide*, 3rd edn, 2013 (978-1-78188-009-8), obtainable from www.style.mhra. org.uk, price £6.50, US $13, €8; an online version is also available from the same address. Quotations and references should be carefully checked. Any quotations in Portuguese must be accompanied by an English translation. All articles are subject to independent and anonymous peer review by experts in the field; authors receive written feedback on the editors' final decision, including guidance on any necessary revisions. *Portuguese Studies* regrets that it must charge contributors with the cost of corrections in proof which the Editors in their discretion think excessive. Copies of books for review should be sent to The Reviews Editor, *Portuguese Studies*, Department of Spanish, Portuguese and Latin American Studies, King's College London, Strand, London WC2R 2LS, UK.

Portuguese Studies and other journals published by the MHRA may be ordered from JSTOR (http://about.jstor.org/csp). The journal is also available to individual members of the Modern Humanities Research Association in return for a composite membership subscription payable in advance. Further information about the activities of the MHRA and individual membership can be obtained from the Honorary Secretary, Dr Barbara Burns, School of Modern Languages and Cultures, University of Glasgow, Bute Gardens, Glasgow G12 8RS, or from the website at www.mhra.org.uk.

Disclaimer: Statements of fact and opinion in the content of *Portuguese Studies* are those of the respective authors and contributors and not of the journal editors or of the Modern Humanities Research Association (MHRA). MHRA makes no representation, express or implied, in respect of the accuracy of the material in this journal and cannot accept any legal responsibility or liability for any errors or omissions that may be made.

ISSN 0267–5315 (print) ISSN 2222-4270 (online) ISBN 978-1-78188-038-8
© 2013 THE MODERN HUMANITIES RESEARCH ASSOCIATION

PORTUGUESE STUDIES VOL. 29 NO. 2

INTERNATIONAL DIMENSIONS OF PORTUGUESE LATE COLONIALISM AND DECOLONIZATION

CONTENTS

Preface

History has long been an integral and vital discipline in Lusophone Studies. Thus, we are pleased to present the current number, 'International Dimensions of Portuguese Late Colonialism and Decolonization' as this year's thematic issue. Although not designed as a response to 'Formal and Informal Empire' (28.2), it does constitute an apposite follow-up. We are grateful to our Guest Editors for preparing and presenting this body of research from the project, '"Portugal is not a small country": The End of the Portuguese Colonial Empire in a Comparative Perspective', which analyses the imperial endgame from a variety of angles. Furthermore, examining the Portuguese case from an international perspective can only contribute positively to the *desiderata* of cross-fertilization in our field.

The volume is completed by another regular feature, 'Lusophone Studies: A Cumulative Area Bibliography, 2011–13', compiled by Emilce Rees. From readers' comments, we know that it serves a very useful purpose. We also recognize, however, that a reviews section should find a regular place in the journal, and we intend to address this in the very near future.

THE EDITORS

Introduction

The International and the Portuguese
Imperial Endgame: Problems and Perspectives

Miguel Bandeira Jerónimo and
António Costa Pinto

ICS-UL/King's College London and ICS-UL

The present volume, *International Dimensions of Portuguese Late Colonialism and Decolonization*, offers a multifaceted approach to the role played by international factors and processes in Portuguese late colonialism. In identifying and assessing some of its main manifestations, it explores their relation with metropolitan and colonial historical events and dynamics. Its six original articles examine the ways in which Portugal (and its authoritarian regime) interacted with the fundamental transformations that characterized the international arena after World War II, especially those impacting on imperial and colonial formations, on their late evolution, and eventual demise.[1] The chronological boundaries of this volume correspond to the major transformations of the international regime that resulted from the War, that is, from the constitution of the United Nations system (and in acknowledging the important changes brought after 1945 one must stress the fundamental legacy of the League of Nations in relation to imperial and colonial questions)[2] to the zenith of the decolonization process in Portuguese Africa, the formal dissolution of its colonial empire.[3]

Despite evident differences in scope, method and research concerns, these contributions nonetheless manifest a common analytical framework. They

---

[1] These articles are the product of the Research project entitled *'Portugal is not a small country': The End of the Portuguese Colonial Empire in a Comparative Perspective* (FCT-PTDC/HIS-HIS/108998/2008).
[2] For the United Nations see David W. Wainhouse, *The Remnants of Empire: The United Nations and the End of Colonialism* (New York: Harper&Row, 1964); Evan Luard, *A History of the United Nations: The Years of Western Domination, 1945–1955* (London: Macmillan, 1982); idem, *A History of the United Nations: The Age of Decolonization, 1955–1965* (London: Macmillan, 1989). For the importance of the League of Nations see Susan Pedersen, 'Back to the League of Nations', *The American Historical Review*, 112.4 (2007), 1091–1117. Related to the genealogies of the UN system see Mark Mazower, *No Enchanted Palace: The End of Empires and the Ideological Origins of the United Nations* (Princeton, NJ: Princeton University Press, 2009).
[3] See Norrie MacQueen, *The Decolonization of Portuguese Africa: Metropolitan Revolution and the Dissolution of Empire* (London and New York: Longman, 1997); António Costa Pinto, *O Fim do Império Português: A Cena Internacional, a Guerra Colonial, e a Descolonização, 1961–1975* (Lisbon: Livros Horizonte, 2001).

Portuguese Studies vol. 29 no. 2 (2013), 137–41
© Modern Humanities Research Association 2013

examine the historical evolution of the engagements between Portugal and
other international actors, including other states, international organizations,
intergovernmental and non-governmental organizations, trades unions, found-
ations, churches and missionary bodies, and corporations. This variegated set
of relationships is addressed, and contextualized, in the light of the different
periods of post-World War II dynamic developments. How these shaped the
evolution of Portuguese late colonialism in a context of global decolonization
(highlighting, for instance, the relationships between them and anticolonial,
nationalist movements); how Portuguese authorities assessed the global and
local transformations entailed by Cold War dynamics and the changes in the
geopolitical strategies and normative arguments deployed by other states,
including imperial ones; and how they perceived and reacted against the potential
impact of these developments in the planned continuation of the Portuguese
imperial polity — these are some of the questions that unify the contributions
to this volume. In order to provide answers to these and other important
questions, the articles explore, in different ways, a combined analysis of the
international (for example, the effects of the change in the international regime
and of the bipolarization of the international system, and respective competing
modernities),[4] the metropolitan (for example, the nature and the functioning of
the authoritarian political regime and the formulation of its African policies),[5]
and the colonial (for example, the emergence of political liberation movements
and the specificities of the *late* colonial state and administration),[6] aiming to
bring together diverse histories and historiographies (international, national,
imperial and colonial).

In this sense, these contributions contribute to the ongoing debates about
the study of late colonialism and the *endgames* of European colonial empires.[7]
Studies of the Portuguese colonial empire and its demise are scant, and
rarely incorporated into international studies. And when they are, there is a
tendency to persist in two *explicative* and *interpretative models*, which largely

---

[4] See Odd Arne Westad, *The Global Cold War: Third World Interventions and the Making of our
Times* (Cambridge: Cambridge University Press, 2005).
[5] *História da Expansão Portuguesa*, ed. by Francisco Bethencourt and Kirti Chaudhuri, vol. v
(Lisbon: Círculo de Leitores, 1999).
[6] Patrick Chabal, 'Emergencies and Nationalist Wars in Portuguese Africa', in *Emergencies and
Disorder in the European Empires after 1945*, ed. by Robert F. Holland (London: Frank Cass, 1994), pp.
234–49; Miguel Bandeira Jerónimo and António Costa Pinto, 'A Modernizing Empire? Politics, Culture
and Economy in Portuguese Late Colonialism', in *The Ends of European Colonial Empires: Cases and
Comparisons*, ed. by Miguel Bandeira Jerónimo and António Costa Pinto (forthcoming, 2014).
[7] For two recent important syntheses see Martin Shipway, *Decolonization and its Impact: A Com-
parative Approach to the End of the Colonial Empires* (Oxford: Blackwell, 2008); Martin Thomas,
Bob Moore and L. J. Butler, *Crises of Empire: Decolonization and Europe's Imperial States, 1918–1975*
(London: Hodder Education, 2008); *Elites and Decolonization in the Twentieth Century*, ed. by Jost
Dülffer and Marc Fey (Basingstoke: Palgrave Macmillan, 2011); and Miguel Bandeira Jerónimo and
António Costa Pinto, *The Ends of European Colonial Empires*. For an exploration of international
dimensions see John Kent, *The Internationalization of Colonialism: Britain, France and Black Africa,
1939–1956* (Oxford: Oxford University Press, 1992) and *International Diplomacy and Colonial Retreat*,
ed. by Kent Fedorowich and Martin Thomas (London: Frank Cass, 2001).

replicate the dominant historiographical trends in the study of the nineteenth-century *new imperialism*: the metropolitan and the peripheral or nationalist ones. Until recently, for instance, international and transnational factors tended to be neglected; and when addressed they tended to be subsumed in diplomatic, bilateral interstate exchanges.[8] Furthermore, both these models neglect the diverse and dynamic nature of colonial contexts and actors, and tend to amalgamate this complexity into a-historical, monolithic units. The first analytical model attributes pre-eminence to metropolitan socio-political calculus and decision-making processes,[9] while the second emphasizes colonial nationalism and processes of socio-political mobilization in colonial contexts.[10] Both types and sets of factors are generally privileged as crucial to explaining European late imperial and colonial *modus vivendi*. As stated above, the majority of studies of the Portuguese case tend to replicate this propensity, failing to integrate several distinct scales of analysis, exploring their historical interrelation, their connections and co-constitution, and mobilizing the related different explanatory factors: geopolitics and *international* relations, domestic politics and imperial policies; and African policies and the colonial situation. The integrated study of the *intersections* of international constraints and opportunities, of metropolitan and imperial pressures, strategies and decisions, and of the colonial *situations* is fundamental. No proper study of late colonialism and the demise of colonial empires can fail to acknowledge factors such as the interrelation and co-constitution between the nature and *modus operandi* of imperial authority and forms of colonial sovereignty, and their relation with colonial societies; the origin and scope of socio-political mobilization of metropolitan constituencies regarding imperial and colonial issues, namely their appreciation of the political, economic, social and cultural *costs* and *benefits* — at international, metropolitan and colonial levels — of the continuity or dismantling of the empire; and, finally, the degree of international recognition (not only politico-diplomatic) of the political legitimacy of colonial sovereignty, evolving since the nineteenth century.[11] They also tend to miss the benefits, and empirically ponder the disadvantages and problems, of

[8] For the *interpretative models* regarding nineteenth-century *new imperialism* see Michael W. Doyle, *Empires* (New York and London: Cornell University Press, 1986), pp. 141–349 and Andrew Porter, *European Imperialism, 1860–1914* (London: Macmillan Press, 1994).
[9] Inter alia, notwithstanding important differences, see Rudolf von Albertini, *Decolonisation: The Administration and the Future of the Colonies, 1919–1960* (New York: Doubleday, 1971 [1966]); Miles Kahler, *Decolonization in Britain and France: The Domestic Consequences of International Relations* (Princeton, NJ: Princeton University Press, 1984); and Jacques Marseille, *Empire Colonial et Capitalisme Français: Histoire d'un Divorce* (Paris: Albin Michel, 1984).
[10] Inter alia, notwithstanding important differences, see Thomas Hodgkin, *Nationalism in Colonial Africa* (New York: New York University Press, 1957); and the original and, at many levels, highly influential, Frederick Cooper, *Decolonization and African Society: The Labor Question in French and British Africa* (Cambridge: Cambridge University Press, 1996).
[11] This is a still crucial suggestion made by Prosser Gifford and William Roger Louis, in the 'Introduction' to their edited volume, *Decolonization and African Independence: The Transfers of Power, 1960–1980* (New Haven, CT, and London: Yale University Press, 1988).

the comparative exercise, a fundamental issue that still needs to be further developed by international literature.

This volume aims to address and tackle some of these questions. On the one hand, all the articles explore the analytical and empirical relevance of international factors in late colonialism and the end of the colonial empire. For example, they assess the impact of the new international normative regime upon the political legitimacy of the Portuguese imperial stand and on political decision-making processes, not only at the diplomatic level, but also at the imperial and colonial levels. The study of the historical constitution of political and diplomatic decision-making processes by Portuguese political and ministerial elites regarding the international, metropolitan and colonial developments of imperial and colonial issues — decoupling *essentialized* narratives that replicate the coeval official discourse — is a fundamental topic that still needs deeper study.[12] On the other hand, these texts place the Portuguese case within the *global* pattern of decolonization (with a special emphasis on the African continent), underlining some specificities, similarities and differences with other cases, and, more importantly, signalling and enabling comparative avenues of enquiry. The multifaceted approach of these texts and the diversity of themes and processes they deal with can open up important comparative possibilities. In political formations suffused with doctrines of *exceptionality*, the comparative exercise is indeed the best antidote.

Based on broad and extensive enquiries in Portuguese and foreign archives, and demonstrating an intensive and extensive use of international bibliography (thus overcoming a longstanding problem of Portuguese historiography),[13] the authors offer a synthesis of the existing literature and a summary of the main current approaches, arguments and findings regarding their own case-studies, while identifying key avenues for future research.[14]

* * * * *

Accordingly, in 'Internationalism and the *Labours* of the Portuguese Colonial Empire (1945–74)', **Miguel Bandeira Jerónimo** and **José Pedro Monteiro** investigate the historical engagement between Portugal and the modalities of imperial internationalism, taking the case of *native* labour in the colonial empire as their main subject. In 'The United States and Portuguese Decolonization', **Luís Nuno Rodrigues** surveys the transformation of US policy towards

---

[12] For example see, among others, Robert H. Jackson, 'The Weight of Ideas in Decolonization: Normative Change in International Relations', in *Ideas and Foreign Policy: Beliefs, Institutions, and Political Change*, ed. by Judith Goldstein and Robert O. Keohane (Ithaca, NY: Cornell University Press, 1993), pp. 111–38.

[13] Already emphasized by António Costa Pinto, *O Fim do Império Português*.

[14] In particular, the lacuna in comparative research on the international dimensions of Portuguese late colonialism during the Cold War: i.e. the relations between the newly independent African countries, the Soviet Union and the socialist countries, and the liberation movements fighting against Portuguese colonialism.

Africa, and towards the Portuguese Colonial Empire in particular, from the Truman to the Ford administrations, including an assessment of the political, economic and socio-cultural determinants of its main characteristics, in a Cold War context. In 'Live and Let Live: Britain and Portugal's Imperial Endgame (1945–75)', **Pedro Aires Oliveira** provides an in-depth analysis of the relationship between Britain and Portugal in a period marked by mounting international and colonial pressure towards the formal disintegration of imperial polities. In 'Cold War Constraints: France, West Germany and Portuguese Decolonization', **Ana Mónica Fonseca** and **Daniel Marcos** address the causes and motivations — domestic, imperial and geopolitical — of the supportive role played by France and by the Federal Republic of Germany in the Portuguese overall strategy in opposition to decolonization drives. In 'South Africa and the Aftermath of Portugal's "Exemplary" Decolonization: The Security Dimension', **Filipe Ribeiro de Meneses** and **Robert McNamara** offer a detailed view of the engagement of South Africa with Portuguese late colonialism, with the dynamics of the transfer of power, and with the perceived impact of decolonization at international and regional levels. Finally, in 'Portugal and the UN: A Rogue State Resisting the Norm of Decolonization (1956–74)', **Bruno Cardoso Reis** explores the characteristics of Portuguese political culture and regime and the diplomatic strategies that the Portuguese formulated, especially in relation to the United Nations.

Internationalism and the *Labours* of the Portuguese Colonial Empire (1945–1974)

Miguel Bandeira Jerónimo and
José Pedro Monteiro

ICS-UL/King's College London and ICS-UL

Introduction

The history of the dynamic engagement, and historical co-constitution, between international processes and imperial projects has been frequently ignored by the literature on the Portuguese case. The analysis of the evolving interconnectedness between twentieth-century internationalism and the nature and *modus operandi* of the Portuguese colonial empire in the post-World War II years, particularly in respect of the politics and policies of native labour, is the core subject of this work.[1]

From the nineteenth century right up to the end of the Portuguese empire, the question of native labour was at the forefront of two interrelated historical processes, both crucial to its existence.[2] First, the question of native labour was central to the configuration of a new imperial political economy associated with the protracted abolition of the transatlantic slave trade and also with the tentative recreation of *new Brazils in Africa*. Native forced labour was the backbone of the reorganized colonial economy. Characterized by a strongly racialized civilizational rhetoric, the imperial projects of nineteenth-century Portugal placed the formation of a 'system' of native labour — legalized, organized and managed by the empire-state — at the core of their concerns.[3] Simultaneously, the regulation of native labour was fundamental to a novel imperial moral economy. Native labour was the primordial element of the

---

[1] This work is a product of the research project *'Portugal is not a small country': The End of the Portuguese Colonial Empire in a Comparative Perspective* (FCT-PTDC/HIS-HIS/108998/2008). These ideas form the core of the international research project *Internationalism and Empire: The Politics of Difference in the Portuguese Colonial Empire in Comparative Perspective (1920–1975)* (FCT-PTDC/ EPH-HIS/5176/2012).

[2] For more see Miguel Bandeira Jerónimo and José Pedro Monteiro, 'Das "dificuldades de levar os indígenas a trabalhar": o "sistema" de trabalho nativo no império colonial português', in *O império colonial em questão, séculos XIX–XX: poderes, saberes e instituições*, ed. by Miguel Bandeira Jerónimo (Lisbon: Edições 70, 2012), pp. 159–96.

[3] Miguel Bandeira Jerónimo, 'The "Civilisation Guild": Race and Labour in the Third Portuguese Empire, *c.* 1870–1930', in *Racism and Ethnic Relations in the Portuguese-speaking World*, ed. by Francisco Bethencourt and Adrian J. Pearce (New York: Oxford University Press, 2012), pp. 173–99.

Portuguese Studies vol. 29 no. 2 (2013), 142–63
© Modern Humanities Research Association 2013

Portuguese 'civilizing mission' and therefore was a dominant constituent of the idioms and repertoires of imperial legitimation enacted at home and abroad. Second, the issue of native labour — especially the recruitment, distribution and use of forced labour within the imperial frontiers — was one of the key subjects around which the relationship between the Portuguese empire-state and various international bodies formed and evolved from a historical point of view.

This double centrality of the native labour question — as repertoire of colonial rule and administration, and as instrument of international legitimation of the country as an imperial civilizing power — turned it into a fundamental subject in the history of the empire's engagement with international bodies, which entailed important international and transnational processes. Their understanding is crucial to the assessment and proper evaluation of the international dimensions of the formation and demise of the Portuguese empire. These processes were marked by several important aspects.

First, the debate around native labour promoted the shared, and contested, formulation of concepts, norms and languages (e.g. about the distinction between slavery and forced labour; about the *sacred trust, trusteeship*; and later on, about the '*good colonial government*', native welfare or development).[4] Concurrently, it entailed the definition of common instruments of policy analysis and policy making, exemplified by the emergence of questionnaires, legislation and international regulatory instruments, which enabled the circulation of *comparable* information about the *modus operandi* of imperial projects. Among other important aspects, this contributed to the *internationalization* of imperial and colonial affairs (partially determining the relations between states and empires); it promoted the gradual emergence of more closely examined and debated concepts of colonial sovereignty and administration (therefore providing evidence and reasons for critical appraisals of the functioning of imperial polities, calling for reform or outright independence, later on); and it conditioned the formulation of (inter)imperial and (inter)colonial policies by transforming their rationale and scope. This aspect also enables a reference to another one: the circulation of imperial idioms and imaginaries, of models and repertoires of colonial rule since the nineteenth century, and the constitution of imperial intersections, i.e., processes of imitation, competition and innovation between empire-states (for instance, the understudied relation between the French and Portuguese *Indigénat* regimes). The degree of interimperial similarity between colonial modalities of legislation and administration increased. The role played by international, interimperial and transnational institutions is illustrative of some of the abovementioned

---

[4]   Michael Callahan, *A Sacred Trust: The League of Nations and Africa, 1929–1946* (Brighton: Sussex Academic Press, 2004); Neta Crawford, *Argument and Change in World Politics: Ethics, Decolonization, Humanitarian Intervention* (Cambridge: Cambridge University Press, 2002); Veronique Dimier, 'On Good Colonial Government: Lessons from the League of Nations,' *Global Society: Journal of Interdisciplinary International Relations*, 18.3 (2004), 279–99.

processes. For instance, the workings of the International Colonial Institute (ICI), created in 1892, an interimperial organization that was fundamental to the political, administrative and juridical international and interimperial consolidation of European *new imperialism*, offer an excellent example. The ICI gathered, compared and circulated information on imperial issues, and created an imperial epistemic community, with diverse origins, outlooks, and intents, certainly, but sharing 'normative beliefs', 'causal beliefs', 'notions of validity' and a 'common policy enterprise'. The ICI enabled interimperial comparison and differentiation, but it also empowered shared idioms and repertoires of colonial rule, sometimes leading to common stances in international *fora*, intended to strengthen imperial legitimacy at home and abroad.[5]

Second, the production and gathering of information, fostered by growing international involvement, conditioned the formulation of imperial and colonial normative frameworks and policies. For instance, the changes to the Portuguese native labour codes were related, in their timings as well as their contents, to international pressures that challenged their moral grounds, their ethical and social consequences. These were born out of denunciations of the coercive mechanisms deployed by the colonial state in order to provide labour to colonial interests. Alongside tax exaction, the 'system' of forced labour was *the* pivotal mechanism of colonial extraction, being transformed into a crucial 'state revenue flow'. Sometimes it was the tax exaction mechanism par excellence.[6] International pressures also emerged from another process: the way that the Portuguese empire compared unfavourably with the *standards of civilization* that were being promoted internationally, but not without great disputes and manifest variety, following the Berlin West African Conference (1884–85) and the Brussels Anti-slavery Conference (1889–90). In spite of all its limitations and shortcomings (no punitive legal framework was determined, no actual supervisory or law-enforcement machinery was devised), the rise and widening scope of an *imperial ethics*, promoted by humanitarian impulses of various extraction supervising colonial rule, impacted heavily on the empire's *modus vivendi*.[7] However, the Portuguese authorities appropriated the language,

---

[5] For the ICI see, for instance, Benoit Daviron, 'Mobilizing Labour in African Agriculture: The Role of the International Colonial Institute in the Elaboration of a Standard of Colonial Administration, 1895–1930', *Journal of Global History*, 5 (2010), 479–501. For *imperial intersections* see Frederick Cooper and Jane Burbank, *Empires in World History* (Princeton, NJ: Princeton University Press, 2010), pp. 14–17. For *epistemic communities* see, among others, Peter M. Haas, 'Epistemic Communities and International Policy Coordination', in *Knowledge, Power, and International Policy Coordination*, ed. by Peter M. Haas (Columbia: University of South Carolina Press, 1992), pp. 1–36, esp. pp. 2–5 (p. 3).
[6] See Miguel Bandeira Jerónimo, 'The States of Empire', in *The Making of Modern Portugal*, ed. by Luís Trindade (Newcastle-upon-Tyne: Cambridge Scholars Publishing, 2013); Crawford Young, 'The African Colonial State Revisited', *Governance*, 11.1 (1998), 101–20 (p. 105).
[7] Suzanne Miers, 'Humanitarianism at Berlin: Myth or Reality?' and L. H. Gann, 'The Berlin Conference and the Humanitarian Conscience', both in *Bismarck, Europe, and Africa: The Berlin Africa Conference 1884–1885 and the Onset of Partition*, ed. by S. Förster, W. J. Mommsen, and R. Robinson (Oxford: Oxford University Press, 1988), pp. 333–45 and 321–31; Suzanne Miers, *Britain and the Ending of the Slave Trade* (London: Longman, 1975), pp. 236–91.

if not the expected related consequences, of a *civilizational obligation* connected to this *imperial ethics* that should from then on guide imperial expansion and interventionism. The definition of 'standards of international morality' by which empire could be critically evaluated could be, and were, also used to enhance its legitimate existence and persistence, especially in international *fora*.[8]

The impact that the collection of such information had on imperial and colonial affairs and on the formulation of legal frameworks and policies was therefore related to the practical, instrumental use that the Portuguese empire-state gave to this information. On the one hand, this multiplied moments of self-inspection. The growing international scrutiny over imperial and colonial affairs was connected to an intensification of the monitoring of the workings of all echelons of colonial bureaucracy and to the assessment of the impact of colonial policies, their motivations and consequences. As we will illustrate, the rationalization of the colonial bureaucracy, its assessment of policies and the associated tentative improvement of the imperial informational order throughout the twentieth century are closely related to the international history of the empire. On the other hand, it led to the reinforcement of colonial sovereignty, given the fact that the dynamic evolution of its definition within an international framework — oversimplifying, from a 'nightwatchman state', focused on maintaining an orderly *status quo* and based on an mere extractive rationale towards a 'proactive', 'dense' and 'big state', promoting a *welfare colonialism* — required an ever-growing commitment from imperial actors, expanding their sovereign functions (namely social ones).[9] The participation in these interimperial and international institutional frameworks therefore reinforced the country's external projection as a *modern* and *progressive* colonial power in tune with the intellectual and organizational *esprit du temps*. Moreover, this participation contributed to the overall political strategies developed by an authoritarian empire-state to *rationalize*, or give factual content to, its imperial legitimacy in critical moments. For example, in contexts of recurrent accusations regarding the continued practices of forced labour or, later on, of criticism over imperial resilience in the face of colonial wars and mounting anticolonial pressures, the Portuguese authorities used the 'standards of international morality' to demonstrate the putative humanitarian, progressive, modern and reformist nature of the empire's policies. The constant use of legislation and, later, of *scientific* documents, based on statistics, questionnaires or reports (the 'imperialism of knowledge'), played a major role in the process. They were *evidence* of *good government* but also *evidence* of international integration.[10]

---

[8] Suzanne Miers, *Slavery in the Twentieth Century: The Evolution of a Global Problem* (Walnut Creek, CA: Altamira Press, 2003), p. 23.

[9] John Darwin, 'What was the late colonial state?', *Itinerário*, 23.3/4 (1999), 73–82 (pp. 76–78). See also Miguel Bandeira Jerónimo, 'The States of Empire'.

[10] See Jerónimo, *Livros brancos, almas negras: a 'missão civilizadora' do colonialismo português (c. 1870–1930)* (Lisbon: Imprensa de Ciências Sociais, 2010). For the 'imperialism of knowledge' see

The focus on native labour and, more generally, on the native policies that engineered and administered social, cultural, economic and political difference within the Portuguese colonial empire, therefore constitutes a privileged case study for the understanding of the entanglements between the former and twentieth-century modalities of imperial internationalism, and other international processes. It also allows, and requires, an integrated analysis of international, metropolitan and colonial dynamics, favouring a dialogue between their histories and historiographies. More than merely pointing to the interconnectedness of imperial and international spheres of debate, this article explores the ways in which the processes of production, treatment, circulation and reframing of information and legislative production across the Portuguese imperial bureaucracy and intelligentsia conditioned and were conditioned by the dynamics of several internationally located dynamics, using two historical *observatories*: first, the activities of the special committees on slavery and forced labour coordinated by the Economic and Social Council of UN (ECOSOC) and the *Bureau International du Travail* (BIT), from 1947 to 1958; and second, Ghana's complaint against Portugal at the ILO and the ensuing events, from 1961 to 1974.

To understand the interaction between the Portuguese empire and international institutions with regard to native labour in the post-war years, one must pay attention to the genealogy of this relationship in the interwar years.[11] After the formation of the League of Nations, in 1919, international debates on colonial welfare gained momentum and became institutionalized.[12] The activities of the League on slavery and forced labour during the 1920s were critical for the Portuguese imperial administration. Following on from many other examples — most notably the *Cadbury Case*, concerning the use of forced labour in the production of cocoa in São Tomé — the year 1925 saw the delivery of a report to the League's Temporary Slavery Commission, made by the American sociologist Edward Ross, focusing on unfree and forced native labour conditions in Angola and Mozambique.[13] The accusations against the Portuguese colonial

Frederick Cooper, 'Modernizing Bureaucrats, Backward Africans, and the Development Concept', in *International Development and the Social Sciences: Essays in the History and Politics of Knowledge*, ed. by Frederick Cooper and Randall Packard (Berkeley: University of California Press, 1997), pp. 64–92 (p. 64).

[11] Miguel Bandeira Jerónimo and José Pedro Monteiro, 'Das "dificuldades de levar os indígenas a trabalhar"', pp. 173–82.

[12] Among others, see Frederick Cooper, *Decolonization and African Society: The Labor Question in French and British Africa* (Cambridge and New York: Cambridge University Press, 1996), pp. 21–110; Susan Pedersen, 'Back to the League of Nations', *The American Historical Review*, 112.4 (2007), 1091–1117; *Internationalism Reconfigured: Transnational Ideas and Movements between the World Wars*, ed. by Daniel Laqua (New York: I. B. Tauris, 2011); Mark Mazower, *Governing the World: The History of an Idea* (London: Allen Lane, 2012), pp. 116–53; Daniel Gorman, *The Emergence of International Society in the 1920s* (Cambridge: Cambridge University Press, 2012), pp. 21–108.

[13] Miguel Bandeira Jerónimo, *Livros brancos, almas negras*, pp. 89–139; Kevin Grant, *A Civilized Savagery: Britain and the New Slaveries in Africa, 1884–1926* (New York: Routledge, 2005), pp. 109–34; Catherine Higgs, *Chocolate Islands: Cocoa, Slavery, and Colonial Africa* (Athens: Ohio University Press, 2012).

administrators of crude exploitation and widespread venality were not new, but for the first time they were being aired in an internationally institutionalized political and social forum. It also provoked an organized reaction by the Portuguese, as international channels could be used to combat the impact of international pressures. Backing up the refutation *in situ* of the report's main accusations, a process led by Mozambique's former Governor General, Freire de Andrade, the colonial and metropolitan bureaucracies mobilized their resources and instruments of knowledge production to question the *methodology* and the conclusions of Ross's work.[14] Alongside other cases, such as the accusations of prolonged slavery in the Portuguese colonies made by the *Bureau International pour la Défense des Indigènes*, led by René Claparède, and the critical report made by the former British Consul in Mozambique, G. A. Morton, and delivered to the Temporary Commission in 1924, the *Ross Report* marked an important moment of imperial self-awareness, self-scrutiny and self-monitoring.[15]

The information gathering by the colonial and metropolitan bureaucracies entailed more than the mere refutation of Ross's work. It was also a crucial moment of imperial accountability, in a double sense. On the one hand, it involved the production of information (for instance, reports and questionnaires) designed to provide an *actual* diagnosis of the native labour issue in the empire; this information was then used to promote more informed and possibly more effective legal and policy-making processes in the empire. On the other hand, this information, filtered and reframed, was used to shape the country's participation in international and interimperial *fora* as a *legitimate* partner, actively participating in and conditioning the debates and their outcomes. The *Ross Report* and what it epitomized — the internationalization of imperial accountability — influenced the decisions to ratify the 1926 Convention on Slavery and to promulgate the new *Código do Trabalho Indígena* (Native Labour Code), in 1928, which selectively incorporated some of the international recommendations put forward in the debates over slavery and analogous conditions. The 1928 Native Labour Code (NLC) explicitly repudiated the legal (but not moral) obligation of native people to work — the quintessential principle of former legislation — and forbade forced recruitment for private purposes, in conformity with the 1926 Convention, reflecting debates that had taken place at the International Labour Organization (ILO) and that would eventually lead to the 1930 Convention on Forced Labour no. 29. This critical

[14]   The methodological question is an important one, given the *scientific* aura of the process. Edward Ross, *Report on Employment of Native Labor in Portuguese Africa* (New York: Abbot Press, 1925). For the reaction see, for instance, Oliveira Santos, *Resposta às acusações que o americano Professor Edward Alsworth Ross fez à administração dos portugueses em angola num relatório que enviou à S. D. N. em 1925* (Luanda: Imprensa nacional de Angola, 1926–27). For the entire process see Jerónimo, *Livros brancos, almas negras*, pp. 211–69.
[15]   For the BIDI and G. A. Morton's report see Miers, *Slavery in the Twentieth Century*, pp. 100, 113, notes 5 and 73, pp. 116 and 120.

juncture in international reprobation and, simultaneously, in the expansion of international regimes regarding the native labour question clearly shaped the outcome of reforms.[16]

The Portuguese decided not to ratify Convention no. 29, something they would do only in 1956. Concerns over the existence of forced labour within the empire — partially derived from the processes of self-scrutiny promoted by the *Ross Report* and similar cases — were one of the main reasons for the decision. Others included the existence of an interimperial *entente*, formed and fostered at the ICI between France, Belgium and Portugal (marginalizing the United Kingdom), that was critical of the ILO's African focus and argued for the constant invocation of the *colonial clause*. There was also a prevailing suspicion over the potential impact of 'internacionalismos perigosos' [dangerous internationalisms] regarding imperial affairs, as Count Penha Garcia, an important Portuguese representative at the League and at the ICI, stated in 1932. In the same year, Teixeira de Sampaio, Secretary General of the Ministry of Foreign Affairs, wrote that it was necessary to counter everything that entailed the 'internacionalização em matéria colonial' [internationalization of colonial matters]. One year later he reinforced his view: 'Nas tendências, reveladas sem rebuço, da Sociedade das Nações para a internacionalização das questões [...] reside a meu ver o maior perigo para Portugal em matéria colonial' [in the tendency shown with all clarity by the League of Nations to internationalize [...] lies the greatest danger to Portugal in colonial issues].[17] The Portuguese authorities knew that the expansive nature of the mandates system and of its 'sacred trust' encapsulated new mechanisms that propelled the sharing and circulation of information and were, therefore, potentially threatening to colonial powers.[18]

But the Portuguese authorities also knew that not to cooperate *tout court* with the League's institutions had serious consequences. The recognition of the country as a legitimate imperial power, the possibility of shaping the debates, especially those on the codification of international norms and supervisory

---

[16]   Suzanne Miers, 'Slavery and the Slave Trade as International Issues, 1890–1939', *Slavery and Abolition*, 19.2 (1998), 16–37; Jean Allain, *The Slavery Conventions* (Leiden: Brill, 2008), esp. pp. 31–171; idem, *Slavery in International Law: Of Human Exploitation and Trafficking* (Leiden & Boston, Martinus Nijhoff Publishers, 2012); Susan Zimmermann, '"Special Circumstances" in Geneva: The ILO and the World of Non-Metropolitan Labour in the Interwar Years', in *ILO histories: Essays on the International Labour Organization and its Impact on the World during the Twentieth Century*, ed. by Jasmien Van Daele et al. (Bern: Peter Lang, 2010), pp. 221–50.

[17]   Minute of L. de Sampayo, 31 March 1932; *Arquivo HistóricoDiplomático, Fundo MNE* (AHDMNE), *maço 164*; Bernardo Futscher Pereira, *A diplomacia de Salazar (1932–1949)* (Lisbon: Dom Quixote, 2012), p. 37.

[18]   For the mandates see, among others, Michael D. Callahan, *Mandates and Empire: The League of Nations and Africa, 1914–1931* (Brighton: Sussex Academic Press, 1999); idem, '"Mandated territories are not colonies": Britain, France, and Africa in the 1930s', in *Imperialism on Trial: International Oversight of Colonial Rule in Historical Perspective*, ed. by R. M. Douglas, Michael D. Callahan, and Elizabeth Bishop (Lanham, MD: Lexington Books, 2006), pp. 1–19; Nadine Méouchy and Peter Sluglett, *The British and French Mandates in Comparative Perspectives/Les Mandats francais et anglais dans une perspective comparative* (Leiden & Boston: Brill, 2004).

machinery, and the acknowledgement that the international instruments of knowledge production and information gathering could be turned into an asset of imperial self-awareness and, possibly, of effective reform — all these reasons suggested a different approach. To enhance the empire-state's external and internal efforts at legitimation was crucial. The decision not to ratify Convention no. 29 and the widespread suspicion at the motivations and impact of internationalism did not entail the suspension of the processes of coop-eration on the formulation of instruments of assessment and comparison over colonial labour. The workings of the League's Committees on Slavery during the 1930s benefitted from an active participation by the Portuguese, functioning as a forum for the international reinforcement of its imperial statute (including its claimed progressive nature) and as a resource for the improvement of their rationalizing strategies about colonial administration. As Foreign Affairs Minister, Armindo Monteiro, put it, to know 'os processos de tratar as populações indígenas' [the processes of handling indigenous populations], to study their 'costumes' [customs], 'de os trazer à colaboração voluntária e civilizadora do trabalho' [to bring them to the voluntary and civilizing collab-oration of labour] was to enhance the defence of the colonial empire.[19] When the Advisory Committee of Experts on Slavery started its work, José de Almada, colonial advisor at the Ministry of Foreign Affairs (MNE), asserted that it would be much more convenient to debate slavery and analogous conditions than to 'deixar avolumar a suspeita' [allow the escalation of suspicion] over the absence of actual measures by the authorities 'para *gradualmente* os extinguir' [to *gradually* extinguish them].[20] The debates surrounding the decision to apply an *ethnographic* questionnaire regarding slavery and analogous con-ditions at the lowest echelons of colonial administration in 1936, following the recommendation of the Advisory Committee and based on a model devel-oped by the *Institut Royale Coloniale Belge*, were a telling illustration. The questionnaires were an important tool in information gathering, not only in respect of slavery and analogous conditions but also of broader questions about the social and economic life of native populations and about the administrative personnel in each *circunscrição*. It could therefore be more than a mere infor-mational element. Portuguese metropolitan and colonial bureaucracies under-stood the dangers, but also the opportunities and the possibilities offered by international circumstances.[21]

[19] Letter of Armindo Monteiro, 14 February 1936, in MU-GM-GNP, *série 167, maço nº 5*.
[20] The italics are ours. Minute of José de Almada, 11 April 1935, AHDMNE, *maço 164*. For the problem of slavery and analogous conditions see Frederick Cooper, 'Conditions Analogous to Slavery: Imperialism and Free Labor Ideology in Africa', in *Beyond Slavery: Explorations of Race, Labor, and Citizenship in Postemancipation Societies*, ed. by Frederick Cooper, Thomas C. Holt, and Rebecca J. Scott (Chapel Hill: University of North Carolina Press, 2000), pp. 107–50.
[21] Information no. 37 of the Office of Political Affairs and Civil Administration of the Overseas Ministry, of 6 April 1938; *Inquérito sobre escravatura e servidão* of *Posto Sede* of Novo Redondo, 28 February 1942; idem, of *Posto* of Alto Cuíto, 10 February 1937, all at MU-GM-GNP, *série 167, maço nº 5*.

'Things not to be known abroad that we must keep in mind'

In 1953, Roy Garrison, a correspondent for the newspaper of the American Federation of Labour (AFL), published an article on labour conditions in sub-Saharan Africa. The Portuguese empire, particularly Angola, was also the subject of his appraisal. The Portuguese, he reported, had 'slave labour for dock work' and 'slave labour gets no wages whatever'; Africans were 'forced to come in from their jungle and semi-jungle habitats and work for nothing and under very miserable conditions and with but a rag for clothes and just enough food to sustain them'. In the same year, Luís Esteves Fernandes, Portuguese Ambassador in Washington, replied, underlining the exceptional virtues of Portuguese colonialism, its *hybridism*, and its legal benevolence. But his answer went further. Based on a report written by the *Agência Geral do Ultramar*, his explanation of the workings of the dock labour supply mechanism was very detailed and informative. This alone could be taken as no more than playing the diplomatic game, but the context and the procedures selected by the Portuguese authorities add weight to the matter. The prompt answer from the Portuguese ambassador was closely coordinated within the MNE, and was based on the practice of monitoring the foreign press on labour issues.[22] The historical context was even more important. 1953 was the year when the ECOSOC and BIT's *Ad-Hoc Committee on Forced Labour* delivered its final report, which contained a global analysis of the forced labour issue.

Forced labour and slavery had been at the centre of international debates since 1947. The AFL delivered a memorandum to the ECOSOC urging it to handle both issues. The action was clearly intended to put pressure on the Soviet Union at the outbreak of the Cold War. The days in which forced labour was considered to be exclusively a colonial problem were over. The debate was a product of the entanglement of Cold War dynamics with discussions of colonial legitimacy. Diplomatic and strategic constraints averted the appointment of an international committee until 1950, when a UN Ad-Hoc Committee on Slavery was appointed. One year later, an Ad-Hoc Committee on Forced Labour was appointed, with shared responsibility between the ILO and the UN.[23]

The Portuguese authorities were aware from the beginning of the implications of such an international resurgence of forced labour issues. These problems were hardly confinable to the socialist countries. But they also knew that the terms of the debate had changed since the 1930s. The international critics of empire were growing in number and geopolitical power. In 1948, Esteves Fernandes,

---

[22]   Roy Garrison, 'How workers are treated in Africa', in AHDMNE, *2° piso, armário 52, maço 74*; Letter n° 264 — *Exemplar da American Federationist*, 26 December 1953, AHDMNE, *2° piso, armário 52, maço 74*.
[23]   Minute by José de Almada, 26 January 1951, AHDMNE, *2° piso, armário 49, maço 21*. For the historical context see Daniel Maul, 'The International Labour Organization and the Struggle against Forced Labour from 1919 to the Present', *Labor History*, 4.48 (2007), 477–500, and Suzanne Miers, *Slavery in the Twentieth Century*, pp. 317–38.

then a Foreign Affairs desk officer, warned about the changing international trends affecting colonial issues. Forums like the UN, he stated, were privileged sites to promote and press for colonial reform. The Belgian example was clear: the Belgian authorities were seen to have reformed their *politique indigène* in the Congo due to international pressures. International public opinion could turn its attention to the Portuguese case. In order to prevent and refute *future* accusations, Fernandes strongly suggested that the colonial authorities should provide an accurate diagnosis of the labour situation in the empire. To be sure, the existing legislation was 'perfeita' [perfect], but it was fundamental to assess the actual practices; otherwise, the repercussions could be 'catastróficas' [catastrophic]. Evidence of migratory movements to neighbouring states was one example of the inability of the state to provide attractive labour conditions for its African subjects. Fernandes' recommendation did not fall on deaf ears. In a memorandum written by the *Inspecção Superior dos Negócios Indígenas* (Higher Inspectorate of Indigenous Affairs, ISNI), presumably in 1949, a critical appraisal emerged. The memorandum was a response to a demand made by the MNE, following accusations against the Portuguese empire and a request for information by the UN Secretary General. The issue was thus again at the forefront of international politics and, according to the author, it was obvious that 'nações sem colónias e anti-colóniais' [non-colonial and anti-colonial nations] would use the matter to 'para levar avante a decisão de interferência da ONU nos domínios ultramarinos das nações coloniais' [advance their cause of pushing the UN to interfere in the overseas domains of colonial nations].[24]

Two points must be stressed. On the one hand, this example shows the ways in which international institutions fostered processes of self-scrutiny, and thorough inspection, along the imperial and colonial bureaucratic chains. The processes of internal assessment of imperial and colonial politics and policies, and their historical evolution, were, to a considerable extent, a by-product of international dynamics. They were never the mere result of domestic, metropolitan aspects such as the political culture of the regime. On the other hand, even an organization of which Portugal was not a member and that was seen as anti-colonial by the Portuguese authorities was able to condition Portuguese behaviour, directly or indirectly. As the report stated, 'dos relatórios e documentos arquivados' [the reports and documents stored] at the ISNI contained information 'o que não devemos dizer para o exterior' [not to be known abroad] but that 'convém não ter no esquecimento' [should be kept in mind]. The memorandum offered a perceptive compilation of testimonies by

---

[24] Minute by Luís Esteves Fernandes, 2 March 1948; Memorandum of ISNI, 'Acusações', both in AHDMNE, 2° *piso*, *armário 49*, *maço 21*. All the problems referred are well known in Portuguese historiography. Regarding the migration to São Tomé see, among others, Zachary Kagan-Guthrie, 'Repression and Migration: Forced Labour Exile of Mozambicans to São Tomé, 1948–1955', *Journal of Southern African Studies*, 37.3 (2011), 449–62. Regarding migration in Mozambique see, for instance, Patrick Harries, *Work, Culture, and Identity: Migrant Laborers in Mozambique and South Africa, c. 1860–1910* (Portsmouth, NH: Heinemann, 1994).

colonial administrators, all of them critical of the real situation regarding native labour. The reports on Angola and Mozambique by the Inspector Superior, Henrique Galvão, were cited, as was the 1941 report of the Curador Geral de Angola, which stressed that abuses were rampant, especially in the north-eastern regions and in relation to forced migration to São Tomé e Príncipe. The information provided by the *Curador de São Tomé* in 1945 highlighted the use of violence against *serviçais* (contract workers), a fact known by the British Consul. An article from the South African newspaper *Forward*, describing inhuman conditions in the transport of Mozambican workers, was attached. In view of its important content and potential consequences, the memorandum recommended that the questionnaire should be made known to the governors of each province. The information should be 'kept in mind', and its production and monitoring should continue.[25]

By this time, forced labour was already a crucial topic in ECOSOC debates. The UN Secretary General had already sent a questionnaire but the Portuguese authorities declined to answer. When, in 1951, the Ad-Hoc Committee on Forced Labour started its activity, the Portuguese position did not change. Despite being a member state of the ILO, Portugal ignored repeated requests to answer the questionnaire. The decision was not a consensual one. In 1950, António de Oliveira Salazar, President of the Council of Ministers, had warned against the potential consequences of a reply. In the past, 'o inconveniente' [the inconvenience] of appearing to avoid clarification of 'o problema do trabalho escravo e da situação dos indígenas nos nosso territórios' [the slave labour problem and the situation of the native in our territories] was regarded as preferable to collaboration with an institution that was against the interests of the country (in the matter), and of which the country was not a member. In respect of the questionnaire, Salazar's diplomatic anxieties prevailed, and only when the accusations against Portugal were formalized did Portuguese authorities decide to reply. However, the imperial and colonial bureaucracies did not ignore the process. An ISNI memorandum, written on 21 August 1950 and signed by Alberto Oliveira, replied to the questionnaire regarding slavery. Even though the Portuguese government routinely refused to answer the UN, versions of possible replies were drafted, demonstrating that the refusals to answer (the questionnaire) were far from pre-determined. This also demonstrated that the importance of these questionnaires went far beyond the mere necessity to organize information to counterbalance external accusations.[26]

As the Portuguese administration knew, the work of the committees was mainly juridical. The possibility of permitting actual inspections in the colonies by investigative bodies was unrealistic. But even the legislation, contrary to the Portuguese authorities' longstanding claim, was far from perfect. Late

---

[25]   Memorandum of the ISNI, 'Acusações', AHDMNE, *2° piso, armário 49, maço 21.*
[26]   Observations of the President of the Council, 18 September 1950; Memorandum by Alberto Oliveira, ISNI; both in AHDMNE, *2° piso, armário 49, maço 21.*

in the 1940s, the possibility of ratifying Convention no. 29 had become a recurrent subject of inter-ministerial correspondence. In 1950, José de Almada summarized the problem: 'Uma convenção ratificada' [A ratified convention] was an international act that 'sai fora do âmbito dos limites territoriais' [goes beyond the territorial boundaries] and its application required 'fiscalização internacional' [international supervision]. This had serious consequences with relation to 'um assunto tão grave como é o do trabalho indígena nas colónias' [such a sensitive issue as the colonial native labour]. The recognition of this fact led the Portuguese to avoid the ratification of such instruments. The Colonial and Corporations & Social Welfare Ministries did not oppose the ratification, but the MNE showed 'sempre uma resistência sistemática' [always a systematic opposition]. In 1953, Fortunato de Almeida, a Foreign Affairs official, disagreed with Almada, but recognized that his objection had a point. Referring to the 1949 ISNI memorandum, he stated that if the convention was ratified and the country allowed the persistence of 'a situação' [the occurrences] reported in it, there would be negative consequences. 'Há pois de sanear e moralizar o que se passa nos territórios ultramarinos, sobretudo em Angola onde ainda vigora o tal sistema do "contracto", em muitos aspectos peor do que a própria escravatura' [There is then a need to clean up and moralize what is going on in the overseas territories, especially in Angola where the so-called 'contract' regime still remains in force, in many respects worse than slavery itself]. 'Se não for feito como trabalho prévio [If it is not done in advance], the ratification was 'inconveniente' [inappropriate]. Another way to moralize labour conditions was to replace the NLC, and this option was a real one, as an ISNI memorandum had suggested in March 1951. Both options were postponed. But the important connection established between international scrutiny, internal information gathering and political decision making was there, even if other concurrent factors were obviously at play.[27]

The final report of the Ad-Hoc Committee on Forced Labour was particularly critical of the dispositions regarding the moral obligation to work within the NLC, and echoed the allegations of the Byelorussian delegate as well as the memorandum delivered by the Anti-Slavery Society (ASS), which focused on Angola, particularly on the sugar plantations and migration to São Tomé and Mozambique. The migration conditions of Mozambican workers to South Africa were also subjected to the Committee's attention. In reply to its critics, the Portuguese government refuted the accusations of scarce labour supply in Angola on the basis of the licence registrations issued by the provincial government. The days when only legislation and the putative civilizational intents of its preambles were invoked to counterbalance international criticism

---

[27]   Minute by José de Almada, 25 January 1950, AHDMNE, *2° piso, armário 49, maço 21*; minute by Fortunato de Almeida, 11 February 1953, AHDMNE, *2° piso, armário 51, maço 33*; Note, 17 March 1951, *Compilação de Pareceres da Inspecção Superior de Administração Ultramarina, 1951*, Arquivo Histórico do Instituto Português de Apoio ao Desenvolvimento (AHIPAD).

were over. The old arguments of the natives' putative inability to match the 'dever moral de trabalhar' [moral duty to work], of their responsibility should they 'embaraça ou dificulta' [hinder or impede] the improvement in their 'condição social' [social condition], and on their role in the obstruction of 'desenvolvimento e progresso material' [development and material progress] of the overseas provinces, persisted. But the international momentum regarding forced labour constrained Portuguese politics and policies, pushing forward internal processes of information gathering, self-inspection and policy evaluation and transformation. The internal debates about how to cope with the problem intensified.[28]

The ratification of several ILO instruments by the Portuguese empire, in the late 1950s, needs to be understood in the wider historical framework, which conjoined several actors — from States to non-governmental organizations (NGOs). These events show us that the international dimensions of the Portuguese empire went far beyond simple bilateral relations. The decision to ratify Convention no. 29 in 1956 must be understood by taking into account the *cumulative* but not necessarily linear historical effect of processes that entailed several institutions and actors, with different motivations and rationales, ranging from the internal critical remarks of Henrique Galvão to the manoeuvres of the special committees and the impact of France's decision to apply the ILO's conventions to its colonial territories, therefore weakening the influence of the longstanding colonial *entente*. The role played by international organizations, trade union movements, philanthropic associations, missionary societies, and by numerous individuals that, more or less instrumentally, participated in international debates about colonial labour and aimed to promote its reform, must be assessed in a combined manner. These were also part of the international dimensions of the Portuguese late colonial state. The history of the interaction between these actors and the Portuguese state also reveals the diversity of positions within the regime. Some advocated a deeper integration of the empire into the international normative framework. Others, like José de Almada and Salazar, emphasized the potential negative consequences.

The ratification had obvious consequences: for example, the possibility of prohibiting international *in situ* supervision became harder to achieve. And perhaps as important was the fact that ratification entailed a significant change in the *political* value of information. Before 1956, none of the specifically colonial conventions of the ILO had been ratified; after 1956, things changed. When the first reports over the *actual* application of Convention no. 29 to the colonies had to be produced, in 1958, the *Direcção Geral da Administração Política e Civil* of the Overseas Ministry urged all Governors General: 'Convirá que haja o maior cuidado na elaboração do relatório' [there should be the greatest care in the

---

[28] *Report of the Ad Hoc Committee on Forced Labour* (Geneva: Imprimeries Réunies SA, 1953), pp. 62–63. Information of Inspecção Superior da Administração Colonial, 14 February 1953, AHDMNE, *2° piso, armário 51, maço 33.*

elaboration of the report]. All reports denied the existence of forced labour. The Governor General of Guinea, instrumentally or not, confused legislation of the *Código do Trabalho Indígena* (articles 295 and 296 were interpreted erroneously). The secretariat of the Government of Angola emphasized the difficulties that emerged during the elaboration of the report, citing the lack of statistical data, or of knowledge of legislation and of the recommendations of international organizations. Despite all the problems, the intensity and the scope of informational exchange and policy assessment within the empire-state changed profoundly — the newly ratified mechanisms of international cooperation, inspection and supervision saw to that.[29]

'The most efficient and prestigious international organization'

The growing integration of Portugal at the ILO, which coexisted with a more troubled interaction with the UN, faced an important challenge associated with the increasing incorporation of newly independent states within international organizations.[30] The decision to ratify the ILO Convention no. 105 regarding the abolition of forced labour in 1959 enabled the Ghanaian government to file a complaint against the Portuguese Government, on 25 February 1961, based on the general argument that Portugal did not fulfil the obligations attached to the convention on overseas territories. A month after the Baixa do Cassange revolt inaugurated a period of insurgency that marked the beginning of the colonial war in Angola, followed by the events in Luanda in February, the Portuguese faced a new challenge.[31] This was a momentous event in the long process of international scrutiny of the Portuguese empire's *modus operandi*, particularly in relation to the use of African manpower. It mobilized a broad range of actors, from Protestant missionaries to international trade unions, human rights movements and African nationalist leaders, whose action, coupled with the ILO effort, led to a widespread demand for international accountability of the empire. The Portuguese authorities regarded this complaint as just one more

---

[29]   Minute of Soares da Fonseca, 2 May 1955, *Arquivo Histórico Diplomático, Fundo Gabinete dos Negócios Políticos* (AHDGNP), GNP-RRI-0721-00507; *Relatórios para a Comissão de Peritos para a Aplicação de Convenções e recomendações (1948–1951), Arquivo Histórico Ultramarino* (AHU), AHU-MU-GM-GNP, *Série 170, Pasta 1*; Letter of the *Direcção Geral de Administração Política e Civil*, 25 September 1958; Report of Governor General of Guinea, 1958; Minute of Manuel Cruz Alvura, 14 March 1958, all in AHU-MU-GM-GNP, *série 170, maço 3*. See also Cristina Rodrigues, 'Portugal e a Organização Internacional do Trabalho (1933–1974)' (unpublished PhD thesis, Universidade de Coimbra, 2012), pp. 183–89.

[30]   For Portugal and the UN see, among others, Fernando Martins, 'Portugal e a Organização das Nações Unidas: uma história da política externa e ultramarina portuguesa no pós-guerra (Agosto de 1941–Setembro de 1968)' (unpublished MA Thesis, FCSH-UNL, 1995).

[31]   For the event at Baixa do Cassange see Alexander Keese, 'Dos abusos às revoltas? Trabalho forçado, reformas Portuguesas, política "tradicional" e religião na Baixa de Cassange e no Distrito do Congo (Angola), 1957–1961', *Africana Studia*, 7 (2004), 247–76; Diogo Ramada Curto and Bernardo Cruz, 'Terrores e saberes coloniais: notas acerca dos incidentes na Baixa de Cassange', in *Império colonial em questão*, ed. by Jerónimo, pp. 3–35.

piece in an international plot, which involved Moscow and newly independent countries like Liberia, which in the same month had urged the UN Security Council to debate the situation in Angola.[32] Despite Portuguese allegations of a politically motivated manoeuvre on the part of Ghana, the ILO established an independent enquiry commission to deal with the case.[33]

Ghana's allegations were ideologically charged and some of the accusations were vague and inaccurate. But they stressed the apparently immutable nature of Portuguese native labour practices: colonial administrators were active agents in recruitment; venality abounded; workers were underpaid and subjected to compulsory migration movements. Legislation was depicted as morally and socially unacceptable, given that it crystallized the segregation between 'civilized' and indigenous labour. These allegations were sustained by witnesses, foreign experts like Basil Davidson, nationalist leaders such as Amílcar Cabral, and by Portuguese legislation itself. Joined by the United Arab Republic, Ghana received the *informational* support of the ASS, the International Confederation of Free Trade Unions and the *Ligue International des Droits de l'Homme*, among others. As the process unfolded, the evidence provided by Ghana regarding labour conditions increased, but it also faced serious obstacles. The commission required precise information and would only recognize as valid the evidence related to events *after* the day when the Convention entered into force.[34]

The Portuguese authorities reacted diversely. First, they established contacts with other delegations within the ILO in order to present their own viewpoint. As it became clear that the BIT would not dismiss Ghana's allegations — as Wilfred Jenks, the ILO's Assistant Director-General, stated this was impossible in 'na situação do Mundo actual' [the world's current situation] — they prepared a strategy that focused on a 'juridical' approach to the problem. Ghana's initiative, by contrast, was portrayed as 'political'. Silva Cunha, a colonial expert, professor and future Overseas Minister, was sent to Geneva by the Overseas Ministry to study alternative courses of action. The Portuguese decision to file a complaint against Liberia in the same year appears to have been the solution, working perhaps as a strategy of diplomatic diversion, ideologically motivated and with a strong symbolic significance. But another type of response was in order. Even a 'juridical' approach required material evidence and support. A memorandum from the Office of Political Affairs and a note by Admiral Sarmento Rodrigues, Governor General of Mozambique,

---

[32] David Wainhouse, *Remnants of Empire: The United Nations and the End of Colonialism* (New York: Harper & Row Publishers, 1964), pp. 30–42.

[33] For the developments see José Pedro Monteiro, 'Portugal, a Organização Internacional do Trabalho e o trabalho nativo: a queixa do Estado do Gana' (unpublished MA Thesis, FCSH-UNL, 2012), pp. 21–49.

[34] ILO, *Report of the Commission Appointed under Article 26 of the Constitution of the International Labour Organization to Examine the Complaint Filed by the Government of Ghana concerning the Observance by the Government of Portugal of the Abolition of Forced Labour Convention, 1957 (n.º 105). Official Bulletin, Vol. 45, n.º 2, Supplement II* (Geneva: ILO, 1962), pp. 124–25.

suggested that the legal provisions contained within the convention were probably not consistently applied. Rodrigues pointed to the cases of the rice and cotton cultures, which could justify 'damaging accusations'.[35]

The Commission started its own investigation. Its main sources were a bibliographic and legislative assessment, interviews with witnesses and *in situ* inspections in Angola and Mozambique. While rejecting the provision of data to the Trusteeship Council, the Portuguese agreed to do so to specialized agencies: the ILO was viewed as the 'menos irresponsável' [least irresponsible] of all the UN specialized agencies, as Ribeiro da Cunha stated. Moreover, the complaint was an opportunity to improve the country's reputation. Part of the strategy entailed the instruction of the representatives of private colonial companies, enrolled as witnesses, in a meeting in Lisbon, who were told to declare that the Portuguese authorities were in tune with international labour standards.[36] The Commission wanted non-state *witnesses*, not just colonial officials, and was not easily mollified. For instance, the director of the Native Affairs office in Mozambique was insistently questioned about Decree 566-D-7, issued in 1947, which had provisions that were incompatible with a free labour model. In Angola, his counterpart had to answer why a large proportion of Luanda prisoners (30%) had been convicted of not fulfilling the moral obligation to work.[37]

After the guarantee of 'non-politicization' given by Wilfred Jenks to Salazar and Adriano Moreira, the commission's request to visit Angola and Mozambique was accepted. All the evidence suggests that the Portuguese prepared for this unprecedented international inspection in detail. An instruction issued by the Angolan Departamento de Negócios Indígenas (Native Affairs Directorate) in October 1961, one and a half months before the visit, asked all the district governors to report if the convention's provisions were being met and what measures should be taken in order to be so. The majority claimed conformity with the agreement. However, in the Zaire District, according to a previous visit, the governor said 'o sistema de trabalho que se estava seguindo ali era ilegal' [the labour system being practised there was illegal] and caused 'o êxodo dos trabalhadores' [the exodus of workers]. In Lunda and Malange, 'a maior dificuldade consistirá em conseguir (julgo impossível) que os actuais trabalhadores recrutados se digam voluntarios' [the greatest difficulty will be (and I think it impossible) to get the present recruited workers to say they are volunteers]. Damage control was executed systematically. In the end, the Commission's assessment was positive, despite important requests for

---

[35]   Minute by Ribeiro da Cunha, 29 April 1961, *Apontamento sobre a visita de Wilfred Jenks*; minute by Silva Cunha, April 1961; Note, s.d., *Estudo Convenção nº 29*; all in AHDGNP, GNP-RRI-0790–12432. Letter from Sarmento Rodrigues to Overseas Minister, AHDGNP, GNP-RRI-0790–12433.

[36]   Minute by Ribeiro da Cunha, *Apontamento sobre a 5ª sessão da Comissão de Peritos em Política Social nos Territórios Não Metropolitanos em Genebra entre 9 e 21 de Dezembro de 1957*, AHDMNE, *2º piso, armário 7, maço 562*; s.a., s.n., AHDGNP, GNP-RRI-0790–12529; minute by Costa Morais, 10 August 1961, AHDGNP, GNP-RRI-0790–12433.

[37]   ILO, 'Report', pp. 153–54, 177.

further explanation, related to the *Sociedade Agrícola do Cassequel* and to the protection of Mozambican workers in South Africa. To praise a degree of compliance with international labour standards and the related endorsement of a narrative of reform that implicated the Portuguese was the major goal. But criticism regarding the Portuguese development model, which went far beyond forced labour issues, emerged. Late colonialism's *repressive developmentalism* was also under the spotlight.[38]

The case and consequences of the Ghana complaint were not the only driving forces behind the 1961 and 1962 reforms, namely the *Indigenato* Regime and NLC abrogation. But the role of the ILO, and its agencies, was certainly decisive. The pressure towards compliance with international labour standards was part of the *international* pressure towards imperial reform. Before the complaint, the ILO Committee of Experts on the Application of Conventions and Recommendations questioned the resilience of a native labour code that preserved the principle of a moral obligation to work and the persistence of a compulsory cultivation regime (for instance, of cotton). The latter's suspension and the creation of a labour inspectorate in May 1961 were related to, even if not determined by, long-standing ILO recommendations. The same can be argued in relation to the NLC abrogation. When the Commission published its report, the NLC was still active. The end of the *Indigenato* regime on 6 September 1961 entailed the suppression of the NLC (given the suppression of the general juridical regime in which it existed), which would legally happen on 27 April 1962, with the publication of the Rural Labour Code (RLC), that concerned only non-specialized African workers. For the Portuguese the Commission's report was significant, as it provided evidence of imperial and colonial reform and international integration, both important instruments and examples of legitimacy, usable in its own propaganda.[39]

The outcome of Ghana's complaint defined Portugal's future relations with the ILO, in a period marked by the extension of war to Mozambique and Guinea. Apart from promoting reforms, the complaint enabled the continued

---

[38]   *Relatório Direcção Serviços de Negócios Indígenas*, 28 October 1961; *Despacho nº 33 do governador-geral de Angola de 17 de Agosto de 1961, Curadoria Geral dos Indígenas da Província de Angola*; both in AHDGNP, GNP-RRI-0790–12530; Armando Almeida e Cunha, *Relatório Convenção nº 29 Trabalho Forçado de Setembro de 1962*, AHU, MU-GM-GNP-*série 135, maço nº 38*. For the repressive developmentalism of Portuguese late colonialism see Miguel Bandeira Jerónimo and António Costa Pinto, 'A Modernizing Empire? Politics, Culture and Economy in Portuguese Late Colonialism', in Miguel Bandeira Jerónimo and António Costa Pinto, *The Ends of European Colonial Empires: Cases and Comparisons* (forthcoming, 2014). For *Cassequel* see Jeremy Ball, '"The Colossal Lie": The Sociedade Agrícola do Cassequel and Portuguese Colonial Labor Policy in Angola, 1899–1977' (unpublished PhD thesis, University of California, Los Angeles, 2003). For more on this see Jerónimo and Monteiro, 'Das "dificuldades de levar os indígenas a trabalhar"', pp. 187–91.

[39]   *Recomendações da Convenção de Peritos sobre Aplicação de Convenções e Recomendações da OIT*, April 1961, AHDGNP, GNP-RRI-0721–00507; ILO, 'Report', pp. 247. Alexandre Ribeiro da Cunha, 'A projecção do sindicalismo em África', in *Colóquios de Política Internacional*, 3 (Lisbon: Junta de Investigações do Ultramar, 2nd edition, 1960). For the case of cotton see, among others, Mary Anne Pitcher, *Politics in the Portuguese Empire: The State, Industry, and Cotton, 1926–1974* (Oxford: Clarendon Press, 1993).

monitoring of overseas provinces' labour policies by the Committee of Experts. Replying to its questions about the conformity of the new code with the recommendations transmitted in 1962, Ribeiro da Cunha declared that all the dispositions previously criticized had been revoked.[40] But this was not enough. In the following year, three requests were made to the authorities by the Committee of Experts: the creation of a public and independent institution responsible for the employment service; a rise in the wages of African workers; and the expansion of the powers of labour inspectorates. These demands persisted until the end of the empire, causing diverse reactions in the Portuguese authorities and government. In 1963, Afonso Mendes, the director of the newly created *Instituto do Trabalho, Previdência e Acção Social de Angola* (ITPAS) [Angola Labour, Welfare and Social Action] argued that it was necessary to create an employment service and to abrogate private recruitment. In sharp contrast to his 1958 appraisal of the ILO, in which its anti-colonial and class-struggle influences were highlighted, he now praised the work carried on by the organization, the 'mais eficiente e conceituada Organização Internacional' [most efficient and prestigious international organization]. Following ILO guidelines, Mendes advocated the establishment of a free, public scheme of labour organization. The abolishment of recruitment would raise the rural workers' wages, which were averaging a third of those of European workers with the same occupation. The RLC had already made provision for the constitution of an employment service. However, other voices were against this solution. In 1965, in a reply to the Committee of Experts' observations, Rodrigo Baião, an ITPAS officer, raised serious reservations about the abolition of recruitment. The putative psychological characteristics of the African worker (an old trope) and the difficulties in organizing a transport system were considered to be the main obstacles to the establishment of such a solution.[41]

Despite some efforts by Portuguese officials to promote reform — always with divergences inside the metropolitan and colonial bureaucracies and provoking the reaction of local interests — international criticism against the Portuguese empire within the ILO did not stop. Angolan clandestine trade unions were also active in the ILO. The *União Nacional dos Trabalhadores Africanos*, linked to the MPLA, already known for its propaganda action in Luanda, in 1959, during the meeting of the ILO's African Advisory Committee, sent a representative to Geneva in 1965 in order to persuade the International

[40]   Minute by Ribeiro da Cunha, 20 July 1962, AHDGNP, GNP-RRI-0790–12529.
[41]   Afonso Mendes, *Serviços de Colocação, 1963*; Rodrigo Baião, *Relatório Convenção n° 105*, 20 August 1965; both in AHU, MU-GM-GNP, *série 135, maço 138*. See also Afonso Mendes, *A Huíla e Moçâmedes: considerações sobre o trabalho indígena* (Lisbon: Junta de Investigações do Ultramar, 1958), p. 192; idem, *O trabalho assalariado em Angola* (Lisbon: Instituto Superior de Ciências Sociais e Política Ultramarina, 1966), esp. 421–35 (for the ITPAS); and José Maria Gaspar, *Problemática do trabalho em África* (Lisbon: Instituto Superior de Ciências Sociais e Política Ultramarina, 1965), esp. pp. 201–11 (for the system of labour recruitment). For a critical analysis of these and other related issues see Frank Luce, 'A History of Labour Law in Angola' (unpublished LL.M Thesis, University of Toronto, 1990), pp. 155–97.

Labour Conference delegates to join a campaign against the labour system in Angola, according to the Portuguese authorities. In 1966, the United Arab Republic announced that would propose the exclusion of the Portuguese state from the ILO due to its forced labour regime. In 1966, the ILO Governing Body asked the Committee of Experts to write a special report on what the Portuguese had achieved in respect of the recommendations of Ghana's complaint Commission. Once again, the Portuguese overseas provinces, and the labour regime therein, were under international scrutiny. Supported by statistical data and legislative information provided by Portuguese authorities, the Committee of Experts insisted on demanding a transition to a *completely* free labour system. The creation of an employment service and policies to raise wages were seen as imperative. Portuguese answers were diverse and elucidative of the disputed nature of the debate. The Angolan ITPAS endorsed all the Committee's recommendations. The Mozambican ITPAS, on the other hand, argued that the employment service was 'inútil, superflue et contra-indiqué' [useless, superfluous and counter-indicated]. Regardless of official claims, there was an increase in recruitment licenses in Angola between 1963 and 1965. In Mozambique, the total number of recruited workers between 1962 and 1963 was more than one hundred thousand. Furthermore, the statistical data about the evolution of wages was unclear and the information regarding the workings of the labour inspectorates was imprecise. Given these shortcomings and in accordance with the protocols related to Ghana's complaint, annual information about the evolution of recruitment and wages in *Diamang*, the *Sociedade Agrícola do Cassequel*, the *Junta Autónoma de Estradas de Angola* (Angolan Road Authority) and the Angolan port authorities was demanded by the Committee of Experts.[42]

The impact of the complaint was still resonating. In a report sent to the ILO that dealt with the period of 1967–69, the Portuguese authorities recognized this fact and protested against the ways in which this supervision exceeded the scope of Convention no. 105. As a result, the Portuguese government decided to suggest 'direct contacts', a possible new procedure for evaluating compliance since 1968, with the organization. The result was a report regarding the colonial reality vis-à-vis forced labour made by Pierre Juvigny, a former director of the UN Minorities' Subcommittee, which resulted from an *in situ* inspection of employment conditions and services of recruitment and inspection in Angola and Mozambique, in 1970. The general conclusions were favourable to Portugal, finding no coercion, although the system of recruitment continued to be assessed critically. The continued existence of professional recruiters was

---

[42] Minute by Ministry of Foreign Affairs, 6 July 1965; Maria Monteiro, *Movimentos Sindicais Angolanos*, 13 July 1965; both in AHU, MU-GM-GNP, *Série 18, L.5.8*; *Observações da Comissão de Peritos, 1966*, in Arquivo Histórico da Direcção Geral do Emprego e Relações de Trabalho do Ministério da Economia (AHDGERT-ME), *Pasta da Convenção nº 105*. For Diamang see Todd Cleveland, 'Rock Solid: African Laborers on the Diamond Mines of the Companhia de Diamantes de Angola (Diamang), 1917–1975' (unpublished PhD thesis, University of Minnesota, Minneapolis, 2008).

noted. In the district of Huambo, 470 agents worked for seventeen recruitment companies, supplying Umbundu labour to coffee plantations in the north. Juvigny saw no problem with this arrangement, however, which assisted the Portuguese claims and arguments, something extremely important in a period of acute colonial conflicts. Cancelling of the use of professional recruiters in the ports of Lobito, in the railways of Luanda, in Cassequel and in Diamang on the eve of Juvigny's arrival certainly contributed to his appraisal of the situation. 'On-site scrutiny by the ILO again had a positive effect', it was claimed, although a perverse one.[43] For instance, the negative impact of counter-insurgency measures in the labour market was not assessed in the report.[44] In 1971, the Portuguese government issued two decrees, 323/71 and 324/71, which made provision for the total abolishment of the recruitment system within five years. A year-by-year reduction of 20% of the authorized recruiters was promised, following early efforts made by Afonso Mendes. But these measures did not preclude international criticism. In June 1972, the ILO's policy-making body approved a resolution, essentially related to the question of freedom of association, which accused the Portuguese authorities of disregarding the ILO's fundamental principles. The ILO also expressed political opposition to Portuguese colonialism and pressed for decolonization, aligning itself with UN declarations. In 1974, a group of African states (Togo, Central African Republic, Guinea-Conakry) proposed Portugal's expulsion from the ILO, but the regime change in metropolitan Portugal in April 1974 aborted the process.[45]

Conclusion

The political and diplomatic importance of the native labour question as a matter of international dialogue and dispute between the empire-state and international society is clear, involving as it did a complex of relations between actors and institutions interacting at multiple levels that cannot be understood with an ordinary, and still predominant, focus on diplomatic, bilateral official exchanges.[46]

[43] *Relatório enviado pelo governo português à comissão de Peritos para os anos 1967–1969* (1970), AHDGERT-ME, *Pasta da Convenção n° 105*; *Rapport de Pierre Juvigny, représentant du Directeur général du Bureau International du Travail, sur les contacts directs avec le gouvernement du Portugal au sujet de l'application de la convention (no. 105) sur l'abolition du travail forcé* (Geneva: BIT, 1971); Cristina Rodrigues, 'Portugal e o OIT (1933–1974)', pp. 194–95; Frank Luce, 'Armed Struggle, the ILO and the Labour Institute: Suppressing Forced Labour in Angola', paper at the conference *Slavery, Migration and Contemporary Bondage in Africa*, Wilberforce Institute, September 2009 (p. 31).
[44] Luce, 'A History of Labour Law in Angola', p. 204.
[45] *Relatório enviado pelo governo português à comissão de Peritos para os anos 1970* (1971), AHDGERT-ME, *Pasta da Convenção n° 105*; see also 'ILO: The Exercise of Civil Liberties and Trade Union Rights in Angola, Mozambique and Guinea (Bissau)', quoted in Frank Luce, 'Armed Struggle, the ILO and the Labour Institute', p. 33, note 54; for the expulsion proposal see AHD/MU/GM/GNP/RRI/0770/00290-001.
[46] James Duffy, *A Question of Slavery: Labour Policies in Portuguese Africa and the British Protest, 1850–1920* (Oxford: Oxford University Press, 1967); Miguel Bandeira Jerónimo, *Livros brancos*; Monteiro, 'Portugal, a OIT e o trabalho nativo'.

Forced labour had long attracted international critical attention to the Portuguese empire. Coming from missionary societies, national and transnational movements, official representatives, international institutions, occasional travellers and social scientists, the recurrent criticism over the workings of the empire, and specifically its native policies, conditioned the development of Portuguese colonial policies, patently shaping the relationship between the empire-state and international actors. The *international* was never merely made by interstate exchanges. International history requires much more than the identification and *narrative* organization of the relics of the 'official mind'. The 'official mind' focused on the *international* was not confined to the corridors of the MNE. The imperial 'official mind' also entailed the *peripheral* diplomatic and strategic spheres of intervention. Moreover, the relevance of the 'official mind', irrespective of the way in which it is conceived, needs to be confronted, and explained, by the cultural, politico-ideological and socioeconomic determinants of diplomatic manoeuvres and imperial and colonial policies. The black boxes of political decision-making at metropolitan, imperial/colonial and international levels must be tentatively opened using different sources and methods, different languages and geographies, and addressing different subjects.[47]

The historical interconnectedness between international organizations and the Portuguese empire-state, particularly with reference to its politics and policies of native labour, was a dynamic process. The alternation between, and the coexistence of, moments of dispute and moments of cooperation was evident. From the period of a predominant interimperial agenda, in the 1920s and 1930s, to an era of a global questioning of the legitimacy of colonialism, the importance of internationalism in the delineation of Portuguese imperial and colonial projects is undeniable. Imperial internationalism was a major factor of the international dimensions of Portuguese colonialism. The evolution of this process was characterized not only by the changing international *zeitgeist* regarding the nature and scope of imperial scrutiny but also by the autonomous role of international institutions, which tended to expand their activities. Despite moments of criticism impacting on the Portuguese colonial empire, the participation of the country in international *fora* was also marked by instances of dialogue and reform that served to enhance its international legitimation and, later, to strengthen the resistance to multiple decolonizing pressures. Even in moments of refusal to ratify international instruments of collective imperial supervision, as we have seen, the internationalized idioms and repertoires of imperial internationalism were nonetheless taken into account in the processes

---

[47]   See Ronald Robinson and John Gallagher, with Alice Denny, *Africa and the Victorians: The Official Mind of Imperialism* (London: Macmillan, 1961). For a proper widening of the notion see John Darwin, 'Imperialism and the Victorians: The Dynamics of Territorial Expansion', *English Historical Review*, 112.447 (1997), 614–42. See also Paul Kennedy, *The Realities behind Diplomacy: Background Influences on British External Policy, 1865–1980* (London: George Allen & Unwin, 1981), *maxime* 'The Diplomacy of Imperialism', pp. 17–139.

of information production and collection, thus interfering in policy making procedures that characterized the Portuguese imperial venture, until its demise.

As in other cases, colonial reform, sometimes merely a legal simulacrum, was an instrument of imperial consolidation and rationalization — central to the constitution of the *late colonial state* — that was also strategic to reinforcing imperial legitimation and sovereignty. The international validation of reform enhanced the state's legitimacy, despite the fact that the political and timetable *décalage* of Portuguese imperial disintegration made things harder. Labour reforms in British and French empires took place within a rather more cooperative context at the ILO.[48] Portuguese claims of sovereignty were not only derived from a *legal* possession of the territories; they were also conditioned by the Portuguese empire's ability to present itself as a polity able to administer its subject populations according to what were the negotiated and debated normative international standards. The moments of reform were closely connected to efforts to adjust Portuguese legislation and practices to the latter, in order not only to prevent international criticism but also to meet patterns and standards of international legitimation and accountability. If 'international institutions enabled states to survive and flourish', as Mark Mazower has recently argued, the case for a similar reasoning can be made, with obvious objections, *a propos* their impact on the Portuguese colonial empire. Among other examples, the political, diplomatic, economic and scientific-technical instrumental and strategic use given by the Portuguese empire-state, in different historical contexts and with diverse motivations and rationales, to its participation in international institutions supports this assertion, as this article has demonstrated.[49]

[48]   Martin Shipway, 'Reformism and the French "Official Mind": The 1944 Brazzaville Conference and the Legacy of Popular Front', in *French Colonial Empire and the Popular Front: Hope and Disillusion*, ed. by Tony Chafer and Amanda Sackur (Basingstoke: Macmillan, 1999), pp. 131–51 (p. 131). Frederick Cooper, *Decolonization and African Society*, pp. 361–83; Jerónimo and Pinto, 'A Modernizing Empire? Politics, Culture and Economy in Portuguese Late Colonialism'. See also Daniel Maul, *Human Rights, Development and Decolonization* (New York: Palgrave Macmillan), pp. 152–227.
[49]   Mark Mazower, *Governing the World*, p. 422.

The United States and Portuguese Decolonization

Luís Nuno Rodrigues

ISCTE-Instituto Universitário de Lisboa

Introduction

In late 1943, George Kennan, United States *chargé d'affaires* in Lisbon, sent a long telegram to the State Department trying to convince Washington of the right strategy to take in negotiations with the Portuguese government for the concession of facilities in the strategically located islands of the Azores. The creation of an American military base in the Azores had been considered by the Joint Chiefs of Staff as 'fundamental' in terms of US projection of power through the Atlantic Ocean to Europe, Africa, and the Middle East. Kennan believed that 'unless we are willing to connive at the overthrow of Dr. Salazar [...] we must gain his confidence. In order to do that, we needed to have some kind of *quid pro quo* to offer to Salazar.' In his opinion, the most important offer would be 'assurances to respect Portuguese sovereignty in all Portuguese possessions' and also 'not to retain the facilities after the war without the agreement of the Portuguese Government'.[1] A few days later, the US government followed Kennan's suggestion: 'it is the Department's feeling that there are several important considerations to which you may in your discretion wish to draw Dr. Salazar's attention. First among these in importance is the assurances to respect the sovereignty of Portugal and its entire colonial empire, assurances that have thus far been withheld.'[2]

This decision paved the way for the US–Portuguese agreement, signed in November 1944. The agreement authorized the US to site a military base on the island of Santa Maria 'for the purpose of facilitating the movement of American forces to the theater of war in the Pacific.'[3] In exchange, the United States agreed to restore full Portuguese sovereignty over East Timor, the only territory of the Portuguese Empire that had been occupied by a foreign power (Japan) during World War II. The terms of this agreement would set the tone for US–Portuguese relations in the following decades: on the one hand,

[1] *Foreign Relations of the United States. Diplomatic Papers* (hereinafter FRUS), 1943, vol. II (Washington, DC: US Government Printing Office, 1964), pp. 558–61.
[2] FRUS, 1943, vol. II, pp. 561–62
[3] *United States Treaties and other International Agreements* (hereinafter UST), vol. 2, Part 2 (Washington, DC: US Government Printing Office, 1951), pp. 2124–32.

Portuguese Studies vol. 29 no. 2 (2013), 164–85
© Modern Humanities Research Association 2013

the United States needed the Azores base, whose strategic importance was reinforced with the onset of the Cold War; on the other hand, the Portuguese government considered the maintenance of the Portuguese empire as a 'sacred' and 'historical' mission and also as fundamental for the political survival of the regime led by Oliveira Salazar since 1932.[4]

The Early Cold War

In the early years of the Cold War, Portugal and the United States signed several agreements authorizing American forces to remain in the Azores base, now established on the island of Terceira. The Truman administration never regarded the existence of the Portuguese colonial empire as an obstacle to the establishment and maintenance of a good relationship with Lisbon, even when other European powers were already starting their processes of decolonization. Despite being an authoritarian regime, Portugal was easily integrated into the new international system. The Soviet veto of Portugal's membership of the United Nations, in 1946, was largely offset by Portuguese participation in the Marshall Plan and also by the invitation to become a founding member of NATO. The integration into the American sphere of influence was also marked by agreements regarding the Azores, signed in 1946, 1948 and 1951.[5] All these developments meant that the Portuguese colonial empire would be tolerated at least in the short term. When, in 1950, the Department of State prepared a 'Policy Statement' on Portugal, the four major objectives of American policy were defined as: 'to maintain and improve existing cordial relations [...] to ensure continuation and development of the facilities now granted to us in the Azores [...] to encourage Portuguese participation in efforts to achieve economic, political, and military integration in Western Europe and coordination in North Atlantic area [... and] to aid in the economic and strategic development of Portugal's large African possessions.' The self-determination of Portuguese colonies was never mentioned in the document.[6]

In fact, with the beginning of the Cold War, the major concerns of the Truman administration were the containment of the Soviet Union and the restoration of prosperity in Western Europe; the questions of Africa and the dismantling of the old European empires were relegated to a secondary level. The African continent continued to be seen as 'a colonial appendage of Western Europe',[7] and the Truman Administration became more and more reluctant to

---

[4] On US–Portuguese relations during World War II, see Luís Nuno Rodrigues, *No coração do Atlântico: os Estados Unidos e os Açores (1939–1948)* (Lisbon: Prefácio Editora, 2005).
[5] Luís Nuno Rodrigues, 'Crossroads of the Atlantic: Portugal, the Azores and the Atlantic Community (1943–57)', in *European Community, Atlantic Community?*, ed. by Valerie Aubourg, Gérard Bossuat and Gilles Scott-Smith (Paris: Éditions Soleb, 2008), pp. 456–67.
[6] 'Policy Statement Prepared in the Department of State', 20 October 1950. FRUS, 1950, vol. III (Washington, DC: US Government Printing Office, 1977), pp. 1540–48.
[7] Peter Duignan and L. H. Gann, *The United States and Africa: A History* (Cambridge: Cambridge University Press, 1987), p. 285.

demand self-determination for the African colonies of its NATO and Marshall Plan allies, such as Portugal, France, and Great Britain. As the historian Thomas Noer explained, American leaders feared that a rapid decolonization would 'cripple European economic recovery (and the ability to resist Communism) and produce weak and unstable African nations unable to prevent Soviet subversion.'[8] The new Cold War policy of containment was seen as more important than any new initiative in Africa, and this set of assumptions clearly determined the position of the United States towards Portuguese colonialism.

This scenario, however, would change during the 1950s with the gradual emergence of the anti-colonialist movement, symbolized by the Bandung Conference of 1955 and marked by the gradual dissolution of the British and French empires and the Suez crisis, in 1956. Portugal resisted the wave of decolonization that swept through Asia and Africa in the post-war years but began to experience strong pressure from India regarding its colonial enclaves in the Indian subcontinent. The Indian government claimed the Portuguese territories of Goa, Damão and Diu should be integrated into the Indian Union, just as the old French enclaves had. Portugal always refused to negotiate with India, but in the summer of 1954 the Indian Union isolated the land-locked Portuguese enclaves of Dadra and Nagar Haveli, prohibiting the passage through its territory of any Portuguese authorities and military forces, weapons or ammunition destined for these enclaves.[9]

After these events, Portugal sought the support and international solidarity of the United States. On 26 July 1954, the Portuguese Ambassador in Washington met with the Assistant Secretary of State for European Affairs and requested 'uma declaração oficial dos Estados Unidos condenando a agressão da Índia' [an official declaration by the United States condemning the aggression of India], stressing to the US that it would be 'no seu próprio interesse como grande potência e nosso aliado na NATO' [in its own interest as a great power and our ally in NATO] to exercise 'toda a sua possível influência para levar a União Indiana a modificar a sua atitude' [all its possible influence to bring the Indian Union to modify its attitude].[10] But for the first time since World War II, Portugal would be faced with the reluctance of the United States to support its colonial policy, since the Americans refused to make any public statement condemning the action of the Indian Government in the episode of Dadra and Nagar Haveli. On 9 August, on meeting the US Ambassador in Lisbon, Foreign

---

[8]   Thomas J. Noer, 'New Frontiers and Old Priorities in Africa', in *Kennedy's Quest for Victory: American Foreign Policy, 1961–1963*, ed. by Thomas G. Paterson (New York: Oxford University Press, 1989), p. 254.

[9]   Luís Nuno Rodrigues, 'Os Estados Unidos e a questão de Goa em 1961', *Ler História*, 42 (2002), 41–90. See also Pedro A. Oliveira, *Os despojos da Aliança: a Grã-Bretanha e a questão colonial portuguesa, 1945–1975* (Lisbon: Tinta da China, 2007), pp. 95–103 and Sandrine Bègue, *La Fin de Goa et de l'Estado da Índia: décolonisation et Guerre Froide dans le Sous-Continent Indien (1945–1962)*, 2 vols (Lisbon: Instituto Diplomático, 2007), vol. 1, chapter 6.

[10]   *Vinte anos de defesa do Estado Português da Índia (1947–1967)*, 4 vols (Lisbon: Ministério dos Negócios Estrangeiros, 1967–68), II, 35–36.

Minister Paulo Cunha told him, with 'great bitterness', that the Portuguese government was 'tremendously disappointed' by the fact that the United States had not taken a public stance on the 'imperialist aggression' of the Indian Union.[11]

The Portuguese government immediately suspended negotiations for the renewal of the Azores base until the Eisenhower administration approved the so-called Dulles–Cunha memorandum, prepared in 1955. Following another visit by Paulo Cunha to the United States, the two Governments had reached agreement on a joint statement referring explicitly to the existence of 'Portuguese provinces' — instead of colonies — in Asia. The subtle distinction was crucial for the Portuguese, who claimed they did not have an empire or any colonies in Africa or Asia, but instead 'overseas provinces' with the same constitutional status as the 'continental provinces'. A few days after the issuance of this *communiqué*, John Foster Dulles was questioned by the American press on whether the US government considered Goa to be a 'province'. Dulles replied that 'the whole world considers it as a Portuguese Province', adding that Goa had belonged to Portugal for more than 'four hundred years'. The journalist insisted: 'Mr. Secretary, did you say province or colony?' Dulles was clear once again: 'province', was the reply. Later, Dulles was asked if his declarations were a sign of 'support of the United States to the position of Portugal in the controversy about Goa'. Dulles declared only that the United States was interested in seeing the problem solved by 'peaceful means'.[12] The Dulles–Cunha *communiqué* was a good example of the ambiguity of the Eisenhower administration towards colonialism, already attentive to developments in the global Cold War, but as yet incapable of assuming a forthright position regarding Portuguese colonial policies in India.[13]

Kennedy's New African Policy

The election of John Fitzgerald Kennedy as the thirty-fifth President of the United States, in November 1960, was a matter of serious concern for the Portuguese government, led by 71-year-old dictator, Oliveira Salazar. The major problem after Kennedy took office, according to the Portuguese Ambassador in Washington, Luis Esteves Fernandes, would be 'a adopção oficial de uma política anticolonial subordinada ao princípio da libertação de

---

[11] FRUS, 1952–1954, vol. VI (Washington, DC: US Government Printing Office, 1986), pp. 1744–45.
[12] *Vinte anos de defesa do Estado Português da Índia (1947–1967)*, III, 87–88.
[13] See Odd Arne Westad, *The Global Cold War: Third World Interventions and the Making of our Times* (Cambridge: Cambridge University Press, 2005); Kathryn C. Statler and Andrew I. Johns, *The Eisenhower Administration, the Third World, and the Globalization of the Cold War* (New York: Rowman & Littlefield, 2006); Thomas Borstelmann, *The Cold War and the Color Line: American Race Relations in the Global Arena* (Cambridge, MA: Harvard University Press, 2001); John Kent, 'United States Reactions to Empire, Colonialism, and the Cold War in Black Africa, 1949–1957', *The Journal of Imperial and Commonwealth History*, 33.2 (2005), 195–220.

todos os territórios dependentes' [the official adoption of an anticolonial policy, subordinated to the principle of liberation for all dependent territories].[14] These fears, expressed by Fernandes, would come true in early March 1961. The American Ambassador in Lisbon, Charles Burke Elbrick, received instructions from Secretary of State Dean Rusk to tell Salazar the American government was 'deeply concerned over the deteriorating position of Portugal' both in Africa and in the United Nations, where the newly independent African nations had now a significant weight in the General Assembly. The United States wanted 'to talk frankly and in friendly spirit with Portugal', to influence its government 'to undertake major adjustments in her policies which, as presently constituted, seem to us headed for very serious trouble.' The new administration believed that it was 'increasingly difficult and disadvantageous to Western interests publicly to support or remain silent on Portuguese African policies.'[15]

Dean Rusk also recommended some caution to Ambassador Elbrick. The Secretary of State was 'fully aware' of the 'distasteful nature' of this approach to Salazar and had 'few illusions' that the Portuguese government would change its policies towards the African territories in the near future. Above all, the United States wanted to avoid the appearance of a 'take it or leave it' attitude which could cause a Portuguese 'counter-action, which we do not want' — especially, argued Rusk, if this reaction could somehow affect the American military base in Lajes, Azores, or even Portuguese participation in NATO.[16]

Oliveira Salazar received Charles Elbrick on 7 March 1961. When the Ambassador explained to him the new American policy, he replied that he was 'profoundly concerned' with the 'apparent lack of understanding' by the American government 'as to the dangers which will unquestionably result for the West if the present American policies in Africa are not reversed.' Salazar believed the Soviet Union was 'actively engaged in attempting to bring about the downfall of the two nations of the Iberian Peninsula.' The Russians were 'attacking Portugal via Africa and it would appear that the Americans are ingenuously playing their game.' Salazar also warned Elbrick it was 'manifestly impossible to be an ally of Portugal in Europe and an enemy in Africa.'[17]

This *démarche* marked a real turning point in the relations between Portugal

[14]   Letter from the Portuguese Ambassador in Washington to the Portuguese Ministry of Foreign Affairs, Historical-Diplomatic Archive, Lisbon, Box 288, MNE-SE, PAA. On the new African policy of the Kennedy administration see, among others, Richard D. Mahoney, *JFK: Ordeal in Africa* (New York: Oxford University Press, 1983); Thomas Noer, 'New Frontiers and Old Priorities in Africa', in *Kennedy's Quest for Victory*, ed. by Thomas G. Paterson (New York: Oxford University Press, 1989), pp. 253–83; David A. Dickson, 'US Foreign Policy toward Southern and Central Africa: The Kennedy and Johnson Years', *Presidential Studies Quarterly*, 23.2 (Spring 1993), 301–15; Thomas Borstelmann, '"Hedging Our Bets and Buying Time": John Kennedy and Racial Revolutions in the American South and Southern Africa', *Diplomatic History*, 24.3 (Summer 2000), 435–63; and Phil Muehlenbeck, 'Kennedy and Touré: A Success in Personal Diplomacy', *Diplomacy & Statecraft*, 19.1 (2008), 69–95.
[15]   FRUS, 1961–1963, vol. XIII (Washington, DC: US Government Printing Office, 1993), pp. 895–97.
[16]   FRUS, 1961–1963, vol. XIII, pp. 895–97.
[17]   'Lisbon 572, March 7, 1961', National Archives and Records Administration (hereinafter NA), State Department Central Files (SDCF), 1960–63, Box 1813.

and the United States. The American government had given Salazar formal notice that it had changed its policy towards Portuguese colonialism. One week later, in the aftermath of the first rebellions against Portuguese rule in Angola, the US delegation voted in favour of a UN Security Council resolution on Portuguese colonialism. The Security Council, 'taking note of the recent disturbances and conflicts in Angola resulting in loss of life of the inhabitants, the continuance of which is likely to endanger the maintenance of international peace and security', called upon Portugal to 'consider urgently the introduction of measures and reforms in Angola'. The Security Council also decided to appoint a subcommittee 'to examine the statements made before the Security Council concerning Angola, to receive further statements and documents and to conduct such inquiries as it may deem necessary and to report to the Security Council as soon as possible.'[18] However, the resolution was not approved. There were five votes in favour (among them the United States and the Soviet Union) but six abstentions (including Great Britain, France and China). In Lisbon, the defeat of the resolution was received with jubilation, but even so the American vote caused strong indignation. The colonial war in Angola had begun and the Portuguese government could not accept the 'casual manner' in which the United States dealt with the African problem, which was of 'such vital importance' to Portugal. In late March, Franco Nogueira, of the Ministry of Foreign Affairs, explained to Ambassador Elbrick that the Portuguese government did not understand American tactics 'in publicly attacking Portugal in the Security Council' only one week after making 'private and confidential approaches' to Salazar. Nogueira pointed out that no Portuguese government could survive the loss of the overseas territories, and therefore the result of American policy 'if pursued to its logical conclusion, would produce a neutralized or even a communist beachhead in the Iberian Peninsula.' Since Portugal and Spain were 'inextricably bound together', any political turmoil in Portugal would be 'immediately echoed' in Spain.[19]

The new policy of the United States in the United Nations continued throughout 1961 and part of 1962. The United States delegation (USUN) voted in favour of resolutions concerning Portuguese colonialism in the General Assembly, in April 1961, in the Security Council, in June 1961, and again in the General Assembly, in December 1961 and January 1962. Moreover, the deterioration of Portuguese–American relations was further aggravated by other policies that brought great distress to the Portuguese government. For instance, the American government intensified its contacts with Angolan nationalist groups, especially the UPA, led by Holden Roberto. The contacts with Roberto, although existent before the beginning of the war in Angola, were significantly intensified from March 1961, with the Department of State

---

[18]   *Department of State Bulletin*, April 3, 1961 (Washington, DC: US Government Printing Office, 1961), p. 499.
[19]   'Lisbon 701, March 30, 1961', NA, SDCF, 1960–63, Box 1260.

instructing the Embassy in Leopoldville to maintain close contacts with the UPA. On the other hand, the administration implemented a new arms policy towards Portugal, officially announced to the Portuguese government in August 1961. From that time on the United States refused to sell Portugal military equipment destined to 'non-NATO' purposes, that is, military equipment that could be used in Africa.[20] As Ambassador Elbrick stated after informing the Portuguese government of the new arms policy, this was indeed the 'latest nail in the coffin of United States–Portuguese relations'.[21]

The Cold War and the Azores

But the reports of the death of US–Portuguese relations were clearly exaggerated. The new policy adopted by the Kennedy Administration towards Portuguese colonialism would be short-lived and from mid-1962 a gradual reversal in the attitude of the United States began to take place. Not only did the American delegation in the United Nations begin to abstain or to vote against resolutions on Portuguese territories, but the administration also authorized several sales of military equipment to Portugal. Moreover, the contacts with the Angolan nationalists were significantly reduced and downgraded. From late October 1962 onwards the USUN and the State Department were even forbidden to receive Holden Roberto.

If one needed to single out the single major factor behind this reversal, it must surely be the US military base in the Azores and its indispensability in military and strategic terms. The base in the Portuguese islands was indeed vital to American strategic and security interests during the Cold War and its 'inability [...] to circumvent the need for a few acres of asphalt', as John Kenneth Galbraith once wrote,[22] was the major point conditioning United States policy towards Portuguese colonialism. The importance of the Azores base explains why both the Department of Defense and the Joints Chiefs of Staff regarded with apprehension the initial change of policy followed by the Kennedy Administration regarding Portuguese colonialism and its possible consequences on the future of the American base. The military feared that the anticolonial stance of the Administration could cause a deterioration of relations with Portugal and put at risk the utilization of the base, especially as the agreement that authorized the presence of US forces in the Azores would end on 31 December 1962.

The first major statement made by the Pentagon on this subject came in July 1961, during the proceedings of an interdepartmental 'Presidential Task Force' created by Kennedy to deal with the issue of 'Portuguese Territories' in

---

[20]   See Luís Nuno Rodrigues, *Kennedy–Salazar: a crise de uma aliança. As relações luso-americanas entre 1961 e 1963* (Lisbon: Notícias Editorial, 2002).
[21]   'Lisbon 240, August 16, 1961.' NA, SDCF, 1960–63, Box 1817.
[22]   FRUS, 1961–1963, vol. XIII, pp. 908–10.

Africa. In the report prepared for the Task Force, the Department of Defense considered that retention of military facilities in the Azores was 'vital to our ability to execute required military missions under wartime and emergency conditions.' The loss of the Azores would be 'most serious from a military point of view for the foreseeable future.' It would require a 'major overhaul of United States wartime plans', because the existing war plans could not be carried out 'if access to the Azores were denied'. The Department of Defense saw 'no suitable alternatives for the Azores route'.[23]

These recommendations made their way into the discussion and the final result of the Task Force on Portuguese Territories — National Security Action Memorandum 60, of July 1961 — incorporated the view from the Department of Defense. NSAM 60 included twelve 'recommendations for action' which dealt primarily with the situation in Portuguese Africa, but the Department of Defense pressed for a final recommendation that all other actions should be implemented 'quietly insofar as possible and in a manner [...] to minimize the possibility of losing the Azores; recognizing the grave military consequences which would attend such a loss.'[24]

Apart from the reports and recommendations from the military establishment, the importance of the Azores base would be fully revealed in a crucial episode that occurred two months before the expiration of the existing agreement. In late October 1962, the United States and the Soviet Union came to the brink of war over the Cuban missile crisis. During this episode, the Azores were essential for surveillance of Soviet submarine activity in the Atlantic. Coincidentally, Franco Nogueira, now Minister for Foreign Affairs, was in Washington during the Cuban missile crisis, and both President Kennedy and Dean Rusk asked him for assurances that the Portuguese would not put any restrictions on the use of the Azores base during the 'present emergency'. Kennedy wanted 'some public declaration, even a vague one', but Nogueira replied that in the present state of Portuguese–American relations such a declaration was impossible.[25] Later that day, after receiving Nogueira's report, Salazar only authorized the Portuguese representative in the North Atlantic Council to make a formal statement regarding the Cuban crisis. The Portuguese government, recognizing the existence of a 'serious threat to the United States and therefore to the security of the West', believed that NATO countries should 'state their solidarity with the measures taken by the United States government'. This belief was reinforced by the fact that 'the Portuguese government has always considered, in relation to any attack on positions where the defense of the interests of the West are at stake, that this solidarity should be indivisible.'[26] The last phrase of the Portuguese statement was a clear allusion to the situation in Angola, where the

---

[23] 'Presidential Task Force on Portuguese Territories in Africa. Report. July 12, 1961.' NA, SDCF, 1960–63, Box 1816.
[24] FRUS, 1961–1963, vol. XIII, pp. 901–02.
[25] Franco Nogueira, *Diálogos Interditos*, 2 vols (Lisbon: Ed. Intervenção, 1979), I, 176–83.
[26] 'Lisbon 319, October 24, 1962.' NA, SDCF, 1960–63, Box 1814.

Portuguese government had always considered that the interests of the West were 'at stake.' As Nogueira assured an astonished Ambassador Elbrick a few days later, 'after two or three more Cubas the United States will see the light and support Portugal.'[27]

Besides the importance of the Azores base for US national security and Cold War objectives, other factors should be added to explain the reversal of Kennedy's policies, such as the divisions within the administration regarding foreign policy priorities, Congressional distaste for the anticolonial policies of the Kennedy administration, and the support Portugal received from other European countries.[28] All these factors forced the White House and the Department of State to review the basic principles that had guided its policy towards Africa since early 1961, and from mid-1962 onwards a gradual reversal in the behaviour of the American administration would take place. In the UN Committee on Decolonization, the USUN voted against two resolutions regarding Portuguese territories in the summer of 1962 and against a Fourth Committee (and then plenary) General Assembly resolution in late 1962. It also abstained on the Committee of 24 resolution of April 1963 and on the Security Council resolution of July 1963. Finally, it abstained on a Fourth Committee (and then plenary) General Assembly resolution in late 1963. During this period, the only vote from the US in favour of a resolution concerning Portuguese colonialism came in December 1963, on the most moderate Security Council resolution since March 1961.

The US administration also reversed its policy on the sale of military equipment to Portugal. Despite the maintenance of the official embargo, in 1962 and 1963 there were several sales of military equipment to Portugal and a significant quantity of this equipment ended up in Africa, being used in the Portuguese colonial wars. Since the administration could base its decision for sale on verification from its military attachés in Lisbon that the arms were 'for NATO use,' it did not require any official statements from the Portuguese government on the end-use of these arms and equipment.

The contacts with the Angolan nationalists were also significantly reduced. As mentioned above, the USUN and the Department of State were forbidden to receive Holden Roberto. This fact even led the Angolan leader to write directly to President Kennedy in late 1962. Roberto evoked the 'growing indignation of the Angolan people over the identification of United States policies regarding Angola with the aims of those of Portugal'.[29]

Finally, in April 1962, the United States made a major financial contribution to Portugal, allowing the Export-Import Bank to provide $55 million 'to finance the export of United States steel' for the construction of a bridge across the Tagus

---

[27] 'Official-Informal' letter from Burke Elbrick to William Tyler, 15 November 1962. NA, State Department Lot Files (SDLF), 68D401, Entry 5296, Box 2.
[28] For a deeper analysis of all these factors see Luís Nuno Rodrigues, *Kennedy–Salazar*, chapter 3.
[29] Letter from Holden Roberto to John F. Kennedy, 19 December 1962, NA, SDLF 68D401, Entry 5296, Box 4.

river in Lisbon.[30] Reporting the impact of this loan in Portugal, Ambassador Elbrick noted the 'excellent coverage' given by Portuguese press, radio and TV. The coverage represented 'a rare event and a gratifying deviation from what has become almost customary treatment of United States news.'[31]

The Johnson Administration

During the presidency of Lyndon Johnson, the behaviour of the United States regarding Portuguese colonialism continued to follow the trend started in 1962 and 1963. Gradually, the United States ceased to exert any significant pressure on the Portuguese government to accept the principle of self-determination and silence became the keyword as far as Portuguese colonialism was concerned. Portuguese Africa had virtually become a non-issue within the administration, completely absorbed and submerged by other problems, such as the involvement in Vietnam.

The assumption of the Presidency by Lyndon Johnson reinforced the 'peripheralization' of African issues, and particularly of Portuguese African issues, in Washington. According to Terrence Lyons, the reasons for this situation were, above all, Johnson's 'obsession with fighting the war in Vietnam' and also his 'domestic concerns' with the creation of the Great Society. As a consequence of the American 'overextension in southeast Asia', the administration again relied on the European powers to handle African affairs. Lyons believes that Johnson 'explicitly urged former European colonial powers to take more responsibility in Africa.'[32]

The role of the Vietnam War deserves to be emphasized. Thomas Noer pointed out that the war 'crushed any remaining possibility for renewed efforts to force Portugal to compromise' in Africa. In his view, Vietnam 'effectively subjugated all African issues, including the struggle in the Portuguese territories.'[33] Moreover, the Portuguese government shrewdly turned the Vietnam War to its own advantage. When, in early 1965, Ambassador Anderson met with Franco Nogueira, the Portuguese Minister expressed all his 'understanding and approval' of the American course of action in Indochina. Although in the course of the conversation Nogueira did not 'explicitly draw a parallel between the Vietnam and Portuguese African situations', Anderson reported, there was 'little doubt from what he said that he had this in mind.'[34]

Nevertheless, the United States would try one last time to persuade the

---

[30] 'Financial Assistance to Portugal', 23 March 1962. NA, SDLF, Entry 3093, Box 2.
[31] 'Joint Weeka N° 17', 27 April 1962. NA, SDCF, 1960–63, Box 1815, 753.00 (W)/4–2762.
[32] Terrence Lyons, 'Keeping Africa off the Agenda', in *Lyndon Johnson Confronts the World: American Foreign Policy, 1963–1968*, ed. by Warren Cohen and Nancy Bernkopf Tucker (Cambridge: Cambridge University Press, 1994), pp. 245–78 (pp. 246–48).
[33] Thomas J. Noer, *Cold War and Black Liberation: The United States and White Rule in Africa, 1948–1968* (Columbia: University of Missouri Press, 1985), p. 123.
[34] 'Joint Weeka, February 13, 1965.' NA, SDCF, 1964–1966, Box 2599.

Portuguese government to change its stance on Africa. In October 1965, Ambassador Anderson presented to Salazar the so-called 'Anderson Plan' for a peaceful solution to the problem of Portuguese Africa. According to the final version of the plan, Portugal should accept a date — eight years from the time of agreement — for 'a broadly internationally supervised plebiscite or referendum in Portuguese African territories'. In the referendum, the options would include 'complete independence, autonomous commonwealth status or continued integration with the metropole as part of the Portuguese nation.' The US also considered it essential that 'increasingly free political activity would be permitted in order to permit a meaningful plebiscite'. The Portuguese government should present this proposal to African leaders, 'and thereby initiate a dialogue which might result in meaningful negotiations.' The US and other nations, 'most especially other NATO countries', would encourage 'African acceptance and would urge the fulfillment of the terms of agreement and would also publicly condemn any violation of the terms.' Moreover, the US 'would itself provide and would encourage other NATO allies to provide, if Portugal so requests, economic and technical support.' The United Nations and its specialized agencies should be allowed 'to observe and report on developments and provide assistance'. Anderson concluded that the acceptance of this plan would move the 'resolution of the Portuguese African problem from the battlefield to the developmental and plebiscite channels.'[35]

When Anderson presented his plan to Salazar, the Portuguese leader's response was cautious and noncommittal. Anderson defined his plan as a 'sincere effort to come to grips with what the United States saw as a most serious problem in a manner consistent with the high principles held by all parties involved.' He also stressed that this proposal 'differed significantly from earlier ones and deserved to be viewed objectively and on its merits.' Salazar raised several objections and preferred to discuss the general issue of Portuguese Africa instead of the specifics of the programme. He said that 'Americans in general seem to feel that the civilizing of African peoples to the point of adequately governing themselves can be accomplished in a matter of years', while the 'Portuguese experience does not confirm this but rather suggested that centuries are required.' Salazar dismissed Anderson, stating that the Portuguese government 'had given, is giving and will continue to give serious consideration to the proposal advanced by the United States.' He urged the Ambassador to continue his discussions with the Foreign Minister.[36]

Five months later, in March 1966, Franco Nogueira indicated Portugal's rejection of the plan. Nogueira told Anderson the Portuguese government had given 'much consideration' to this matter but it was impossible 'to make any

[35]   'Summary of Ambassador's April 13 Proposal for New Initiative to Portugal on Question of Portuguese African Territories and Department's June 9 Response.' NA, SDLF 68D401, Entry 5296, Box 7.
[36]   'Transmitting Memorandum of Ambassador Anderson's Conversation on October 22, 1965, with Prime Minister Salazar, Lisbon A-162, November 3, 1965.' NA, SDCF, 1964–1966, Box 2604.

public announcement under any conditions in regard to an ultimate goal of self-determination simply because this would set in motion events which would quickly get out of control.' Nogueira did not doubt 'the good faith of the United States' but he felt that 'any assurances given now would not be binding for any length of time [...] because the pressures both internally and externally on the United States would be so great that before very long they would be back at Portugal either directly or in the United Nations demanding premature action.'[37]

After this conversation, Ambassador Anderson concluded there was 'absolutely no change likely in the immediate future in the attitude and determination of the Portuguese government with respect to their African provinces.' For the future, Ambassador Anderson recommended 'we let this pot simmer on the back burner until some significant event makes a new approach advisable.' Therefore, 'without abandoning our principles looking towards government by the consent of the governed', the Ambassador saw 'no purpose to be gained by unnecessarily precipitating irritations in Portuguese–United States relations.'[38] Anderson even suggested that in the future, the US should be 'as liberal as we can possibly be in permitting Portugal to obtain export licenses for military equipment except lethal weapons and combatant aircraft, so long as Portugal continued to conduct her military operations as defensive measures and continued to respect international frontiers.'[39]

The next relevant document related to Portuguese–American relations was prepared in 1966 by Everett Briggs, then Second Secretary of the American Embassy in Lisbon. The document announced the complete revision of American policy towards Portugal that would occur during the Nixon administration. Briggs proposed a new 'pragmatic' approach to the Portuguese problem rather than the old 'ideological' one. He believed it was no use for American policymakers to insist on self-determination for Portuguese Africa. The 'insistence on self-determination as a practical solution for Portuguese Africa' was completely 'unrealistic'. The administration needed to 'keep the historical record clean' and would officially continue attached to 'the principle of self-determination'. Nevertheless, this could not be the policy followed 'on the field' and 'should not prevent us from adopting a practical policy based on recognition of the trend towards change in Portuguese Africa.' According to Briggs, 'we should seek instead to reorient our thinking and action with respect to the problems of Portuguese Africa and get out of the ideological vicious circle in which we have been trapped for five years.'[40]

---

[37] 'Portuguese Policy Towards African Provinces: Conversation with Foreign Minister on March 2, 1966, Lisbon A-328, March 14, 1966.' NA, SDCF, 1964–1966, Box 2600.
[38] 'Portuguese Policy Towards African Provinces: Conversation with Foreign Minister on March 2, 1966, Lisbon A-328, March 14, 1966.' NA, SDCF, 1964–1966, Box 2600.
[39] 'Year End Policy Assessment — Portugal, Lisbon A-334, March 14, 1966.' NA, SDCF, 1964–1966, Box 2598.
[40] 'United States Policy Towards Portuguese Africa: A Commentary, Lisbon A-425, May 11, 1966.' NA, SDCF, 1964–1966, Box 2604.

Briggs proposed the US recognized that 'even under Portuguese rule a positive trend towards change is finally under way in the colonies.' The administration should consider 'whether our current policies towards Portugal, including specifically our United Nations votes and our military sales restrictions, are effective and are enhancing the rate at which change-for-the-better can occur in the territories.' Finally, the US should find ways 'to assist Portugal to prepare its colonies for a better economic and social future without too much concern for the current political development of the areas.' Briggs considered change to be inevitable, 'for too many children are now attending too many schools and being given the tools of civilization to think that Portugal will be able to contain them indefinitely within the rigid, paternalistic, colonial, system of today.'[41]

Briggs's ideas were obviously subscribed to by the new Ambassador in Lisbon, Tapley Bennett. In early 1967, Bennett confided to Eugene Rostow, the Under Secretary for Political Affairs, that he hoped the US would be able to 'look beyond the aggravation they cause us and avoid slapping them unnecessarily.' In fact, if the administration 'must buffet our hyper-sensitive NATO ally, Portugal, it would be better to use gloves than bare knuckles. Knuckles are not very productive with people like the Portuguese; they merely lick their bruises and resent the treatment.'[42]

'The Whites are here to stay'

In 1968 there were important political changes in both countries. In Lisbon, Marcello Caetano, who represented the more 'liberal' wing of the regime, replaced Salazar. Caetano, however, did not introduce any significant changes in terms of Portuguese colonial policy. The wars continued in Angola, Mozambique and Guinea, despite the promise of constitutional reforms announced by the new government. In Washington, Richard Nixon was elected President, putting an end to eight years of Democratic government under Kennedy and Johnson.

A few months after his inauguration, Nixon ordered the National Security Council to produce a 'comprehensive review of US policy toward Southern Africa'.[43] The final result of this review, National Security Study Memorandum 39, recommended sweeping changes to the policy followed in the previous years. The US had been trying to balance 'economic, scientific and strategic interests in the white states with the political interest of dissociating the US from the white minority regimes and their repressive racial policies.' The attempt to reconcile these opposing perspectives had led, in the previous administrations,

[41]   'United States Policy Towards Portuguese Africa: A Commentary, Lisbon A-425, May 11, 1966.' NA, SDCF, 1964–1966, Box 2604.
[42]   Official-Informal letter from Tapley Bennett, Jr., to Eugene Rostow, 9 January 1967. NA, SDCF, 1967–1969, Box 2441.
[43]   FRUS, 1969–1976, vol. XXVIII (Washington, DC: United States Government Printing Office, 2011), p. 9.

to decisions 'made ad hoc, on a judgment of benefits and political costs at a given moment.' The study presented several options for the future, but the administration eventually chose Option 2, the so-called 'Tar Baby Option'. The basic premise was that 'the whites are here to stay and the only way that constructive change can come about is through them.' Moreover, 'there is no hope for the blacks to gain the political rights they seek through violence, which will only lead to chaos and increased opportunities for the communists.' Therefore, the US should adopt 'selective relaxation of our stance toward the white regimes' in order to 'encourage some modification of their current racial and colonial policies.' Regarding Portugal and Portuguese colonialism, the paper advised the administration to accept 'present Portuguese policies as suggesting further changes in the Portuguese Territories', but continued 'discussions with Portuguese on African policy'. The arms embargo should be maintained but the US should give 'more liberal treatment to exports of dual purpose equipment'. At the same time, the Nixon administration should 'encourage trade and investment in Portuguese Territories' and 'full Export-Import Bank facilities'. Richard Nixon personally believed the US should be 'realistic' in its relations with southern Africa. It was 'obvious that we have to avoid the colonialist label but we must analyze where our national interest lies and not worry too much about other peoples' domestic policies'. It was undisputable to the President that 'the whites can't go home' and that 'they are there to stay'.[44]

Relations with Portugal improved immediately. In fact, even before NSSM's final approval Nixon had already promised Caetano, who visited the US for Eisenhower's funeral, that the Americans were going to support the Portuguese government. Following this conversation, the Nixon administration decided to reduce or suspend US official support for nationalist movements in Portuguese Africa.[45] On January 1970, the administration also approved that 'non-lethal equipment which has dual civilian and military uses will be excepted from the arms embargo on Portugal'.[46] American abstention on UN resolutions on Portuguese colonialism became normal practice. At the same time, the Nixon administration also adopted 'several measures aimed at encouraging US private investment in Lusophone Africa, and facilitate the granting of credits to projects in the Portuguese overseas provinces'.[47]

The relaxation of tensions and the new policies in Washington led Marcello Caetano to accept a resumption of talks on the Azores base, suspended since 1962. In December 1971 both countries reached an agreement extending American base rights until 1974. This agreement marked a big change compared

---

[44]   FRUS, 1969–1976, vol. XXVIII, pp. 34–56
[45]   Witney W. Schneidman, *Engaging Africa: Washington and the Fall of Portugal's Colonial Empire* (Lanham, MD: University Press of America, 2004), p. 112.
[46]   FRUS, 1969–1976, vol. XXVIII, p. 69.
[47]   Pedro Aires Oliveira, 'A política externa do marcelismo: a questão africana', in *Diplomacia & guerra: política externa e política de defesa em Portugal. Do final da Monarquia ao Marcelismo*, ed. by Fernando Martins (Évora: CIDEHUS, 2001), pp. 244–45.

to the previous ones. In exchange for the continued use of the Azores base, the United States agreed to provide unprecedented advantages to Portugal: 400 million dollars in grants and loans from the Export-Import Bank, 15 million dollars a year in Public Law 480 grain shipments, 5 million dollars' worth of 'drawing rights from Government lists of surplus non-military equipment', the loan of a 'hydrographic survey vessel', one million dollars in 'educational assistance' from the Pentagon budget, and 'the waiver of Portuguese support payments for the US military advisory assistance group in Lisbon'.[48]

The White House refused to submit this agreement to the Senate as a Treaty, claiming the Azores base was a NATO facility and the agreement had been signed under the NATO charter. This provoked strong reaction in some sectors of Congress. The Nixon administration was accused of aiding a non-democratic and colonial government. Charles Diggs, Chairman of the Subcommittee on Africa of the House Committee on Foreign Affairs considered this an 'infamous agreement'. In his opinion, the terms of the agreement had only one possible meaning: 'a deliberate decision at the highest level of this Government to announce to the world that the United States stands with Portugal [...] the United States in effect turned its back on its support for self-determination in Africa.' The Portuguese position on the 1971 agreement fuelled this reaction. Marcello Caetano declared publicly: 'the treaty is a political act in which the solidarity of interests between the two countries is recognized and it is in the name of that solidarity that we put an instrument of action at the disposal of our American friends, who are also new allies.'[49]

Two years later, during the Yom Kippur war, the US would use the Azores base to mount a massive arms lift to Israel. During the war, the US armed forces were able to 'rotate 42 flights through Lajes in a 24-hour period'.[50] The use of Lajes was the result of intense pressure on Portuguese officials by Secretary of State Henry Kissinger. The base became particularly significant at that time because all other NATO allies refused the use of their territories or bases to ship military supplies to Israel; Portugal, therefore, was the only NATO country to allow the United States to use its facilities.[51] In December 1973, Kissinger visited Portugal and declared the United States was 'extremely grateful' for Portuguese support during the Middle East crisis, and that both countries

[48] *The Complex of United States Portuguese Relations: Before and After the Coup*, Hearings before the Subcommittee on Africa of the Committee on Foreign Affairs, House of Representatives, 93rd Congress, 2nd Session (Washington, DC: United States Government Printing Office, 1974), p. 2. For the entire agreement see *Issues in United States Relations with Spain and Portugal. Report prepared for the Subcommittee on Europe and the Middle East of the Committee on Foreign Affairs*, US House of Representatives (Washington, DC: Library of Congress, 1979), p. 56.
[49] *The Complex of United States Portuguese Relations*, pp. 2, 184.
[50] *Congressional Research Service, US Military Installations in NATO's Southern Region*, Report prepared for the Subcommittee on Europe and the Middle East of the Committee on Foreign Affairs, US House of Representatives, 99th Congress, 2nd Session, quoted by Simon Duke, *United States Military Forces and Installations in Europe* (New York: Oxford University Press, 1989), p. 245.
[51] Witney W. Schneidman, *Engaging Africa*, pp. 134–35.

would be 'even better friends than we are now'.[52] The Portuguese government took the opportunity to persuade Kissinger to approve or facilitate the sale of anti-aircraft missiles that Portugal needed in Guinea, where it was feared that the PAIGC was on the verge of using missiles of Soviet origin. According to a former Portuguese official, on the eve of the military coup of 25 April 1974 a shipment of missiles for Portugal was being prepared in West Germany.[53]

Again, this policy faced strong opposition in Congress, where critical voices against Portuguese colonialism continued to be heard. Congress approved the 'Tunney-Young' amendment, which made congressional authorization mandatory for sales of military equipment to Portugal.[54] Since mid-March 1974, the Subcommittee on Africa of the House Committee on Foreign Affairs had been holding hearings on 'The Complex of United States Portuguese Relations'. Portuguese colonialism was the main subject of lively discussions in this subcommittee when the military coup of 25 April 1974 occurred, over-throwing Marcello Caetano's government in Portugal and putting an end to the dictatorship that governed Portugal since 1932.[55]

The United States and the End of the Portuguese Empire

The new political and military authorities in Lisbon were divided over the future of the Portuguese colonies. The new Portuguese President, António de Spínola, had written a book in early 1974, outlining his proposal for a 'Federation of States' or 'Lusitanian Community', inspired by the ideas of General de Gaulle. According to Spínola, the Portuguese colonies in Africa should follow a process of self-determination, though not necessarily equivalent to immediate independence or a simple transfer of power to the liberation movements that had fought against Portuguese rule in Africa. Self-determination was supposed to mean a choice between several possibilities: continuation under Portuguese sovereignty, creation of a new political structure (federation or commonwealth) under which the territories maintained strong links to Portugal, or independence. The populations living in the Portuguese territories should choose among these several options, each defended by different political and social groups in the colonies. Therefore, even after the coup in Lisbon, the new Portuguese President refused to recognize PAIGC, FRELIMO or even the three Angolan movements as the sole legitimate representatives of the peoples

---

[52]   *The Complex of United States Portuguese Relations*, p. 54.
[53]   J. Calvet de Magalhães, 'Estados Unidos da América, relações com os', in *Dicionário de História de Portugal*, ed. by António Barreto and Maria Filomena Mónica, Suplemento, vol. VII (Lisbon: Livraria Figueirinhas, 2000), p. 675. See also Witney W. Schneidman, *Engaging Africa*, pp. 135–36.
[54]   Cf. Pedro Aires Oliveira, 'A política externa do marcelismo', p. 243 and also José Freire Antunes, *Nixon e Caetano: promessas e abandono* (Lisbon: Difusão Cultural, 1992), pp. 267–68.
[55]   *The Complex of United States Portuguese Relations: Before and After the Coup*, Hearings before the Subcommittee on Africa of the Committee on Foreign Affairs, House of Representatives, 93rd Congress, 2nd Session, 1974.

in their territories, as the United Nations had already done. In the weeks that followed regime change in Lisbon, Spínola offered the liberation movements an immediate cease-fire with no pre-conditions. The nationalists, he argued, should organize themselves as political associations that could spread their political message and, in a promised democratic environment, make their political campaigns until the final act of self-determination. It was not clear, in Spínola's several statements, how long this process was going to take.

At home, however, there was a lack of consensus regarding decolonization. The majority of the new political parties that emerged in Portugal, and the young officers of the Armed Forces Movement (MFA) that had planned and executed the coup of April 1974, seemed to oppose Spínola's ideas — now regarded as conservative and 'neo-colonialist' — and favoured a rapid decolonization with independence and transfer of power to the nationalist movements.[56] On 10 June 1974, *The New York Times* reported Spínola's difficulties, identifying another major obstacle to his plans: the General had 'pledged to grant the colonies self-determination while the nationalist movements are demanding outright independence'.[57] In fact, PAIGC, FRELIMO and the Angolan movements bluntly rejected Lisbon's proposals for a cease-fire. It quickly became clear the nationalist movements would only accept a cease-fire when the Portuguese authorities declared they were willing to discuss independence and a transfer of power. For them, decolonization should be immediate, not a gradual process of self-determination and, above all, no other parties should be involved in negotiations with Portugal. The movements considered themselves as the only legitimate representatives of the will of their peoples and this legitimacy, they argued, had already been confirmed by the United Nations. In the case of Guinea, the nationalists had already proclaimed the Republic of Guinea-Bissau, in September 1973, and more than eighty countries had since recognized the new independent country.[58]

The international context of the mid-1970s was also decisive to promoting the rapid end of the Portuguese empire. International pressure for Portuguese decolonization had been particularly intense over the 1960s and the first years of the 1970s, with frequent resolutions approved by the UN Security Council and General Assembly. Moreover, the Portuguese military coup and the subsequent process of decolonization occurred at a very particular moment of the Cold War, marked by *Détente*, a political crisis in the United States, and the growing importance and protagonism of Western European countries, governed by parties belonging to the Socialist International.[59] Thus, when the military

---

[56]   Luís Nuno Rodrigues, *Spínola* (Lisbon: Esfera dos Livros, 2010), pp. 283–84. See also Norrie MacQueen, *The Decolonization of Portuguese Africa: Metropolitan Revolution and the Dissolution of Empire* (London: Longman, 1997).

[57]   *The New York Times*, 10 June 1974, p. 65.

[58]   A. E. Duarte Silva, 'O litígio entre Portugal e a ONU (1960–1974)', *Análise Social*, 30.130 (1995), 5–50 (pp. 43–44).

[59]   On the international context of Portuguese transition and decolonization see the recent works of Mario Del Pero, '"Which Chile, Allende?" Henry Kissinger and the Portuguese Revolution.' *Cold*

coup of April 1974 occurred, expectations worldwide were that regime change in Lisbon would lead to the end of the Portuguese empire and the immediate independence of the colonies.

In this context, the Nixon administration was paralysed by its own domestic fragilities. The United States, unlike the UN and the majority of Western European governments, did not exert significant pressure for a rapid decolonization. A briefing paper prepared by the State Department at the end of May 1974 recalled that 'Portugal's provisional government has announced its acceptance of self-determination with all its consequences as a means of solving its colonial problems.' The United States was happy with the policies followed by Spínola, and Ambassador Stuart Scott had already informed the Portuguese leader of 'US sympathy and support for the new government's African policies'. According to this document, Henry Kissinger should cautiously declare that the Nixon administration believed the Portuguese government was being 'sincere in its efforts to resolve the question of the status of its African territories in a manner acceptable to the indigenous populations.' The US should not have a direct intervention in this process: 'we do not believe it would be useful for the US to intervene. We believe the problem to be the responsibility of Portugal.'[60]

Kissinger, however, remained sceptical about the future of the Portuguese empire and about Spínola's ability to control the process of decolonization. In December 1973 he had declared in a State Department meeting that for the Portuguese in Africa 'maybe the way to get out is the way de Gaulle did it'.[61] After the coup, however, his position changed. As the Secretary of State put it, just one day after the events in Lisbon, 'they must be crazy to think they can hold the colonies in a more liberal way', adding that '[if they] follow this path they will lose the colonies.' At a meeting held in Algiers on 30 April, Kissinger asked President Houari Boumedienne of Algeria if he had considered the possibility of 'a transitional period of self-Government and autonomy', but not immediate independence, in the Portuguese colonies. Boumedienne replied that, above all, the 'end result should be clear' and Portugal would have to declare the 'independence' of their territories. Kissinger recalled the 'Portuguese mentality' and added that perhaps the colonies were not fully prepared to take the 'big step' towards independence. The Algerian President insisted he wished to 'accelerate' the whole process but Kissinger suggested that

War History, 11.4 (November 2011), 625–57; Tiago Moreira de Sá, *Os Estados Unidos e a democracia portuguesa (1974–1976)* (Lisbon: Instituto Diplomático, 2009); Pedro Aires Oliveira, *Os despojos da Aliança: a Grã-Bretanha e a questão colonial portuguesa, 1945–1975* (Lisbon: Tinta da China, 2007); Ana Mónica Fonseca, 'The Federal Republic of Germany and the Portuguese Transition to Democracy (1974–1976)', *Journal of European Integration History*, 15.1 (2009), 35–56; António José Telo, *História contemporânea de Portugal: do 25 de Abril à actualidade*, 2 vols (Lisbon: Editorial Presença, 2008), particularly vol. II, chapter 8.
[60] 'Your Meeting With UN Secretary General Waldheim At Noon May 31, 1974', telegram from Secretary of State to the White House, May 30, 1974, in <http://aad.archives.gov/aad/createpdf?rid=6 4981&dt=2474&dl=1345>.
[61] 'Minutes of the Secretary of State's Staff Meeting, Washington, December 3, 1973, 3:10 p.m.', in <http://history.state.gov/historicaldocuments/frus1969–76ve06/d71>.

Algeria could support, as 'the first step, self-Government and autonomy' for a 'transitional' period of two years. It was not an American proposal, Kissinger added, but only a 'working hypothesis'. The Algerian President did not agree and replied the US should instead help Portugal to 'liberate' their colonies and any American initiative in this direction would be 'viewed favourably by the entire African continent.'[62]

For a while, António de Spínola believed he could change the balance in the international arena and win support from the Nixon administration for his colonial policies. He was able to meet Richard Nixon on the Azores, on 19 June 1974, when he asked for US support for his domestic and colonial policies. He warned Nixon that Portugal was being threatened by the Communist Party and by radical officers of the MFA and argued that the US should back him in this struggle. Spínola also told Nixon that, a few days earlier, negotiations between Portugal and PAIGC had been suspended because of disagreement over the future of the Cape Verde Islands, among other reasons. Spínola believed that with US support (for instance, a public declaration of the strategic importance of the Cape Verde Islands for the Western Alliance), as well as the support from other countries influenced by the US, Portugal could force the PAIGC to separate Cape Verde from Guinea-Bissau and to accept a referendum in Cape Verde. Apparently, Spínola was now willing to let Guinea go but he wanted to make sure that Cape Verde would exercise self-determination; this would set the tone for Angola and Mozambique and for the rest of Portuguese decolonization, with Guinea being, in the end, the only exception. Therefore, while the Organization of African Unity (OAU), gathered in Mogadishu in mid-June, was pressing the PAIGC not to separate Guinea from Cape Verde, Spínola was trying to get the US to support his claim that Guinea and Cape Verde were two different situations. If they went together, Spínola explained to Nixon, the Soviet Union could probably establish military bases in the strategically located Cape Verde Islands, and control the 'South Atlantic' from there. Therefore, he solemnly required 'international support' from the US to the effect that the situation in Guinea could be 'separated from the other territories'.[63]

But the Nixon administration already had its hands tied with the Watergate scandal and with congressional pressure over presidential initiatives in the area of foreign policy, after the events in Chile in 1973. There were vague promises of support from President Nixon, but no concrete steps in the following weeks to help Spínola and his decolonization plans.[64] Kissinger, for his part, remained sceptical. At the end of June, he would comment again on the situation in Portugal, conveying to his Spanish counterpart, Pedro Cortina Mauri, the conviction that Portugal would have to grant independence to their

[62] 'Meeting with Houari Boumédiene, Secret, Memorandum of Conversation, April 30, 1974', pp. 8–9, in *Kissinger Transcripts*, KT01126 , NSA online.
[63] António de Spínola, *País sem rumo: contributo para a história de uma revolução* (Lisbon: Scire, 1978), pp. 160–61.
[64] See Tiago Moreira de Sá, *Os Estados Unidos e a democracia portuguesa*, p. 183.

territories. When Cortina Mauri reminded him that the new authorities in Lisbon had promised 'self-determination' but not necessarily independence, Kissinger replied, 'but does that not ultimately lead to the same thing? [...] Once promised, you have to grant independence and the process is usually quicker than people anticipate [...] If I have to make a prediction — and this is not a recommendation — I predict that these territories will be independent in less than two years.'[65]

Kissinger was right in his prediction. In July 1974, a strong political crisis erupted in Lisbon, with the resignation of the provisional government led by Palma Carlos. According to a *New York Times* report, Spínola 'suffered a setback' with the fall of the government, failing 'to change the electoral timetable and hold a quick election for the presidency in the hope of strengthening his own authority'.[66] With the country plunged into its first major post-revolutionary political crisis, Spínola's plans for Portuguese decolonization fell apart completely in a matter of weeks.

Under domestic pressure from political parties and the junior officers of the MFA, and international pressure from the UN, the OUA and Western Europe, Spínola would finally sign Law 7/74 or the Decolonization Law, on 27 July 1974. The text of this document stated that the Armed Forces Movement had 'considered it appropriate to clarify the scope' of its initial programme. The announced principle that 'the solution for the overseas wars is political, not military', presented in the AFM programme, meant, 'according to the Charter of the United Nations, recognition by Portugal of the right of peoples to self-determination.' Secondly, the recognition of the right to self-determination, 'with all its consequences', included 'the acceptance of independence for the overseas territories'. Finally, the Law clarified that the President, after listening to the Junta of National Salvation, the Council of State and the Provisional Government, had the authority to 'conduct actions and to conclude agreements regarding the exercise of the right recognized in previous articles'.[67] A few days before Nixon's resignation, the American embassy in Lisbon reported that the Decolonization Law had finally brought to the Portuguese 'expressions of satisfaction and relief that the long and costly wars were now at end'. After so many years, 'the crux of the overseas problem was now solved.'[68] For the United States, however, the Portuguese decision to give independence to its former African colonies did not represent the end of a process but rather the

[65] 'Secretary's Informal Lunch, Madison Dining Room, Secret, Memorandum of Conversation, June 21, 1974', pp. 2–3, in Kissinger Transcripts, KT01228, NSA online.
[66] *The New York Times*, 10 July 1974, p. 77.
[67] Law 7/74, 27 July 1974, in <http://www1.ci.uc.pt/cd25a/wikka.php?wakka=descono3>.
[68] 'Reaction To Spinola Speech On Portuguese Territories', telegram from the American Embassy in Lisbon to the Secretary of State, 29 July 1974, in <http://aad.archives.gov/aad/createpdf?rid=117085&dt=2474&dl=1345>.

beginning of a large-scale involvement in the Angolan civil war that would start in 1975.[69]

Conclusions

The position of the United States regarding Portuguese colonialism and decolonization followed the general patterns of US African policy during the Cold War. In the early years of American–Soviet rivalry, the Truman administration decided that European recovery and containment of the Soviet Union were by far the top priorities of its foreign policy; the end of colonial empires and African demands for self-determination were relegated to a secondary position. In the specific case of Portugal, US support for maintenance of Portuguese sovereignty over the 'overseas provinces' dated back to World War II and was directly related to the strategic importance of the American military base at the Azores in the contexts of World War II and the Cold War.

During the Eisenhower administration there were some signs of change. The 1950s witnessed the gradual emergence of the anti-colonial movement, symbolized by the Bandung Conference in 1955, and the gradual dissolution of the British, French and Belgium empires. This new strength of anti-colonialism obliged the US to gradually change its position towards Portuguese colonialism. Eisenhower, however, as Peter Duignan mentioned, responded to these challenges 'in a slow and ambivalent fashion'.[70] This ambiguity and ambivalence was fully revealed in the episode of the enclaves of Dadra and Nagar Haveli, with the US refusing to express public support for the Portuguese position, but, in the end, recognizing the Portuguese territories were 'provinces', not 'colonies'.

The changes already announced during the Eisenhower administration would be fully revealed during the early months of Kennedy's presidency. Washington began to fear that African nationalism and the newly independent African nations would be under strong Soviet influence. The fear of 'losing Africa' was decisive in promoting the new African policy in the early days of the Kennedy administration, particularly felt in the relations with Portugal and the Portuguese colonies. Nevertheless, it was the same background of pragmatic Cold War considerations that ultimately justified the abandonment of many new African policies inaugurated by Kennedy, such as the policy toward Portuguese Africa, the Congo, or South Africa. Therefore, taken as a whole, the new African policy announced by the Kennedy administration had few durable consequences. As one scholar has already noted, 'a seemingly bold policy, which gave African affairs a high profile, tolerated ideological diversity and blazed an independent path', was abandoned in the last phase of the Kennedy administration and during the Johnson years, to be replaced by 'a policy which

---

[69]   For US intervention in Angola see Tiago Moreira de Sá, *Os Estados Unidos e a descolonização de Angola* (Lisbon: Dom Quixote, 2011).
[70]   Peter Duignan and L. H. Gann, *The United States and Africa*, p. 286.

largely treated African affairs as a peripheral concern, promoted ideological rigidity, and adapted to Western European sensitivities.'[71]

From 1969, the Nixon administration openly assumed its desire to improve relations with Portugal and with the so-called 'white redoubt' regimes in southern Africa. According to the new principles guiding US policy towards Africa, those regimes were 'there to stay' and therefore the United States should build closer political relations with Lisbon, Pretoria and Salisbury. The 'Tar Baby' option was determinant in the relations with Portugal, with the Nixon administration reducing contacts with African nationalists, increasing arms exports, and signing a new Azores agreement in December 1971.

In the end, the narrative of US–Portuguese relations seems to demonstrate that, despite the growing interest in African affairs since the late 1950s, Europe continued to be the political centre of the Cold War throughout the decades. The fear of losing the strategically located Azores base in a period of several important Cold War episodes, such as the Berlin and Cuban crises, and the Vietnam and Yom Kippur wars, outweighed the concern with African developments and the rhetoric of anti-colonialism that briefly emerged in the late 1950s and the early 1960s. The hesitations and ambivalences of American policy towards Portugal in the period analysed in this article also reflect a larger problem American foreign policy-makers had faced since World War II: the dilemma between European solidarity and African decolonization. In the case of Portuguese–American relations, to use the words of Steven Metz, the early 1960s marked a shift 'from a strictly Eurocentric policy in which the benefits of colonialism to the NATO countries was the primary motive of our African policy to a position that attempted to separate the European and the African aspects of the problem.'[72] But when African demands for self-determination and independence 'clashed with policies considered crucial to United States security relationships with Europe', Kennedy, Johnson and Nixon always decided in favour of European and transatlantic priorities.[73]

---

[71]   David A. Dickson, 'US Foreign Policy toward Southern and Central Africa', pp. 303–05.
[72]   Steven Metz, 'American Attitudes toward Decolonization in Africa', *Political Science Quarterly*, 99.3 (Fall 1984), 515–33 (p. 527).
[73]   Peter J. Schraeder, *United States Foreign Policy toward Africa: Incrementalism, Crisis and Change* (Cambridge: Cambridge University Press, 1994), pp. 14–15.

Live and Let Live: Britain and Portugal's Imperial Endgame (1945–75)

PEDRO AIRES OLIVEIRA

IHC-FCSH-UNL

In an era of profound changes in the colonial world, it was inevitable that the trajectories of Britain and Portugal would at a certain point intersect. Since differences between their colonial philosophies became more pronounced after the Second World War that intersection was likely to result in a clash of interests, opinions and attitudes, especially when certain developments in Britain's foreign and imperial policies impacted on Portugal's increasingly vulnerable position. Historically, Britain's relation with the Portuguese overseas empire was far from having been a simple one. While bound to Portugal by an alliance forged in 1373, its position as the senior member of that relationship was significantly strengthened in the early nineteenth century, thanks to its undisputed economic and strategic primacy.

The fact that Britain was able to exact a high price for the assistance provided to the Portuguese crown during the Napoleonic wars (above all, the opening of the Brazilian ports to foreign trade in 1808), and apply significant pressure to bring about the extinction of the slave trade in their colonies, created a strong anti-British bias among large sectors of the Portuguese ruling classes. Such a feeling was only mitigated by the awareness that their independence in Europe, as well as access to credit and to the know-how and technology of the industrial era, was to a large extent secured by their haughty ally. This may explain why several traumatic episodes — the most notorious being Lord Salisbury's 1890 ultimatum — were, if not forgotten, then at least overcome by the pragmatic instincts of their liberal elites. Portugal's last imperial cycle — the '*Third Portuguese Empire*'[1] — relied heavily on Britain's economic tutelage (at least until the 1940s) and, more crucially perhaps, on the diplomatic and military protection that Britain was ready to provide, in accordance with its own strategic interests in several areas of the globe.

For some Portuguese colonial 'theorists' and administrators, Britain's imperial record was also a source of admiration and, at times, her imperial institutions were emulated in reforms introduced in Portugal's overseas possessions (for example, the High Commissioners' regime in Angola and Mozambique after

---

[1] The expression is borrowed from W. Gervase Clarence-Smith, *The Third Portuguese Empire, 1825–1975* (Manchester: Manchester University Press, 1995).

Portuguese Studies vol. 29 no. 2 (2013), 186–208
© Modern Humanities Research Association 2013

the Paris Peace Conference of 1919). In the inter-war period, it is unsurprising that an authoritarian right-wing dictatorship such as Salazar's *Estado Novo* was clearly more at ease with the continuity of Britain's imperial preponderance than with a new balance of power that might arise from a redistribution of African colonies among the revisionist and fascist powers. Even though the Second World War might (with hindsight) be seen as the event which ultimately sealed the fate of the European colonial empires, the Portuguese rulers were able to find some solace in the fact that Britain was, until 1945, led by such a staunchly imperialist leader as Sir Winston Churchill. Their conviction that Britain would fight hard to preserve its colonial assets gave them animus to face the well-known hostility of the new emerging superpowers towards the old imperial order. If the Soviet Union's anti-colonial stance was something that Salazar regarded as a fact of life, he was less inclined to resign himself to the United States' idea of placing colonial territories under some kind of international supervision.[2] In the final stages of the Pacific War, he was able to secure Roosevelt's agreement on the restoration of Portuguese sovereignty in Timor as the trade-off for the establishment of an American military airfield in the Azorean island of Santa Maria. By exploiting the military and logistic needs of the Atlantic powers, Portugal became one of the first beneficiaries of the reassessment which the Roosevelt administration felt constrained to make of its own anti-colonial views in order to secure other paramount strategic goals.[3]

The focus of this article is the interplay between Britain and Portugal in the three decades that witnessed the dissolution of their respective colonial empires. Operating within an authoritarian framework, Portugal's decision-makers were largely exempt from the pressures that in other European democracies contributed to accelerate the pace of decolonization. They were therefore keen to forge a close (and, seen retrospectively, dangerous) connection between the fate of the dictatorship in the metropolis and the survival of Portugal's rule in the overseas provinces. The following sections examine the destabilizing impact of Britain's colonial retreat upon Portugal's empire and make an effort to explain the motives that prevented successive British governments from assuming a more critical posture towards the *Estado Novo*'s policies. Although strategic calculations may have been paramount in the formulation of Britain's policies, official records suggest that the Foreign Office's historically benign posture vis-à-vis the dictatorship in Lisbon was also a factor to be taken into account. A final section briefly considers how the simultaneous 'regime change' in London and Lisbon in 1974 allowed the UK to play a small but not insignificant role in the final states of Portugal's decolonization.

---

[2] For these American intentions see Paul Orders, '"Adjusting to a New Period in World History": Franklin Roosevelt and European Colonialism', in *The United States and Decolonization: Power and Freedom*, ed. by David Ryan and Victor Pungong (London: Macmillan, 2000), pp. 63–84.
[3] See Luís N. Rodrigues, *No coração do Atlântico: os Estados Unidos e os Açores, 1939–1948* (Lisbon: Prefácio, 2005).

Portugal, Britain and the Euro-African Mirage

Contrary to some expectations, at least among oppositionist circles in Portugal, the defeat of the Axis powers and the victory of a coalition led by the Western democracies and the Soviet Union did not spell the end for Salazar's regime. As a matter of fact, in the following months the increasingly tense relationship between the wartime members of the Grand Alliance would play into the hands of the Portuguese dictator. Not only was Portugal viewed as a bulwark of stability in Western Europe's southern flank but, more important still, its Atlantic archipelagos were perceived as critically important by the Anglo-American military planners in a series of contingency plans for a future confrontation with the USSR.[4]

Unaware of the full extent of Britain's debilitation after the war, Salazar thought that Portugal might still carve out its geopolitical niche in the context of a revitalized *Pax Britannica*. The election of a Labour government in mid-1945 was not seen as an obstacle to this objective. In fact, the relationship with the new Attlee administration started on a very cordial note, with flattering references to the Anglo-Portuguese Alliance in the House of Commons in 1946 and joint Anglo-American backing for Portugal's application to UN membership in that same year. Relying on the advice of Foreign Office (FO) diplomats, the new Labour Foreign Secretary, Ernest Bevin, a former trade unionist, was quite willing to cultivate a friendly relationship with the austere and 'incorruptible' Portuguese dictator. For his part, Salazar was quickly reassured by the basic continuity of Britain's foreign policy under Attlee, as well as by the uncompromising anti-communist stance that characterized Labour's position in the early stages of the Cold War. Even more significantly, Bevin's ideas regarding the future development of Europe as a 'Third Force' in world politics, independent of the US and the Soviet Union, were congenial to Salazar's world view.[5] Now that Germany had ceased to count as a major power in continental Europe, the Portuguese leader felt that the only chance of preserving Europe's standing and 'identity' depended on its capacity to find a way to economic regeneration — and this was something that might only be achieved through the mobilization of one of its last meaningful assets: the natural resources contained in its overseas dependencies. The prospect of such a 'Third Force' being led by Britain, the foremost of the European colonial powers, was all the more attractive to Salazar, who hoped that such a new entity

[4] For the UK relationship with Salazar in the final stages of the war and in the immediate post-war period, see Francisco Seixas da Costa, 'The Opposition to the "New State" and the British Attitude at the End of the Second World War: Hope and Disillusion', *Portuguese Studies*, 10 (1994), 155–76, and David Castaño, *Paternalismo e cumplicidade: as relações luso-britânicas de 1943 a 1949* (Lisbon: Associação dos Amigos do Arquivo Histórico-Diplomático, 2006).
[5] For the 'Third Force' project, see Anne Deighton, 'Entente Neo-Coloniale? Ernest Bevin and the Proposals for an Anglo-French Third World Power, 1945–1949', *Diplomacy and Statecraft*, 17 (2006), 835–52.

might also function as an effective counterpoise to the global 'expansionist' designs of both Washington and Moscow.

Needless to say, there was a great deal of wishful thinking in the way Salazar perceived Britain's capacity to lead such a project in the circumstances of the time. In fact, the establishment of a 'Western bloc' with a defence pact at its core was only one of several policy options which Attlee's government was ready to consider. Throughout 1948, in the light of such developments as the Prague coup, the Berlin blockade, and the hardening of East–West tensions in Europe, it soon became evident that Britain's debilitated economic position forced its government to adopt a more sober view of its ability to undertake major international commitments, and redouble its efforts to persuade the Americans to play a more permanent role in Western Europe's security arrangements.

In the preceding months, Salazar's illusions had been severely shaken in other ways, as he gradually came to realize that Britain was not in a position to assist him in some of his major goals for the immediate post-war era, such as the modernization of the Portuguese armed forces and the launch of a new industrial effort. The only power able to fulfil such demands was the United States. By then, Truman's increasingly anti-communist rhetoric, and his conciliatory attitude towards the survival of European rule in Indochina and other places in Asia, had already helped to assuage some of Salazar's more deep-seated suspicions of Washington's intentions. Two events in 1948 illustrate the erosion of Britain's influence and its replacement by the US as the major foreign interlocutor of Portugal. The first was the signing of a new defence agreement between Lisbon and Washington, in February, which granted the US full transit facilities in the Azores for the next three years (eventually extended for another five). The second was Salazar's belated application to the European Recovery Programme (the 'Marshall Plan') in November, after having tried, without success, to persuade Washington to take on the £40 million of credits which Portugal still held in the Bank of England, as part of Britain's war debt. The two steps were not easy for Salazar to take. The defence agreement was a reminder that the *Pax Britannica* in the Atlantic world, which had served Salazar's regime very well since the 1930s, was giving way to a new, and more uncertain, *Pax Americana*; and participation in the Marshall Plan was resented as a concession to the 'power of the dollar' and to the conditions that the US was trying to dictate to the Europeans, in order to influence and shape the new international system that would emerge in the continent. Even so, Portugal's alternatives were limited. If Salazar had chosen a more autarkic path, this would have meant a situation of isolation in Western Europe, very similar to the one endured by the impoverished Spanish dictatorship of General Franco. Portugal's full cooption to the American sphere of influence occurred early in 1949, when Salazar was persuaded to accept Bevin's invitation to join the new collective defence pact sponsored by Britain and the US. Even if invited at a stage that prevented it having any sort of influence in the drafting of the pact's treaty, Portugal did become the only non-democratic founding member of NATO — an event that came to symbolize the near full rehabilitation of its regime in the post-war order.[6]

Another development that attested to Portugal's growing intimacy with some of the leading Western colonial powers was its participation in several meetings and intergovernmental bodies, both in Europe and in Africa, from the late 1940s to the late 1950s.[7] This was, after all, the period that became popularly known as Africa's 'second colonial occupation', when several European powers took steps to ensure that large-scale development schemes would bolster their colonial productions, and thus contribute to the revitalization of the metropolitan economies.[8] Even if the expectations associated with this 'developmentalist' drive were never quite fulfilled, this was the type of approach that left the Portuguese more hopeful with regard to the entrenchment of colonial rule in subtropical Africa. The ideas of trusteeship revived by the United Nations Charter, and the first steps towards the dismantling of the European empires in Asia, had been perceived with apprehension by the government in Lisbon, for whom India's claims to Goa and the remaining Portuguese enclaves in the subcontinent was anathema. But the enthusiasm with which the British, the French and the Belgians embraced the economic exploitation of their African territories in the late 1940s, and the indulgence now displayed by Truman's administration towards the European colonial empires, were reassuring trends for Lisbon. Salazar's policy was one of allowing for a certain measure of economic modernization of its African colonies, while maintaining a very tight grip on its political life. In some territories, the *mise-en-valeur* envisaged by the regime implied an enormous pressure on the African workforce, whose contribution for some large public works and private sector ventures (agricultural plantations, mining, etc.) was in great demand. Inevitably, situations of crude labour exploitation led to some concerns about social conditions in the Portuguese territories being voiced in international bodies and in the international press as well. Following a pattern familiar from previous epochs, Anglo-Saxon Protestant missionaries and the occasional radical journalist became the whistle-blowers for those human rights abuses, which, predictably, elicited an angry reaction from the Portuguese authorities. In the early 1950s, while British missionaries still preferred to use conventional

[6]   For these developments see Fernanda Rollo, *Portugal e o Plano Marshall: da rejeição à solicitação da ajuda financeira norte-americana 1947-1952* (Lisbon: Estampa, 1994) and António Telo, *Portugal e a Nato: o reencontro da tradição atlântica* (Lisbon: Cosmos, 1996).
[7]   On this inter-imperial cooperation see John Kent, *The Internationalization of Colonialism: Britain, France and Black Africa, 1939-1956* (Oxford: Clarendon Press, 1992); and for Portugal's participation in those efforts, see Pedro A. Oliveira, *Os despojos da Aliança: a Grã-Bretanha e a questão colonial portuguesa, 1945-1975* (Lisbon: Tinta da China, 2007), pp. 55-75.
[8]   See Nicholas J. White, 'Reconstructing Europe through Rejuvenating Empire: The British, French and Dutch Experiences Compared', in *Post-War Reconstruction in Europe: International Perspectives*, ed. by Mark Mazower, Jessica Reinisch and David Feldman, *Past and Present Supplement*, 6 (2011), 211-36.

diplomatic channels to voice their concerns about conditions in Angola, British journalists like Basil Davidson were acquiring some notoriety as outspoken critics of Portuguese colonial methods.[9]

Thus, when Portugal finally joined the UN, in late 1955, there was already a growing awareness in some international circles as to the apparently more retrograde political and social conditions in its African colonies. The fact that the Indian Union had an unresolved dispute with Lisbon over the future of Goa ensured that much of this criticism would not go unnoticed at the UN, where the interests of the old colonial powers were now being challenged by an emerging coalition of Afro-Asiatic and Socialist states. Soon after its admission to the UN, Portugal had to face mounting pressure from several anti-colonial nations, who used Lisbon's refusal to provide the information requested by the Secretary General under Article 73 of the UN Charter as a pretext to castigate its record as a negligent colonial power. Unsympathetic to the motives and rhetoric of the anti-colonial constituency, the UK government was generally supportive of Portugal's refusal to comply with such a request, endorsing its arguments which involved references to 'security' and 'constitutional impediments'. At the same time, though, British diplomats were also willing to impress on their Portuguese counterparts the advantages of a voluntary offer of selective data on the social and economic conditions of its overseas dependencies, in order to deprive its critics of the moral high ground in the charged atmosphere that prevailed after such events as the Bandung Conference and the Suez crisis.[10]

Portugal and Britain, along with France and Belgium, also had an opportunity to exchange views on the increasingly strained positions of their colonial territories in a series of confidential meetings which took place on the eve of every UN General Assembly between 1957 and 1959.[11] These semi-secretive meetings, where political intelligence was shared and common positions for some of the debates were defined, turned out to be the swan song of the sense of unity that prevailed in New York among the old colonial powers. The UK in particular was finding it less convenient to close ranks with its more hard-line European allies, fearing that this might somehow tarnish its credentials as a liberal and enlightened imperial power, as well as compromise its international reputation among other important allies, such as the US, which by now was becoming more apprehensive of the anti-colonial rhetoric of the USSR's new leader, Nikita Khrushchev.[12]

[9]   See Pedro A. Oliveira, *Os despojos da Aliança*, pp. 160–74.
[10]   See, for instance, TNA. CO 936/542. 'The transmission of information under article 73e of the United Nations Charter: Portugal. Brief for United Kingdom Delegation', 15 July 1958.
[11]   British minutes of such meetings can be found in a number of Colonial Office files at the NA under the title 'Quadripartite Talks in Africa', for the period 1957–59. For a general appraisal of those talks, see Pedro A. Oliveira, *Os despojos da Aliança*, pp. 198–208.
[12]   On the UK's strained relationship with the UN in this period see William Roger Louis, 'Public Enemy Number One: Britain and the United Nations in the Aftermath of Suez', in *Ends of British Imperialism: The Scramble for Empire, Suez and Decolonization* (London: I. B. Tauris, 2006), pp. 689–724.

It was therefore not surprising that some of the initiatives associated with the policy of the British Prime Minister, Harold Macmillan, of trying to press ahead with an orderly retreat from empire, were received with some shock by Salazar and his ministers.[13] His famous African tour of 1960, and in particular his 'Wind of Change' speech in Cape Town, was perceived as a deeply disturbing development. Gradually, all the fears that had accumulated in Lisbon ever since the dissolution of the British Raj were fully confirmed. In Salazar's eyes, London had finally capitulated to a line of 'appeasement' of Third World nationalism and seemed poised to succumb to a policy of 'scuttle' which would pave the way for communist ascendancy in the former colonial world.[14] Throughout 1960, events seemed to move at an incredibly fast pace, in French and Belgian colonies especially, but at the UN as well — the 'scramble out of Africa' was in full swing, and Britain was also apparently eager to follow the trend. In New York, Portugal's bid for a non-permanent seat at the Security Council, for example, received only lukewarm support from Britain and other Western states and was predictably defeated. Worse was to come. In December, the UK delegation abstained on a number of General Assembly resolutions that called for a speedy end to colonial rule in Africa, and singled out the Portuguese government in particularly harsh terms. The comment made by the Portuguese ambassador in London encapsulated Lisbon's thinking on what could be expected from post-Suez Britain: 'Mais uma vez se verificou que os británicos não vão atrás do direito nem da lógica, mas obedecem mais à força das realidades práticas. [...] A rendição em África é a linha de conduta. O receio da Rússia e o respeito pela Índia e outros países asiáticos da Comunidade condicionam a atitude' [We see, once more, that the British heed neither law nor logic, but rather give in to the force of practical realities. [...] Capitulation in Africa is their preferred line of conduct. Fear of Russia and respect for India and other Asian countries of the Commonwealth states determine their attitude].[15]

The 'perfect storm': Salazar's Critical Year of 1961

In 1961 the Portuguese regime and its empire were struck by a 'perfect storm' of events: the hijack of a Portuguese liner, the *Santa Maria*, in the Caribbean by a high-profile dissident, Captain Henrique Galvão (January); the assault on the Luanda prisons by a group of Angolan nationalists (February), soon to be followed by the UPA uprising in the northern districts (March); several hostile resolutions presented at the UN (some of them with the blessing of the

[13]   Among the many studies devoted to Macmillan's decolonization policies see, for example, Ronald Hyam, *Britain's Declining Empire: The Road to Decolonization, 1918–1968* (Cambridge: Cambridge University Press, 2006).
[14]   See Pedro A. Oliveira, 'Harold Macmillan, "Os Ventos de Mudança" e a crise colonial portuguesa (1960–1961)', *Relações Internacionais*, 30 (June 2011), 21–38.
[15]   Arquivo Nacional Torre do Tombo. AOS/CD-19. Private letter from General Abranches Pinto to Oliveira Salazar, 22 December 1960.

new Kennedy administration); a failed military putsch in Lisbon orchestrated by Salazar's defence minister, Júlio Botelho de Moniz (April); and finally the loss of Goa to the Indian Union after a swift military operation that met little opposition from the local Portuguese garrison (December).

As these events unfolded, Britain's Conservative government tried to perform a delicate balancing act.[16] On the one hand, the Foreign Office was not insensitive to the predicament of a long-standing ally in Europe and fellow colonial power in Africa. If Portugal was left at the mercy of the forces which aimed at the rapid liquidation of its colonial sovereignty, there was a real chance that a new 'Congolese' scenario might come about in Angola, with ominous consequences for the stability of central-southern Africa, where many thorny issues were still to be resolved in several British territories. Although the dismantling of British rule in Africa was being undertaken with energetic zeal by the new Colonial Secretary, Iain MacLeod, other members of Macmillan's Cabinet were less enthusiastic about the pace of events, not to mention the concessions to the more 'militant' sectors of African nationalism, which many perceived as unjustified.[17] For many high-ranking officials in Whitehall, the manner in which the transfer of power was to be carried out was not a minor issue: the administrating powers should retain a certain measure of control regarding the timetable and, it was hoped, influence the choice of the interlocutors to whom power could be 'safely' handed.[18] But apart from the differences between the more 'radical' and the more 'institutional' approaches to decolonization, the political climate in Britain in the early 1960s was marked by a growing consensus among the main political parties on the inevitability of self-government and black majority rule in Africa. There were several assumptions underpinning such a consensus. One was the notion that Britain's international standing and prestige would be better safeguarded by an orderly and voluntary retreat from its colonial territories, even if there were doubts about the capacity of those territories to stand on their own feet after independence. Since the late 1950s, events in territories such as Kenya or Nyasaland had made it clear that the political costs of maintaining order and suppressing local nationalist activities were just too damaging for Britain's liberal reputation, both at home and abroad. But perhaps even more relevant were the larger strategic considerations which prevailed at this particular juncture of the Cold War, namely the need to counteract the bid for influence which the communist powers were making all across the Third World. For many in the West, including Britain's political

[16]   Britain's official response to the events of 1961 in Angola has been covered by Glyn Stone, 'Britain and the Angolan Revolt of 1961', *Journal of Imperial and Commonwealth History*, 27.1 (January 1999), 111–37.
[17]   On Macmillan's government and the end of empire in Africa, see Philip E. Hemming, 'Macmillan and the End of the British Empire in Africa', in *Harold Macmillan and Britain's World Role*, ed. by Richard Aldous and Sabine Lee (Basingstoke: Macmillan, 1996), pp. 97–121.
[18]   For an overview of how Britain's African decolonization policy gradually evolved in official circles, see Hyam, *Britain's Declining Empire*, and Frank Heinlein, *British Government Policy and Decolonization, 1945–1963* (London: Frank Cass, 2002).

elite, only by making concessions to independence demands and shoring up a 'trustworthy' class of local rulers could the communist inroads into the colonial world be halted. Further weight was given to this approach when the recently installed Kennedy administration announced that the 'modernization' of newly independent nations (or those in the process of acquiring independence), and the 'containment' of Soviet influence in the Third World would become key issues of its foreign policy agenda.

The tensions in the British cabinet regarding both the timing of the withdrawal from Africa and the notion of decolonization as the best option to keep former colonies within the West's sphere of influence would surface in the diplomatic exchanges between London and Lisbon throughout 1961. This was evident in several moments. The first was the Angolan crisis, the impact of which was felt at the UN when the Portuguese response to the events in Luanda and in the northern districts become the subject of heated debates in the Security Council and the General Assembly between March and June, resulting in the passing of several resolutions condemning Lisbon's policies. Those discussions in New York were paralleled by Portuguese accusations of disloyalty directed at the US, not only for having voted against a NATO ally, but also for having played an active role in the eruption of violence in Angola, as evidence gathered by Portuguese diplomats in Leopoldville pointed to the CIA's sponsorship of Holden Roberto, the UPA leader who had masterminded the massacre of Portuguese settlers and their African employees in mid-March.[19]

Fearful of falling out of step with the new Democratic administration, the UK government took care to pursue close consultations with Washington concerning these matters, even knowing that it would not be easy to reach common positions. At the UN, for reasons that had much to do with its still substantial commitments as a colonial power in Africa, the UK delegation was instructed to abstain on several resolutions critical of Portugal. British officials were sceptical of Portuguese claims that their 'assimilationist' policy was the wisest alternative to self-determination; but most of them felt that conditions were definitely not ripe for the speedy retreat that was being urged upon the Portuguese, in part because they feared that this might create a power vacuum and a 'Congo-type' situation. An influential trend inside the Cabinet, led by Lord Home, the Foreign Secretary, and David Eccles, the Education Minister, favoured another sort of approach, one that would take into account the 'specificities' of Portugal's predicament, as well as its leader's 'idiosyncrasies'. In April, Eccles, who knew Salazar well from his time as the wartime representative in Lisbon of the Ministry of Economic Warfare, and Lord Salisbury, former minister and leading arch-imperialist of the Tory party, visited Lisbon in order

---

[19]   On Kennedy's policy towards Portugal see Luís N. Rodrigues, *Salazar-Kennedy: a crise de uma aliança* (Lisbon: Editorial Notícias, 2002). A wider chronological perspective is provided by Witney W. Schneidmann, *Engaging Africa: Washington and the Fall of Portugal's Colonial Empire* (Lanham, MD: University Press of America, 2004).

to take stock of the Portuguese government's position and immediate plans. From talks with Salazar, Eccles learned that he was firmly opposed to 'putting his name on any declaration that might refer to self-determination' or even to accepting an intensification of the assimilationist policy in which Portugal took great pride; the only 'significant' concession he was ready to make was to accept the collaboration of foreign capital in accelerating the colonies' economic development — provided that such collaboration was 'channelled through Lisbon'. This was a far cry even from the moderate line preached by Home. In late May, the Foreign Secretary himself would head a new mission to Lisbon in order to impress upon Salazar the advantage of adopting a different approach to his colonial problems, one that, by presenting a more liberal and reformist face, would rebuff some of the criticism that had recently fallen upon Portugal. Again, Salazar was impervious to such advice.[20]

Back in London, the British Foreign Secretary and his colleagues were finding it increasingly difficult to strike the right line in dealing with Portugal's obduracy. Besides the international aspects involved, the government had also to tackle the pressures emanating from civil rights organizations, as well as from the Labour Opposition. The Angolan revolt occurred at a particular historical juncture that conditioned the way these late imperial emergencies impacted on the metropolitan consciousness. Two years earlier, Britain had been deeply shocked to learn the gruesome details of the Hola Camp massacre, in Kenya, whilst Lord Devlin's Report on the Nyasaland emergency, describing the colony as a 'police state', raised significant concerns among the more liberal-minded sectors of the public. Events in Africa were also attracting more media coverage: decolonization was gathering momentum in some of the British colonies; the French were struggling to find a way out of the Algerian morass; and the former Belgian Congo had become one of the main flashpoints of the Cold War. Even more crucial, in terms of British public opinion, was the situation in the Central African Federation, where the white minority in Rhodesia was adopting an increasingly harsh attitude towards the local black nationalists; and in South Africa, where the Sharpeville massacre of 1960 had triggered a serious crisis between Pretoria and London, leading the former to abandon the Commonwealth the following year.[21]

Events in Portugal and its colonies were also being more closely covered and scrutinized in Britain. Mainstream publications had devoted considerable attention to the *Santa Maria* affair, and the BBC took the decision to reactivate its Portuguese Language Service shortly after the Angolan uprising. The swing in the general mood was perceptible in the coverage provided by centrist newspapers such as *The Times* or *The Economist*, which ran editorials

---

[20]   Glyn Stone, 'Britain and the Angolan Revolt of 1961', pp. 116–25.
[21]   On this point see Nicholas J. White, *Decolonisation: The British Experience since 1945* (London: Longman, 1999).

expressing serious misgivings about the *Estado Novo*'s colonial policies.[22] But, understandably, it was from those sectors of the British left that had made anti-imperialism one of their hallmarks that a more vigorous reaction emerged. By late 1960, Labour and Liberal MPs, some of them affiliated with the Movement for Colonial Freedom, together with several anti-Salazarist émigrés in the UK, had established the Committee for Freedom in Portugal and the Colonies.[23] Their initiatives (press conferences, meetings, letters to newspapers) would be complemented by a modestly staffed but efficient campaign by members of the Baptist Missionary Society, which had seen some of its missionaries expelled from Angola by the Portuguese authorities, allegedly because of their ties with the UPA 'terrorists' in the Congo districts. Pronouncements critical of Portugal were also made by bodies such as the British Council of Churches and the World Council of Churches.[24]

This public outcry was enough to ensure a sustained parliamentary interest in the Angolan situation throughout 1961. In several debates in the House of Commons, Macmillan's government was questioned on a number of aspects of its policy vis-à-vis Portugal, especially in the diplomatic and military fields. For the Labour Opposition, which had relatively few areas of marked disagreement with the Conservatives in terms of domestic policy, 'minor' foreign policy issues provided a safe ground on which to score points against their opponents — a pattern that would resurface in the early 1970s, when another 'thorny' question related to the Portuguese colonial wars came to the forefront of British politics, namely the Wiriyamu massacre in Mozambique (addressed below). The cooperation between the two allies in NATO, both in terms of joint military exercises and arms supplies, came under tight scrutiny, with harsh words being employed by some Labour MPs to castigate Macmillan for his 'hands-off' policy over Angola.

But, again, the government never lost sight of deeper strategic realities. While a feeling of comradeship towards a fellow colonial power would hardly have prevented it from emulating the more righteous conduct of the US at UN debates, for instance, the option of adopting sanctions which could alienate Portugal from NATO was never seriously considered. The most that Macmillan was prepared to concede was a selective arms embargo (announced in the House of Commons in early July), banning the sale of military equipment to Portugal's African dependencies but not to its metropolitan territory, allowing it to fulfil its NATO obligations — a solution similar to that adopted by the

[22] See, for instance, *The Times*, 'In a clearer light', 28 June 1961, and *The Economist*, 'Our job in Angola', 8 July 1961.
[23] On the British left and decolonization see Stephen Howe, *Anticolonialism in British Politics: The Left and the End of Empire, 1918–1964* (Oxford: Clarendon Press, 1993); and for the links between the anti-imperialist left in Britain and the Portuguese political expatriates there, see Pedro A. Oliveira, 'Generous Albion? Portuguese anti-Salazarists in the United Kingdom, *c*. 1960–74', *Portuguese Studies*, 27.2 (2011), 175–207.
[24] See *The Times*, 'Churches appeal to Portugal. World Council deplores Angola attacks', 23 June 1961; *The Times*, 'Church protest on Portugal planned', 20 October 1961.

Kennedy administration, but one that Hugh Gaitskell, the Labour leader, did not hesitate to describe as 'a farce'.[25]

Salazar's dangerous year, however, would not end without a traumatic episode for Portugal's imperial mystique — the fall of the so-called *Estado Português da Índia*, the most cherished relic from the Age of the Discoveries. This would also prove to be one of the most testing moments for the Anglo-Portuguese Alliance, for reasons that are not difficult to grasp. Caught between its residual treaty obligations towards Portugal and the political ties with a key member of the Commonwealth, the UK never harboured any doubts as to the inconvenience of taking sides on this particularly thorny dispute.[26]

Although this could hardly have come as a surprise, the Portuguese were apparently hopeful that the UK might still use its diplomatic influence with Nehru to dissuade him from resorting to force to settle the ongoing dispute, or at least to make him realize that he would have to pay a high price for taking such a course. Salazar's belief in Nehru's willingness to retain his prestige as the international champion of pacifism led him to adopt a strategy based on the assumption that the prospect of a symbolic military resistance in Goa would be sufficient to deter the Indian premier from considering a military assault on the colony. When, in late 1961, this did not prove to be the case, Salazar had to content himself with the hope that heroic bloodshed in Goa would, at least, maintain the façade of defending the empire at all costs, from 'Minho to Timor'. If this gamble were to acquire a modicum of credibility, British assistance was important, at least in terms of facilitating transportation of Portuguese reinforcements to Goa, via some of the UK's bases between the Mediterranean and the Indian Ocean. But a formal appeal to the Old Alliance again met with Britain's refusal to take sides, even if Macmillan proved ready to make a last-minute *démarche* in New Delhi, in order to dissuade Nehru from resorting to violence. This, along with other approaches made by the Americans, was totally ineffective. On 17 December 1961, India's armed forces launched 'Operation Vijay', a swift assault against Goa involving 45,000 troops, backed up by armed vehicles and aerial and naval forces. The resistance offered by the Portuguese garrison (no more than 3,500 poorly equipped men) was minimal; the Indian *blitz* was over in 36 hours, with few casualties on either side. The media operation organized by the Portuguese Government to depict the invasion of Goa as a brutal act of aggression by India ended in failure.[27]

At the UN the crisis attracted the attention of the member-states for little more than a week, and, predictably, a Security Council draft resolution 'deploring' the use of force by India, calling for an immediate cease-fire, and urging both parties to settle their differences peacefully, was vetoed by the Soviet Union.

[25]   *The Times*, 'NATO arms for Portugal', 5 July 1961.
[26]   See Simon C. Smith, 'Conflicting Commitments: Britain and Portuguese Possessions in India, 1947–1961', *South Asia*, 20.1 (1997), 17–34.
[27]   For a detailed description of 'Operation Vijay' see Maria Manuel Stocker, *Xeque-mate a Goa*, 2nd edn (Lisbon: Texto Editora, 2011).

Although the British Representative in New York was instructed to vote with the Americans, he was not urged to take a strong line against Nehru; evidently policy makers in Whitehall were already thinking about Britain's relationship with India beyond the Goa crisis.[28]

The Portuguese government's reaction to Britain's apparent lack of solidarity was heated. In the days that followed the invasion, students protested at the British and American embassies, the Union Flag was burned in the streets of Lisbon, and demonstrators plastered the walls of the capital's main square with anti-British and anti-American slogans. In the press, usually subject to strict censorship, a host of editorials criticized 'Britain's duplicity' and evoked other unhappy moments in Anglo-Portuguese relations, such as Lord Salisbury's ultimatum of 1890.[29]

This backlash against the Alliance, and Salazar's apparent willingness to undertake a revision of the treaties (as expressed in his address to the Portuguese National Assembly on 3 January of the following year),[30] provided the pretext for a global re-assessment of the Anglo-Portuguese connexion in Whitehall, which resulted in a memorandum submitted to the Cabinet by the Foreign Secretary. 'If another situation like Goa should arise', wrote Home, 'we might well face the same embarrassment without even the reason of our Commonwealth commitments to explain our inaction.' Therefore, Britain should approach the Portuguese in a friendly manner and persuade them to accept a new and more realistic *modus vivendi*. To 'sweeten the pill', it could reaffirm its commitments to the defence of metropolitan Portugal and the Atlantic islands, including the Cape Verde archipelago, whose strategic importance had recently been stressed by the Minister of Aviation and military planners.[31] The Cabinet's reaction to Home's suggestion was not enthusiastic, though. In the aftermath of the Goa crisis, there were doubts in Whitehall about the very survival of Salazar's regime.[32] While the fate of the regime hung in the balance, ministers felt that it might not be very wise to engage in conversations that would most likely end in a solemn reaffirmation of the alliance.

In the meantime, in Lisbon a cooler atmosphere had also settled in. Apparently, Salazar was inclined to follow the advice of the more Anglophile elements of his foreign policy establishment, who did not relish the idea of burning the bridges that connected Portugal to its oldest ally. After all, Portugal still had a major asset in its dealings with the Atlantic powers, the Azorean bases, the strategic importance of which had just been highlighted by a new crisis over Berlin (soon to be followed by another one over Cuba). In 1962, Salazar did not hesitate to

---

[28]   TNA PREM 11/3837. Telegram 5937 from the FO to Sir Patrick Dean, 20 December 1961.
[29]   TNA FO 371/160 728. Dispatch by Sir Archibald Ross, 28 December 1961.
[30]   Salazar's speech, reproduced in *Vinte anos de defesa do Estado Português da Índia, 1947–1967*, 4 vols (Lisbon: MNE, 1968), IV, 378–93.
[31]   TNA CAB 129/109. C. C. (62). Memorandum 'The Anglo-Portuguese Alliance', 10 April 1962.
[32]   See the FO paper 'Possible overthrow of the regime in Portugal', first drafted in December 1961 but in final version only in August 1962. TNA FO 371/166 996.

play this trump card to ensure that both the Americans and the British would display a more moderate stance at the UN. The bilateral agreement for the lease of the Azorean bases, due to expire that year, was not renewed — and this meant that the Americans (and the British) would only enjoy the facilities in the Atlantic islands on a precarious, day-to-day, basis.[33]

Live and Let Live: Britain and Portugal's Wars in Africa

Throughout the next decade, Anglo-Portuguese relations would evolve according to a relatively stable pattern.[34] One might say that this was a classic situation where the two allies 'agreed to disagree'.

After coming to terms with the idea that a 'premature' decolonization of some of its African countries was better than a gradualist approach, which entailed the risk of alienating local nationalists, Britain had become irrevocably committed to the liquidation of its African empire, even if that meant confronting the white settler lobby in the Central African Federation and other die-hard imperialists in the UK itself. Among its policy makers and diplomatic elite, a consensus had emerged as to the desirability of keeping Britain in line with the normative trends that had conferred an almost universal acceptance on the concepts of self-determination and racial equality. If Britain wanted to retain its role as one of the moral leaders of the 'free world', and maintain a degree of cohesion in the new 'multicultural' Commonwealth, then an overly close association with an unrepentant colonial power like Portugal was indeed problematic. Nevertheless, the strategic imperatives of the Cold War, particularly in the 'core' Euro-Atlantic area, also meant that a certain measure of prudence was advisable when the interests of a fellow NATO member were at stake. One might also take into account the fact that Britain's strategic 'ambivalence' — i.e., the preference of its political elites for an international role that encompassed various dimensions (the 'special relationship' with the US, the Commonwealth and 'Europe')[35] — was congenial to the *Estado Novo*'s interests. Besides their common membership in NATO, the UK and Portugal were also partners in the European Free Trade Association (EFTA), a loose association of states which London had sponsored in the late 1950s as an alternative to the European Economic Community (EEC).

From the Portuguese point of view, the British connection was still deemed an important factor in their foreign relations, even if now deprived of much of its former significance. Apart from the aforementioned institutional links,

---

[33]   On these aspects, see Rodrigues, *Salazar–Kennedy*. Britain's facilities in the Azores were tacitly renewed whenever Lisbon and Washington reached an agreement for the use of the bases by the US air force.

[34]   For a general overview see Glyn Stone, 'Britain and Portuguese Africa, 1961–65', *Journal of Imperial and Commonwealth History*, 28.3 (2000), 169–92.

[35]   On Britain's strategic 'ambivalence' see Frank Heinlein, *British Government Policy and Decolonization*, and David Sanders, *Losing an Empire, Finding a Role* (Basingstoke: Macmillan, 1990).

there was still a relevant commercial and economic dimension in their relationship, and in fact the UK remained Portugal's main trading partner until the early 1970s. To this one might also add the 'sentimental' ties that were much cherished by significant sectors of the Portuguese ruling classes — notwithstanding the disappointment that many felt about Britain's alleged concessions to Afro-Asiatic nationalism. Also, there was a small but influential pro-Salazar lobby in Britain.

As already mentioned, Portugal also held some trump cards for rebuffing possible British pressures. In this respect, one should note that by the mid-1960s Salazar had gained some leverage in the context of the Rhodesian crisis, Britain's last imperial conundrum in Africa. Following years of carefully nurtured contacts with some of the leaders of the Central African Federation, the Portuguese dictator finally decided to place his bet on Ian Smith and give him his full support in the run-up to the Unilateral Declaration of Independence (UDI) in November 1965.[36] Taking advantage of Mozambique's location, the Portuguese authorities allowed their ports, pipelines and railways to deliver crude oil to the rebel colony, thus contravening the second round of sanctions imposed on Salisbury by Harold Wilson's government. Some of the most notorious breaches of the sanctions had been occurring at Beira, using the pipeline connecting the Mozambican port to the Rhodesian refinery at Ferukua, near Umtali. At one point, the British authorities resorted to a blockade of the port of Beira, establishing a permanent presence by the Royal Navy — the Beira Patrol — in Portuguese territorial waters, much to the chagrin of Salazar's government.[37] After a while, though, an almost farcical arrangement came into force: the Portuguese managed to divert their supply routes to Rhodesia through the Lourenço Marques and Limpopo Railway, with the active collaboration of some of the major oil multinationals (including Shell and BP), while the British maintained the Beira Patrol in the Mozambique Channel, thus keeping up the façade of their sanctions policy. Both Lisbon and London found this arrangement satisfactory. The Portuguese were heavily engaged in counter-insurgency operations in three of their African colonies (Guinea, Angola and Mozambique) and obviously wished to avoid a dispute with a fellow NATO ally; for their part, the British realized that any increased pressure upon Portugal, by extending their sanctions to Mozambique, for instance, would immediately raise questions as to why the same penalty was not also applied to South Africa — a regional player that successive British governments preferred not to confront for fear of upsetting the very substantial strategic and economic interests established there.[38]

[36]   This relationship is documented in Pedro A. Oliveira, *Os despojos da Aliança*, pp. 324–47 and in Luís Barroso, *Salazar, Caetano e o 'Reduto Branco': a manobra político-diplomática de Portugal na África Austral, 1951–1974* (Lisbon: Fronteira do Caos, 2012).
[37]   See Richard Mobley, 'The Beira Patrol: Britain's Broken Blockade against Rhodesia', *Naval War College Review*, 4.1 (2002), 63–84.
[38]   See Andrew Cohen, 'Lonrho and Oil Sanctions against Rhodesia in the 1960s', *Journal of Southern African Studies*, 37.4 (December 2011), 715–30.

Although marked by a significant degree of continuity with previous Conservative policies, Labour's attitude towards Portugal should not be perceived as a crude exercise in *realpolitik*. Under Wilson's premiership, Britain stuck to its selective arms embargo on Portugal, with the various orders placed by Portuguese firms being examined on an ad hoc basis by several departments in Whitehall. If a certain amount of British military equipment eventually found its way to Portuguese Africa, it is no less true that the contribution of Britain's defence industry to Portugal's war effort was relatively modest when compared with the role played by the French, the West Germans, or even the Americans.[39]

Some British firms were also sidelined by the Portuguese government in 1968 when the time came to select the consortium that would be in charge of building the Cabora Bassa dam, in western Mozambique, a mammoth project that came to symbolize Portugal's determination to remain in Africa and strengthen its ties with the neighbouring white minority regimes of Salisbury and Pretoria. Although it was recognized in Lisbon that the British consortium led by the English Electric Company had presented a solid proposal, the government preferred to award the contract to ZAMCO, a consortium whose core firms were from South Africa, France and West Germany, while the credit facilities were assured by a syndicate led by the Banque National de Paris et des Pays-Bas. The potential embarrassment of a British involvement in the scheme became all too evident at a later stage, when a Swedish firm decided to withdraw from ZAMCO, and the participation of Barclays Bank in the financing of the project, through its South African branch, was vigorously denounced by a civic campaign carried out by the Dambusters Mobilizing Committee.

In the early 1970s, a more relaxed atmosphere was again discernible in the relationship between London and Lisbon, something made possible, on the one hand, by Salazar's incapacitation in 1968 and his subsequent replacement by the 'modernizing' Marcello Caetano, and, on the other, by the election of a Conservative government, under the premiership of Edward Heath, in 1970.

Although the change of premier in Lisbon was not followed by a decisive departure from the policies pursued by Salazar, Caetano was at least keen to repair the damaged relationships with London and Washington. At the same time, he was willing to pursue a more decentralized policy for the colonies, under the slogan of an 'autonomia progressiva e participada' [progressive and participatory autonomy]. In British diplomatic circles there was hope that his reformist agenda might gradually bring Portugal closer to mainstream European politics, including (an acceptance of) self-determination for the African colonies and a move towards the EEC, now about to evolve into a larger association that would include former EFTA members like the UK. Edward Heath's government

---

[39]   See Ana Mónica Fonseca and Daniel Marcos, 'French and German Support for Portugal: The Military Survival of the "Estado Novo" (1958–1968)', *Portuguese Studies Review*, 16.2 (2008), 103–09. See also their contribution in the present volume.

was also marked by a more pragmatic approach when pondering the timing of Portugal's disengagement from Africa, much in line with the thinking that prevailed in Washington under the Nixon administration. The Foreign and Commonwealth Office was optimistic about Portugal's ability to conduct a gradual imperial retreat, with an unmistakable *neo-colonial* flavour; it was also amenable to the exploration of business opportunities, particularly in Angola, where the discovery of oil in Cabinda, in 1967, and other developments in the agricultural and mining sectors, had opened up encouraging prospects for some British firms and corporations.

But all things considered, though, this *rapprochement* should not be exaggerated. As Caetano's initial promises of reform gave way to a more *continuiste* colonial policy it soon became clear that a closer partnership with Portugal would most likely be fraught with problems. His endorsement, in November 1970, of Spínola's military raid in Conakry, with the purpose of overthrowing Sékou Touré and capturing the PAIGC leadership (*Operação Mar Verde*), highlighted, once more, Portugal's near-pariah status on the international stage, and caused significant embarrassment in British diplomatic circles. Even if patrician politicians like Sir Alec Douglas-Home, Heath's Foreign and Commonwealth Secretary, and other Tory party members, might express some sympathy towards Caetano and his predicament in Africa (something that might be partly explained by their own impatience with the assertive posture of Afro-Asiatic leaders at Commonwealth summits and at the UN), the fact was that Portugal's uncompromising stance against decolonization prevented it from being fully embraced by sympathetic Western governments.

This was eloquently demonstrated by two critical episodes in 1973: first, the events which surrounded Caetano's official visit to London, linked to the 600th anniversary of the Anglo-Portuguese Alliance; second, the UN General Assembly's consideration of admission for the 'state of Guinea-Bissau', whose independence had been proclaimed unilaterally by the PAIGC. In the first case, Heath's government was evidently wrong-footed by the timely reporting of a massacre of some 400 African civilians in the province of Tete, western Mozambique, at the hands of Portuguese commandos. This atrocity, which had occurred in late 1972, made headlines in *The Times* just a few days before Caetano's arrival in London, in July 1973, and inevitably set the tone for his brief visit. With the memory of the My Lai massacre still fresh in everyone's mind, this was just the kind of incident that could easily mobilize the attention of the media and galvanize anti-*Estado Novo* activists in the UK — as indeed it did. A heated debate in Westminster, and the sense of outrage expressed by large sectors of the public, eventually persuaded the Conservative government to distance itself from the clumsy attitude of denial adopted by the Portuguese (regarding first the existence of the massacre itself, and then its scale).[40]

---

[40]   Norrie MacQueen and Pedro A. Oliveira, 'Grocer Meets Butcher: Marcello Caetano's London Visit of 1973 and the Last Days of Portugal's Estado Novo', *Cold War History*, 10.1 (2010), 29–50.

But it was Guinea-Bissau, more than Mozambique, that proved to be the Achilles Heel of the Portuguese empire. The PAIGC's decision to hold an election for a constituent assembly in its 'liberated areas', less than a year after the assassination of its widely respected leader, Amílcar Cabral, and then launch a campaign for the diplomatic recognition for its new 'state', was a bold initiative that crowned a host of military achievements (such as the neutralization of Portugal's air supremacy in the territory, thanks to the introduction of Soviet surface-to-air rockets). By presenting its case at the UN, and immediately receiving the support of a significant number of member-states, the PAIGC posed an important challenge to Portugal's colonial theology, undermining as it did the doctrine of an 'integral' pluricontinental empire.[41]

At the UN, even though the PAIGC request was not exactly a thorny issue for the UK delegation, as it did not meet the common criteria which Britain followed to recognize new regimes, a sense of unease was evident in government circles when the matter came under discussion with other European powers. Although all but one of its eight fellow EEC partners decided to abstain on the resolution which hailed Guinea-Bissau's 'accession to independence', all of them made it known that they reserved the right to establish formal contacts with the PAIGC in the future. When instructing the UK Mission to justify its veto, Douglas-Home took care to emphasize the critical differences between the two countries' approaches: 'We agree that you should make a balancing explanation of the vote. Our objective will be to make it clear that we are not defending Portugal in Africa but our own principles of international law. You should say therefore that we have frequently made clear that the Portuguese should press ahead with all practical speed in granting self-determination and independence. We again urge them to demonstrate to the international community that they are making real progress.'[42]

Well informed of Portugal's deteriorating position in Guinea, Heath's government was even engaged in a last-minute effort to bring together Portuguese and PAIGC representatives at the negotiating table. This discreet mediating role allowed for a secret meeting of a low-ranking Portuguese official in London with a troika of PAIGC cadres in February 1974 — something that went against the hard-line Portuguese rhetoric of refusing to engage in talks with 'terrorists'. The meeting failed to produce any palpable results, but its revelation twenty years later indicates how unconvincing Caetano sounded to his allies when he re-stated Portugal's ability to sustain its military effort in Africa.[43]

---

[41]   Norrie MacQueen, 'Belated Decolonization and UN Politics against the Backdrop of the Cold War: Portugal, Britain and Guinea Bissau's Proclamation of Independence', *Journal of Cold War Studies*, 8.4 (2006), 29–56.

[42]   TNA. FCO 65/1395. Telegram from Douglas-Home to UK Delegation at the UN, 24 October 1973.

[43]   The meeting was revealed in a cover story published by the Portuguese weekly *Expresso* in 1994, the details of which are reproduced in José Pedro Castanheira, *Quem mandou matar Amílcar Cabral?* (Lisbon: Relógio d'Água, 1995).

Portugal's Endgame in Africa

The nature of the UK's involvement in the hazardous process of Portugal's extrication from Africa was, to a certain extent, conditioned by an unexpected coincidence — Labour's victory in the general election of February 1974 and the overthrow of Caetano's government in Portugal, less than two months later. For reasons that are almost self-explanatory, this simultaneous 'regime change' opened up new perspectives for the revitalization of the bilateral relationship and allowed London to play a small but not insignificant role in several stages of Portugal's decolonization.[44]

In its previous spell in opposition, the Labour Party had adopted a posture more critical to the continuation of the *Estado Novo*'s colonial policy: Caetano's visit to London in 1973 had given Wilson a pretext to move towards the stance more commonly associated with the 'anti-imperial' elements of his own party. Labour's ties with the leader of the Portuguese Socialist Party in exile, Mário Soares, were also strengthened on that occasion, and in the run-up to the general election a pledge was made in several party documents concerning the adoption of a firmer line towards the liberation of southern Africa, as soon as Labour returned to government.

Hence, the advent of a more liberal, if still undefined, regime in Lisbon, under the aegis of a military junta headed by General António de Spínola, opened the door to close diplomatic cooperation between the two countries. Soares and the Socialists became key protagonists in the post-coup politics in Portugal, and the British authorities were able to forge a wide range of contacts throughout the political spectrum in Lisbon. Portuguese officials and the military held the UK's decolonization record in high esteem and were eager to learn from what they perceived as the British experience of ending an empire in a relatively orderly fashion, as well as from their ability to build strong links with former colonies through the Commonwealth.

For the British, as well as for Soares, who in this respect articulated the consensus of the 'moderate' parties set up after the Revolution, the restoration of democratic freedoms in Portugal, and a relatively smooth transfer of power in Africa, depended upon the new regime's ability to put an end to the wars — even if this meant sacrificing some 'liberal niceties' in the agreements to be negotiated with the liberation movements. Any delay affecting the transition of power was generally seen as likely to bring about a breakdown of order, a renewal of the confrontation between the Portuguese army and the guerrillas, or even desperate counter-coups by the white settlers. All efforts were therefore to be directed towards avoiding a destabilization of the political process in

---

[44]   For a general overview of Portugal's decolonization and revolutionary process, see Kenneth Maxwell, *The Making of Portuguese Democracy* (Cambridge: Cambridge University Press, 1995) and Norrie MacQueen, *The Decolonization of Portuguese Africa: Metropolitan Revolution and the Dissolution of Empire* (London: Longman, 1997).

Portugal due to events in Africa — this was the paramount goal of the civilian actors in Portugal, as well as of the more 'progressive' wing of the MFA. The 'romantic' stand taken by Spínola, the unelected President of the Republic, who in the early stages of his short mandate tried to impose an alternative based on a plebiscite rather than the direct transfer of power to the liberation movements, was therefore perceived as unrealistic both in Whitehall and in the mainstream British press.[45]

In the months following the coup, the British authorities tried to assist Portugal in its efforts to reach an agreement regarding the future of Guinea, the colony where a military collapse seemed most likely to occur. Wilson and his Foreign Secretary, James Callaghan, a former Labour spokesman for colonial affairs, refrained from offering their good offices for any type of mediating role, but in May 1974 London become the venue for the first round of negotiations between Portuguese representatives and the PAIGC, while the British Embassy in Algiers provided secure communication channels to the Portuguese delegation when the Algerian capital hosted the ensuing round of talks. Apart from this, the UK's only significant moves in the early stages of Portugal's decolonization were its decision to withhold recognition of the PAIGC self-proclaimed 'state' until the independence agreement had been signed; and its request to the members of the UN's ad hoc commission set up in the previous year to investigate the Wiriyamu atrocities to conduct its inquiries in a discreet manner, at least while the thorny negotiations between Lisbon and the liberation movements were still being carried out.[46]

Of all the former Portuguese colonies, Mozambique — with its independence set for June 1975 by the Lusaka Agreement of September 1974 — was probably the one whose future had the most direct impact on British interests. The reason for this was, naturally, the situation in Rhodesia, where Ian Smith's government was still refusing to come to terms with the principle of majority rule. Given FRELIMO's commitment to the aspirations of Black Nationalism in Rhodesia, it was easy to predict a change in the attitude of the future Mozambican state with regard to its compliance with the UN sanctions that targeted Salisbury. The closure of Mozambique's ports to Rhodesia's foreign trade would not in itself render the international embargo effective, but would at least make the efforts undertaken by the white regime to circumvent the sanctions more expensive, and at the same time allow London to discontinue the Royal Navy's Beira Patrol. Given that the Lusaka Agreement (September 1974) had made no provisions whatsoever for the calling of elections, the UK's priority was to establish a working, and, if possible, an amicable, relationship with FRELIMO — an objective somewhat facilitated by the links which several

---

[45]   On British perceptions of Spínola's plans, see Pedro A. Oliveira, *Os despojos da Aliança*, pp. 411–23. On press comments see, for example, *The Times*, 'Dismantling an Empire', 24 May 1974, and *The Economist*, 'The unendurable burden', 27 April 1974, and 'Straying to the left', 11 May 1974.
[46]   See Pedro A. Oliveira, *Os despojos da Aliança*, pp. 417–26.

Labour ministers had forged with the Mozambican nationalists in various campaigns and anti-colonial bodies.

The first contacts between British officials and Samora Machel in Dar es Salaam indeed marked the beginning of an auspicious relationship between the two countries, as FRELIMO soon made clear its willingness to seal the Mozambican border with Rhodesia — a gesture that entailed severe harm to the country's economy, leading the UK to offer it some financial assistance in the form of 'development aid'. While acknowledging FRELIMO's debts towards some of the communist powers, British diplomats did not regard the absorption of Mozambique into the Soviet or the Chinese sphere of influence as inevitable. They were confident that Machel's 'pragmatism' would prevail over the more ideologically minded stances of other figures of the movement and, ultimately, pull the country into the direction of a 'non-aligned' stance, akin to the one adopted by the majority of OAU member states.[47]

The UK's approach to the decolonization of Angola makes an interesting contrast with Mozambique. In Angola, the fragmentation of the nationalists into three rival groups, each with its own distinct leaderships and external allies, as well as the dynamics of the Cold War and of regional conflicts, made the formulation of a coherent policy rather more difficult. However, while proclaiming a policy of 'neutrality' towards Angola's movements, a pro-UNITA bias became evident in Whitehall, at least from late 1974 until the eve of independence in Luanda, in November 1975. Contrary to what happened with FRELIMO and PAIGC, the MPLA seems to have failed to build a truly effective network of sympathizers within the British Labour Party, before and after the military coup in Lisbon. In some official circles, its historical leader, Agostinho Neto, was regarded as a weak and dogmatic politician, who at the time of the collapse of the Portuguese dictatorship faced a significant internal challenge (Daniel Chipenda's 'Eastern Revolt'), which he was only able to overcome by increasing his dependence on his Soviet patrons.

Jonas Savimbi, on the other hand, seemed a more promising figure. Besides enjoying the support of Kenneth Kaunda, one of Britain's key allies in the region, he was a charismatic leader who seemed most likely command the vote of Angola's most populous ethnic group, the Ovimbundu, in any future electoral contest. Additionally, the victory of a Soviet-backed movement in Luanda would almost certainly strengthen the hand of the more hard-line sectors in Rhodesia and South Africa, thereby undermining the prospects for the regional détente recently launched by Kaunda and Vorster. FCO papers concerning this period reveal various British governmental initiatives in favour of UNITA until the outbreak of the civil war in Angola, from invitations to Savimbi to visit London with all expenses paid, to the discreet encouragement

---

[47]   See TNA. FCO 45/1729. Minute of a meeting chaired by Martin Reid, head of CSDA, on the UK's future policy towards Mozambique, 3 March 1975, and FCO 45/1732. 'British policy towards Mozambique', by Stanley Duncan, 19 March 1975.

given to several private firms or businessmen to provide different forms of assistance to UNITA.[48]

This UNITA bias was eventually redressed when it became clear that Neto's movement would be able to proclaim Angola's independence in Luanda, on 11 November 1975. By then, not only did the MPLA government meet the criteria demanded by British recognition policy, but South Africa's intervention in the civil war alongside UNITA significantly altered the political outlook of the Angolan crisis. A rationale similar to that employed by the Attlee government in 1949, regarding the advantages of recognizing Mao's regime, was then put forward by several officials: the existence of formal diplomatic relations with Luanda would facilitate a dialogue with the MPLA, which in the long run might evolve towards a more 'pragmatic' posture and reduce its dependence upon the Soviet Union.[49] Translated into policy, this determined the UK's recognition of the Luanda government in February 1976, simultaneously with other EEC countries.

Such a gesture was insufficient, however, to inaugurate a period of 'constructive engagement' with the MPLA regime. In fact, British–Angolan relations were hindered by various incidents in the ensuing years, such as the trial of several British mercenaries who had fought in the FNLA ranks in the last stages of Angola's first civil war by a 'revolutionary court' in Luanda. The few British investments in the country, such as the Benguela Railway (owned by Tanganyika Concessions), were irreparably affected by the revival of the conflict with UNITA in the early 1980s, and British oil companies failed to secure a stake in the exploitation of Angola's rich reserves for years to come. By the end of the decade, it was difficult to predict a bright future for Western and British interests in Angola.

Final Remarks

In more than one way, the Angolan fiasco encapsulates several strands of Britain's attitude towards Portugal's end of empire. The British government's complacent stance towards the authoritarian regime of Salazar and Caetano meant that in 1974 its intelligence on the leadership of the main Angolan nationalist movements was poor; on the other hand, its initial preference for Savimbi's UNITA testifies to the importance of the Commonwealth dimension and the anti-Soviet orientation of its foreign policy; and its efforts to come to terms with the MPLA regime after November 1975, and persuade the more ideologically oriented Americans to do the same, highlight the pragmatic

---

[48]   TNA. FCO 45/1694, including the programme for the visit of Jonas Savimbi to the UK on April 1975, and the record of a meeting between UNITA's leader and the Parliamentary Under Secretary of State for Foreign and Commonwealth Affairs.

[49]   TNA/FCO 15/1688. Paper: 'Angola', from the Central and Southern Africa Department, 19 December 1975.

approach which was in evidence in other Cold War junctures. But, as this article has aimed to demonstrate, it is not easy to define in clear-cut terms Britain's policy with regard to Portugal's colonial predicament: a mixture of expediency and principled behaviour was present in several moments. Despite sharing with Portugal a similar determination to hold on to its imperial status in the post-war years, its ruling elite operated within a very different political culture. Even though historians nowadays tend to emphasize certain violent episodes that cast doubt on a 'Whig' version of Britain's decolonization (Malaya, Kenya, Aden), it is probably fair to say that its imperial disengagement was conducted so as to allow for the peaceful attainment of independence by a significant number of its colonies. The notion that Britain's international standing might benefit from its being perceived as a principled power which accepted the universality of self-determination was a powerful idea shaping the policy-making process in London. A more conventional strategic calculus, however, was ever-present in Whitehall: the need to preserve the cohesion of the 'Western alliance' was a paramount goal in Britain's foreign policy, even if it meant preserving the allegiance of an unrepentant colonial power like Portugal. Indeed, whenever it was felt that this goal could somehow be jeopardized, a cautious attitude was likely to prevail. Throughout the 1960s, for instance, this was translated into an absence of formal contacts with African nationalists and a neutral or sympathetic attitude at the UN. It would be wrong to place Britain on the same footing as other European powers who felt less embarrassed about assisting the *Estado Novo* regime and its wars in Africa. After 1974, the UK would benefit from a number of fortunate coincidences that allowed it to reap significant rewards in the decolonization of some Portuguese territories (particularly Mozambique). But in other places, such as the far-flung territory of East Timor — brutally occupied by Suharto's Indonesia in 1975 with the blessing of the US and Britain — a less principled notion of the 'national interest' eventually paved the way for an old style *realpolitik* approach.[50]

Instituto de História Contemporânea, Faculdade de Ciências Sociais e Humanas, Universidade Nova de Lisboa, 1069-061 Lisboa

[50]   For the intricacies of the US and the UK's involvement in East Timor's aborted decolonization in 1975, see Brad Simpson, '"Illegally and Beautifully": The United States, the Indonesian Invasion of East Timor and the International Community', *Cold War History*, 5.3 (2005), 281–315 and Pedro A. Oliveira, 'Entregue aos lobos: o Reino Unido e a invasão de Timor-Leste', *Relações Internacionais*, 13 (2007), 139–56.

Cold War Constraints:
France, West Germany and
Portuguese Decolonization

ANA MÓNICA FONSECA AND DANIEL MARCOS

CEHC, ISCTE-IUL and IPRI-UNL

Introduction

In this article, we will analyse the particular role that France and West Germany played in supporting Portugal's resistance to decolonization. Faced with the refusal of the United States to support his colonial policy at the beginning of the 1960s, Oliveira Salazar had to turn to his European Allies. The fact that both France and West Germany were willing to respond positively to this request is explained by the particular context these two countries were experiencing, in a world constrained by the Cold War. They decided to support Portugal in its resistance to decolonization mainly for reasons related to the Cold War and the importance that both Paris and Bonn attached to the particular role played by Portugal in this context. For France, supporting the Portuguese regime was seen as a way of defying the Western superpower and protecting its own interests in Africa; for the Federal Republic of Germany, it was a matter of keeping Portugal inside the Atlantic Alliance.

During the 1960s, these were the objectives behind Franco-German support of Portuguese colonial policy, which were reflected in the military cooperation and political assistance to the *Estado Novo* regime.

Cold War and Decolonization

If World War I helped to create local resistance movements against colonialism, it was World War II that destroyed the colonial system itself. In the Far East, occupation by the Japanese destroyed the French, British and Dutch imperial systems and the European powers proved unable to rebuild their imperial structure in those territories.[1] Nor can we ignore the impact that the United Nations Charter had in the process of dissolving the colonial structure and ideal. The endorsement of Wilsonian values, this time reflected by the approval of the Declaration of Human Rights in 1948, reinforced the post-war transnational

---

[1]   Odd Arne Westad, *The Global Cold War: Third World Interventions and the Making of our Times* (Cambridge: Cambridge University Press, 2005), pp. 86–87.

Portuguese Studies vol. 29 no. 2 (2013), 209–26
© Modern Humanities Research Association 2013

discourse. Although the Charter and the Declaration of Human Rights did not include enforcement mechanisms, they acted as an important source of legitimation of colonial peoples' efforts to build their societies independently of the European powers.[2]

Everything pointed towards a rapid disaggregation of the colonial empires. The first major state to obtain its independence was India, in 1947. With the Cold War under way, there was, however, no substantial interference from the superpowers in this process. The Indian nationalist movement had been growing since the 1930s and became more active during World War II, despite harsh British repression. The United Kingdom's inability to forge alliances with the Indian elites intensified the process of transfer of power, sealing the end of Britain's 'jewel in the crown'.[3]

In other regions of Asia and Africa, the Dutch, French and Portuguese were not so sensitive to the nationalist elites. If Indira Ghandi and Jawaharlal Nehru were able to secure independence for India, Ho Chi Min in Vietnam and Sukarno in Indonesia were strongly repressed. Furthermore, the United Kingdom decided to keep control of Malaya and Singapore, as well as its African territories. In this first decolonization wave in Asia, within a completely chaotic and fast-changing environment, the beginning of the Cold War was something unprecedented, both for the anticolonial and imperial actors, and even for the United States and the Soviet Union. Concerned with the evolving situation in Western Europe, both superpowers took time to adjust to events in Asia. Although understanding the radical nature of some movements, the US hesitated to openly support their European allies' maintenance of their colonial empires. The American objective was to encourage their allies to improve the economic and social conditions of the dependent territories, putting aside outdated conceptions of development.[4]

Mao Tse-Tung's coming to power in China, in 1949, and the beginning of the Korean War, in 1950, contributed to combining firmly the Cold War dynamics and the process of decolonization. In Vietnam, China began supporting Ho Chi Min's forces fighting the French, leading the US to unquestioningly support their European allies, at least in those areas that, like Indochina, were of strategic interest for the West. From this moment on, the Cold War was a factor in European resistance to decolonization.[5] By the end of the Korean War, the developments in Asia and Africa were seen mainly through the Cold War lens, both by the United States and the Soviet Union, which was followed,

---

[2] Mark Philip Bradley, 'Decolonization, the Global South and the Cold War, 1919–1962', in *The Cambridge History of the Cold War*, ed. by Odd Arne Westad and Melvyn Leffler, vol. I: *Origins* (Cambridge: Cambridge University Press, 2010), pp. 464–85 (p. 472).

[3] William Roger Louis and Ronald Robinson, 'The Imperialism of Decolonization', *The Journal of Imperial and Commonwealth History*, 22.3 (1994), 462–511.

[4] Bradley, p. 473.

[5] Martin Thomas, *Crises of Empire: Decolonization and Europe's Imperial State, 1918–1975* (London: Hodder Education, 2008), pp. 48–49.

immediately, by China and all the other Third World countries. Basing itself on a theory of modernization, according to which the economic and social development of the population and the preservation of the liberal system was the best way of preventing communist infiltration, the United States tried to persuade the European colonial powers and the newly independent countries to follow the North American model. In the case of the colonial powers, the 1948 Marshall Plan was the clearest example of this policy, even having a special programme (Point IV) dedicated to the developing countries, very similar to that applied in Europe. This reflected the need to implement a policy which had a direct economic and social impact, but it largely ignored Third World concerns regarding its own political evolution towards self-determination. From the Western point of view, abandoning the colonial empires seemed to be out of question.[6]

Later on, during the Eisenhower administration, the United States continued to insist that their European allies should invest in the political and economic development of their colonies. At the same time, they tried to draw the newly independent countries to their political bloc, not understanding that a possible interest by these countries in the American economic model did not correspond to an extension of cooperation at the political and diplomatic levels. Moreover, and mindful that the Cold War was conducted mainly in Europe, and in Germany in particular, the North American political elites ended up by focusing mainly on European issues, leaving Third World problems behind. Thus, they tended to be more sensitive to the appeals of the European colonial powers, which argued that they needed their empires in order to stimulate their own economic recovery.[7]

The intensification of the bipolar conflict and the growing impact it had on Third World disputes prompted the formation of an alternative position regarding decolonization. In Bandung, in 1955, the main anticolonial leaders defined a new transnational ideological base, which would allow the Asian and African peoples to be protected from the bipolar rivalry. Thus, Bandung created an alternative international order, built by countries which had their colonial past as common ground. As the Cold War reached stalemate in Europe, the superpowers spread their ideological competition towards the Third World, which proved to be fertile ground.[8]

In fact, during the 1960s, the United States, the Soviet Union and also China saw the newly independent Third World countries as stages on which their dispute was to be fought. Despite the post-colonial Third World leaders' insistence on non-alignment, they were dragged into this ideological conflict,

---

[6] John Kent, 'United States Reactions to Empire, Colonialism, and the Cold War in Black Africa, 1949–1957', *The Journal of Imperial and Commonwealth History*, 33.2 (2005), 195–220.

[7] Bradley, p. 477.

[8] Michael Latham, 'The Cold War in the Third World, 1963–1975', in *The Cambridge History of the Cold War*, ed. by Odd Arne Westad and Melvyn Leffler, vol. II: *Crises and Détente* (Cambridge: Cambridge University Press, 2010), pp. 258–80 (pp. 258–59).

which was fought between different development models. Thus, Cold War competition was magnified in the post-colonial regions of Asia and Africa, mainly because it overemphasized local conflicts, which had much more to do with local factors than with ideological differences.[9]

Portugal and the Colonial Issue in the Cold War

Two major events characterized the political and social scene in the second half of the twentieth century. After the end of World War II, the world was divided between two superpowers and their spheres of influence. However, even more than the Cold War it was the emergence of new states, formed as a consequence of the European colonial empires' disaggregation in Asia and Africa, which undoubtedly characterized world history, influencing international politics up to the present day. The most recent developments in decolonization studies allow us to understand that the Cold War was not just the political context that characterized the independence process of most peoples of Africa, Asia and Central America. Each of these two phenomena to some extent explained the other.[10]

In order to understand the interconnection between the Cold War and decolonization we must avoid confusing these two political, economic and social processes. A superficial analysis of the Soviet and North American documents may lead us to conclude that the decolonization process of the second half of the twentieth century was just another element of the bipolar rivalry. However, it is now clear that decolonization was a broad political process, which did not simply begin after World War II. As well as being deeply rooted in local factors preceding the Cold War, it undeniably followed that conflict, extending beyond its end.

Nevertheless, particularly after the 1950s, the bipolar rivalry affected the decolonization process at different levels, mostly because the United States and the Soviet Union (and, later, China) tried to export to the new emerging states their own model of political, economic and social organization.[11] This underlines the fact that the Cold War cannot be considered as merely a cause of the decolonization process, but also as a political conflict which framed it ideologically, helping to delay or accelerate the long process of political and social transformation that swept Asia and Africa in the second half of the twentieth century. It could be said that the relation between the Cold War and decolonization reflects the progressive domination of international society and politics by the ideological competition between the two superpowers.[12]

---

[9]   Latham, pp. 279–80.
[10]   Michael Graham Fry, 'The United Nations Confronts the United States in 1958', in *A Revolutionary Year: The Middle East in 1958*, ed. by Wlm. Roger Louis and Roger Owen (Washington, DC: Woodrow Wilson Center Press, 2002), pp. 143–80 (p. 143).
[11]   Bradley, pp. 464–70.
[12]   Odd Arne Westad, 'The New International History of the Cold War: Three (Possible) Paradigms', *Diplomatic History*, 24.4 (2010), 551–65.

The transformation that occurred in the international system after World War II forced the Portuguese regime to make some changes in the way Portugal presented its colonial policies to foreign countries. Salazar's ingrained distrust of US power, due especially to US anti-colonial positions, made him anticipate that an attack on the colonial empires was imminent. However, Lisbon saw a way to improve relations by exploiting the strategic importance of the Portuguese Atlantic islands, particularly the Azores. The invitation to Portugal to become a founding member of NATO clearly showed that the US wanted her involvement in the Western Alliance, despite being a dictatorship. This allowed the *Estado Novo* to pursue its traditional goals in foreign policy: the Atlantic vocation and a preferential alliance with a maritime power that would contribute to the maintenance of the colonial empire. The integration of Portugal into the North Atlantic Pact gave the regime equal status with the other European powers.[13]

After 1951, Salazar changed the Constitution, trying to replace the classic imperial idea that dated to the interwar period. Portugal reinforced its assimilationist conception of colonialism, designating its colonies Overseas Provinces, which would join with the European territories to form a nation that was 'una e indivisível' [united and indivisible]. However, this reform maintained the *Estatuto do Indígena* [Native Statute], denying citizenship to the majority of the colonized peoples.[14] Overall, we can say that the reorganization of the Portuguese colonial empire after World War II reflected a belief that Portugal could only survive as an intercontinental bloc. For the Portuguese political elites there was no space in the Cold War world for small countries because the world tended towards the constitution of great territorial blocs, economically strong and politically united. In other words, in this world 'as nações mais pequenas se sentem oprimidas' [the smaller nations feel oppressed] and tend to be absorbed by powerful countries or blocs.[15]

Thus, from the end of the 1940s the *Estado Novo* regime tried to frame Portuguese resistance to decolonization as a Cold War issue. In the developments in the Dutch and French empires in Asia, Salazar saw the pernicious hand of the Soviets. According to Portuguese diplomatic rhetoric, it could be expected that the same Soviet strategy would be extended to Africa too: in Salazar's own words, the Soviet Union was preparing to 'set fire to the African continent'. In his opinion, the only way to avoid such an event was through the establishment of European–African cooperation, with the support of the United States.[16]

---

[13] Nuno Teixeira, 'Entre África e a Europa: a política externa portuguesa, 1890–2000', in *Portugal contemporâneo*, ed. by António Costa Pinto (Lisbon: Dom Quixote, 2004), pp. 87–116. See also António Telo, *Portugal e a NATO: o reencontro da tradição atlântica* (Lisbon: Edições Cosmos, 1996).

[14] Valentim Alexandre, 'O império colonial', in *Portugal contemporâneo*, ed. by Costa Pinto, pp. 67–86.

[15] Alberto Franco Nogueira, *A luta pelo Oriente* (Lisbon: Centro de Estudos Políticos e Sociais, 1957), p. 97.

[16] 'Breves considerações sobre política interna e internacional: a propósito da inauguração do Estádio de Braga' (28 May 1950), in A. Oliveira Salazar, *Discursos e notas políticas*, vol. IV (Coimbra: Coimbra Editora, 1961), pp. 459–78.

The great importance that the regime attached to its colonial empire motivated it to resist the decolonizing movement by use of force. Particularly after 1955, with Portugal's admission to the UN, her colonial policy came under strong attack from the international community. The *Estado Novo*'s refusal to decolonize and its decision to defend the empire by force favoured a diversification of Portugal's traditional alliances. In fact, the new US policy towards Africa, defined after the Suez Crisis, which favoured an exit of European powers from the continent, created a period of increased tension in American–Portuguese relations. Pressure from the US led Portugal to react, by refusing to renew the Azores agreement. This situation endured from 1962 to 1971 and ultimately increased the distance between Washington and Lisbon.[17]

By the end of the 1950s, Portuguese foreign policy was gradually shifting from a strong relationship with the Atlantic powers (the UK and US) towards a new relationship with the continental countries (France and the Federal Republic of Germany), which had already recovered economically and politically from World War II. By becoming closer to France and West Germany, Portugal sought to make good the loss of the political and military support given until then by the US and NATO, by turning its back on its Atlantic tradition and embracing a European continental stance. It is within this context that we understand French and West German relations with Portugal during the 1960s.[18]

This shift reflects Portugal's major concern regarding its colonial policy. As the United States was unable, for either domestic or external reasons, to guarantee support to the maintenance of the Portuguese colonial empire, Lisbon's only alternative was to adopt a more pragmatic and flexible foreign policy. It would always be sympathetic with Western values, as long as that stance did not threaten Portuguese interests in the Third World. Whenever her sovereignty was put to the test outside Europe, Portugal would search for alternative support, assuming an autonomous position towards the Atlantic powers, as a way to safeguard Portuguese colonial policy. Simultaneously, the disposition of France and West Germany towards Portugal can be understood as a reflection of the search for a 'progressive autonomy' of the Western countries from the United States.[19]

---

[17]   António Telo, 'As Guerras de África e a mudança nos apoios internacionais de Portugal', *Revista de História das Ideias*, 16 (1995), 347–69 (p. 368).

[18]   Ibid.

[19]   John Lewis Gaddis defines progressive autonomy as something that the countries within each bloc tried to obtain, especially at the end of the 1950s. In the Soviet bloc, the main example is the People's Republic of China. In the Western bloc, de Gaulle's France shows the progressive difficulty that the US had in controlling their allies. Gradually, the 'weak were discovering opportunities to confront the strong'. John Lewis Gaddis, *The Cold War* (New York: Allen Lane, 2005), pp. 119–55.

French and West German Attitudes to the
Portuguese Resistance to Decolonization

The above mentioned diversification of alliances in Portuguese foreign policy was only possible due to the good will of France and the Federal Republic of Germany (FRG) towards Portuguese colonial policy. On the one hand, France and Portugal had shared since the 1930s a common position regarding their colonial empires, namely assimilationist principles. During World War II, there was even some ideological rapprochement by Portugal with the Vichy regime, which contributed to an understanding between the two countries.[20] Surprisingly, perhaps, this understanding was not broken after the liberation of France, and the two countries' cooperation continued until 1974, based on shared common interests in Africa. Portugal had a hard-line policy of resisting decolonization, while France saw Africa as one of its strategic areas of influence.[21]

West Germany, on the other hand, had been founded in 1949 as a direct consequence of its occupation after World War II. The firm resolve of Chancellor Konrad Adenauer to bind the FRG to the Western bloc characterized the first years of its foreign policy. In 1955, the FRG was finally admitted to NATO and recognized as an autonomous international actor. Due to Germany's sensitive position (a divided country in a divided Europe), Bonn's main concern was with the stability of the Western bloc. The conservative elites ruling the country had always demonstrated a particular respect and admiration for Salazar, who represented the spirit of 'old Europe', particularly for his conservative, Catholic character.[22] Besides this personal dimension, West Germany was particularly interested in the political stability of Portugal and the maintenance of the regime, in order to avoid any possibility of a communist takeover, which might spread to Spain.[23]

These were the two starting points for the role these countries played in the Portuguese resistance to the decolonization process. As mentioned above, France and Portugal had in common a colonial empire, which would face the same type of challenges; although they found somewhat different answers to these challenges, they had a similar view of their interests in the Third World. West Germany, for its part, was mainly concerned with the international impact of the Portuguese colonial problem, which led Bonn to develop an ambivalent policy towards it.

---

[20]   Cf. Helena Pinto Janeiro, *Salazar e Pétain: as relações luso-francesas durante a II Guerra Mundial (1940–1944)* (Lisbon: Edições Cosmos, 1998), p. 203.
[21]   Amaral da Silva Lala, 'L'Enjeu colonial dans les relations franco-portugaises, 1944–1974' (unpublished doctoral thesis, Institute d'Études Politiques de Paris, 2007), p. 28.
[22]   Ana Mónica Fonseca, 'A República Federal da Alemanha e a política colonial do Estado Novo no início da década de 1960', in *Outros horizontes: encontros luso-alemães em contextos coloniais*, ed. by Fernando Clara (Lisbon: Edições Colibri, 2005), pp. 65–78.
[23]   Ana Mónica Fonseca, *A força das armas: o apoio da República Federal da Alemanha ao Estado Novo (1958–1969)* (Lisbon: Instituto Diplomático, 2007).

French and Portuguese cooperation on the colonial issue[24]

For both Portugal and France, the beginning of the decolonization movement after World War II was perceived as a threat to their role in world affairs, leading both countries to resist granting self-determination to their colonies. Therefore, the approval of the United Nations Charter, as well as the Marshall Plan initiatives regarding the developing of European dependent territories, was treated with great suspicion by both the Paris and Lisbon governments. This situation allowed the beginning of a technical and economic cooperation between the two countries in international forums such as the African Commission for Technical Cooperation.[25]

Additionally, for Portugal, France's traditional Christian and colonial heritage was perceived as an alternative to the American cultural supremacy in the Western alliance. However, what could be seen as a perfect conjunction for cooperation was affected by the different nature of the political systems in each country. Portugal witnessed with deep sorrow France's departure from Indochina in 1954, from Tunisia and Morocco in 1956, and Algeria in the early 1960s.[26] Contrary to what happened in democratic France, however, Portuguese resistance to decolonization was mainly explained by the authoritarian nature of its regime. It was the *Estado Novo*'s political elites and Salazar himself who decided to resist by force any move towards self-determination in the Portuguese empire, mainly because it was inconsistent with the nationalist ideology of the regime.[27]

Despite these differences, France and Portugal came to share common interests right up to the end of the Portuguese colonial empire. Together, they tried to avoid the attacks that both countries suffered in the UN (France until leaving Algeria, in 1962; Portugal until the end of the *Estado Novo*, in 1974). For France, supporting Portugal meant helping a country in its dispute with the United States over its colonial policy, and, most importantly, assisting a country that had an important presence in Africa, a region that France considered of strategic importance. These were the main reasons why Portugal and France deepened their political and military cooperation, in the final years of the Portuguese empire.[28]

Nevertheless, the first years of the Gaullist era in France were followed with some concern by the Salazar regime. In 1958, Charles de Gaulle came to

[24]   An earlier version of this topic was published in *Portuguese Studies Review*, 16.2 (2008), 103–19 (pp. 106–11).
[25]   Commission de Coopération Technique Africaine (CCTA). Amaral da Silva Lala, pp. 60–88.
[26]   Amaral da Silva Lala, p. 80 and Sandrine Bègue, *La Fin de Goa et de l'Estado da Índia: décolonisation et Guerre Froide dans le Sous-Continent Indien (1945–1962)*, vol. I (Lisbon: Instituto Diplomático, 2007), pp. 555–57.
[27]   António Costa Pinto, *O fim do império português: a cena internacional, a guerra colonial e a descolonização, 1961–1975* (Lisbon: Livros Horizonte, 2001), p. 86.
[28]   Daniel Marcos, *Salazar e de Gaulle: a França e a questão colonial portuguesa (1958–1968)* (Lisbon: Instituto Diplomático, 2007), pp. 235–46.

power broadly defending authority, order and strong governmental control, regarded by the Portuguese regime as a positive change. However, the revision made by de Gaulle to French colonial policy, testified by the independence of French Guinea and the other colonial territories and by developments in the Algerian War, terrified the Portuguese government. The regime saw this change in French policy as the end of an advantageous cooperation between their countries, similar to the situation when Britain relinquished its empire in Asia and Africa.[29]

Nevertheless, this did not happen. The recognition of the right to self-determination and, therefore, to decolonization by the new French government did not mean the end of cooperation between Portugal and France, despite Salazar's own rejection of that course of action. For de Gaulle, ending the colonial bond with the African possessions was crucial to the new politics he wanted to pursue: the reinforcement of France as a European power with nuclear capability and, to some extent, militarily independent of American protection. As John Lewis Gaddis put it, France's goal 'was nothing less than to break up the bipolar Cold War international system.'[30]

The relations between Portugal and the French government should be seen in this context. De Gaulle tried to take advantage of the Portuguese refusal to decolonize, realizing that the isolation of Salazar's regime, despite French cooperation, could strengthen its own position in the Western World. In fact, at the beginning of the 1960s, Portuguese colonial policy was strongly condemned in the United Nations due to Portugal's obstinate refusal to leave Africa.[31] This was the beginning of a tense period in Portuguese–American relations. In early 1961, after the war started in Angola, the new Kennedy administration sought to pressure the Portuguese government into transforming its colonial policy, paving the way to self-determination. Also in the UN, and for the first time, the American administration voted against Portugal and in favour of Third World countries in a set of resolutions that condemned the beginning of the war in Portuguese Africa.[32] Thus, it is possible to say that de Gaulle saw in these circumstances the 'ideal occasion' to, once again, 'tackle north American power, accusing it of a lack of solidarity towards its European allies'.[33]

That is why, when the Portuguese Foreign Minister, Marcello Mathias,[34] met

---

[29]   Daniel Marcos, 'Portugal e a França na década de 1960: a questão colonial e o apoio internacional', *Relações Internacionais*, 11 (2006), 31–45 (pp. 34–35).
[30]   John Lewis Gaddis, *The Cold War* (London: Penguin Books, 2005), p. 138.
[31]   Three resolutions were approved by the General Assembly of the United Nations in December 1960, condemning Portuguese colonial policy and demanding the decolonization of the non-self-governing territories. For a detailed description of all the UN resolutions regarding Portuguese colonial policy, see A. E. Silva, 'O litígio entre Portugal e a ONU (1960–1974)', *Análise Social*, 130 (1995), 5–50.
[32]   Luís Nuno Rodrigues, *Salazar-Kennedy: a crise de uma aliança* (Lisbon: Editorial Notícias: 2002).
[33]   Daniel Marcos, *Salazar e de Gaulle*, p. 232.
[34]   Marcello Mathias (1903–1999) was Foreign Minister between 1958 and 1961. After leaving the Ministry he was appointed Ambassador in Paris, where he remained until 1971.

de Gaulle in Paris, in October 1960, de Gaulle promised to help the Portuguese struggle to keep the African territories. Informed by Mathias that Portugal would resist granting independence to its colonial possessions, 'at any cost', the General's reply was clear: France would 'never do anything that could harm the Portuguese ideas towards its colonial possessions.'[35] With this statement, French–Portuguese cooperation was clearly reinforced. In the UN, for example, French support to Portugal during 1961 was in line with the words of de Gaulle. If, as described above, the United States supported the Third World countries' resolutions against Portuguese colonial policy, France always chose to follow an abstentionist position, a pattern that continued until 1974.

French commitment to Portugal did go further, to the point that France even tried to influence US policy on the Portuguese question. In May 1961, the representatives of France, the United States and the United Kingdom met in London to discuss, among other issues, Angola. On this occasion, the division between France and the US became clearer. The French position was based on the conviction that Portugal was capable of containing the nationalist uprisings. Thus, the attitude towards Portugal should be persuasive, applying only light pressure on Salazar to accept decolonization. According to the French, the adoption of a softer position had the advantage of concealing from the USSR and the Third World the existence of divisions inside the Western Alliance regarding the colonial issue.[36] At the end of May, during President Kennedy's visit to Paris, de Gaulle insisted that the Western World should not 'offend' Portugal, by publicly attacking its colonial policy, because that would only 'instigate unrest in Angola'. By so doing, the French president was inviting his American counterpart to follow France's aim to 'progressively encourage' Portugal to grant independence to the colonies.[37] In this sense, this moderate attitude towards the Angolan question should prevent the withdrawal of Portugal from the Western Alliance, and avoid political instability or even the establishment of a communist regime in the Iberian Peninsula, which would certainly be the case with a sudden loss of the empire.

France's sympathetic attitude towards Portuguese colonial policy led the two countries to reinforce their already solid military cooperation. In fact, some senior Portuguese military chiefs were former students of the French War Academy, with a thorough knowledge of French military equipment. France thus became one of the first options when US military supplies started to become scarce. During the 1960s, Portuguese–French military cooperation allowed Portugal to obtain equipment which was indispensable to its African war effort: aeroplanes, helicopters, trucks, ships and submarines. In addition to the *Nord-Atlas*, *Broussard* and *Harvard T-6* aeroplanes bought even before the Colonial

[35]   Maurice Vaïsse, *Documents diplomatiques françaises, 1960* (Paris: Imprimerie National, 1996), pp. 457–58. The Portuguese diplomat constantly reminded the French representatives that Angola might turn into another case of instability in Africa, just as the Belgian Congo did.
[36]   Daniel Marcos, *Salazar e de Gaulle*, pp. 84–95.
[37]   Maurice Vaïsse, *Documents diplomatiques françaises*, pp. 669–70.

War had begun, Portugal acquired from France, from 1963, the prestigious *Allouette III* helicopter.[38]

Nevertheless, political circumstances forced France to impose some restrictions on military supplies to Portugal. In 1962, the French government was forced by the deterioration of the Portuguese international position to limit the type of military equipment sold to the country. According to the French Prime Minister, Michel Debré,[39] France should sell to Portugal only 'strictly defensive' material such as cargo planes and other means of transport, whilst the sale of equipment 'capable of being used in counter-guerrilla warfare' should be refused.[40]

However, the negotiations between Portugal and France for the construction of eight warships, four submarines and four escort vessels in 1963–64, reflected, more than ever, the impact of political considerations on military cooperation. In this case, Portugal had to deal with the resistance of some French ministries, mainly Finance (concerned with the stability of the French currency) and Foreign Affairs, but encountered favourable attitudes at the Defence Ministry. The Portuguese Navy had been attempting to buy warships from its French counterpart since 1958, and some preliminary contact took place in 1960. Nonetheless, the beginning of the Colonial War in Angola postponed the talks until 1963, when the negotiations were resumed. Once again, what seemed to be strictly military talks were constrained by the political background. Also in this same year, the French government presented to Portugal a proposal for the establishment of a military base in the Azores that would enable the French Armed Forces to test their ballistic equipment. As we shall see, both issues were related, and the Portuguese government had to exploit French strategic and military needs in order to overcome any political resistance.

Portugal's main objective was to obtain French financial support for the construction of the warships. France's first proposal, although favourable to the Portuguese government, was not welcomed by Marcello Mathias, the Portuguese Ambassador at the time. In his words, Portugal's wish was that 'os pagamentos começassem o mais tarde possível, que se escalonassem pelo mais longo prazo possível e que a taxa de juro fosse a mais baixa possível' [the payments should start as late as possible, they should be spread over the longest term possible, and the rate of interest should be as low as possible]. Furthermore, he was not afraid to threaten the French with the possibility of the Azores negotiations being called off.[41] It was a high-risk move, but Portugal did accomplish its purposes. France agreed to build eight warships, with the financial operation being supported by French enterprises. Beyond this, the Portuguese Armed

---

[38] Daniel Marcos, *Salazar e de Gaulle*, pp. 153–59.
[39] Debré (1912–1996) was Prime Minister between 1959 and 1962.
[40] Archive du Ministère des Affaires Étrangère de France (AMAE), Europe/Portugal (1961–1970)/Vol. 90: 'Note from the Foreign Ministry', 1 June 1970.
[41] Instituto dos Arquivos Nacionais/Torre do Tombo, AOS/CO/MA-5, 'Telegram from the Portuguese Embassy in Paris', 1964.

Forces also obtained guarantees from the French government to supply ammunition to the ships for fifteen years. As Mathias wrote to Salazar, this agreement was extremely important to Portugal because it showed how good the relations between these two states were. Despite the international criticism of Portuguese colonial policy, France 'não hesitou em provar-nos a amizade das nossas relações' [did not hesitate to prove to Portugal its friendship] and 'a sua convicção que a nossa política em África não nos conduza a uma catástrofe' [its conviction that our policy in Africa will not lead us to a catastrophe].[42]

With regard to the establishment of a French military base in the Azores, this also turned out to be a very profitable deal for the military needs of the Portuguese Armed Forces in Africa. The signing of the agreement on 7 April 1964 was a way for Portugal to return France's 'amizade e lealdade' [friendship and loyalty]; at the same time, for Portugal it was an opportunity 'que nos assegure uma certa forma de estabilidade tanto no apoio político como militar da França' [that should assure us a certain sort of stability in both political and military support from France].[43] With this sympathetic attitude, Lisbon managed to force France to ignore the restrictions imposed on military exports to Portugal since 1962, receiving authorization to import military equipment needed by its Armed Forces, particularly rockets.[44]

With these developments, 1964 was the high point of the Portuguese–French political and military cooperation. From then on, the military relations between the two countries stagnated, although we cannot say that they got worse. Until September 1968, when Salazar left the government, there were no further significant developments in French–Portuguese relations. Despite the French military lobby's desire to increase cooperation with Portugal, the acquisition of twelve *PUMA* helicopters in 1969 was probably the most important Portuguese purchase in the second half of the 1960s. Nevertheless, France continued to support Portugal politically in the United Nations.[45]

West Germany and the Portuguese colonial issue[46]

Contrary to what happened with France, the main element of Portuguese–West German relations was military cooperation. Initiated after the FRG's admission to NATO, in 1955, this cooperation began with the establishment of a training base for the West German Air Force in southern Portugal, at the end of 1960. This base, to be installed in Beja (Alentejo), would serve for training in long-distance flights and was part of a larger system of bases designed for logistics

[42]   IAN/TT, AOS/CO/MA-5, 'Communications from the Portuguese Embassy in Paris', 29 February 1964.
[43]   'Letter from Marcello Mathias to Oliveira Salazar', in *Correspondência Marcello Mathias/Salazar, 1947/1968*, ed. by Joaquim Veríssimo Serrão (Lisbon: Difel, 1984), pp. 465–66.
[44]   Daniel Marcos, *Salazar e de Gaulle*, pp. 202–06.
[45]   Amaral da Silva Lala, pp. 323–401.
[46]   An earlier version of this topic was published in *Portuguese Studies Review*, 16.2 (2008), 103–19 (pp. 111–17).

support in Europe, in case of war. In return for establishing this base on Portuguese territory, it was agreed between Lisbon and Bonn that the German Armed Forces would purchase large quantities of ammunition and hand grenades produced by Portuguese military manufacturers (especially the Fábrica Nacional de Braço de Prata — FNBP). One of the most important elements of this agreement was the commitment by the German Defence Ministry that 'as fábricas portugueses estariam sempre ocupadas com encomendas satisfatórias' [the Portuguese factories would always be kept busy with sufficient orders].[47] That is, these industries would always be kept operative and thus able to produce weapons and ammunitions for the Portuguese Armed Forces as well. As a consequence of this commitment, Lisbon had to pay only the production costs, since the maintenance expenses were already covered by the German agreement. The respective Ministers of Defence, Júlio Botelho Moniz and Franz Joseph Strauss, signed the final agreement for the establishment of the Beja Airfield in December 1960.[48]

However, only three months after the signature of this long-term agreement, the colonial wars erupted in Angola, completely changing the nature of this otherwise regular cooperation between two NATO Allies. Confronted with the Portuguese refusal to recognize the right to self-determination by its colonial possessions, the Federal Republic found itself divided as to what position to take. On the one hand, the strategic importance of Portugal to the Atlantic Alliance was something that Bonn could not ignore. It recognized the importance of supporting a NATO ally that was strongly anti-communist and that controlled one of the main elements of Western — and most importantly, West German — security, namely the Azores. At the same time, the West German leaders feared that, in the event of the *Estado Novo* losing its empire, the whole regime would fall apart, creating a power vacuum which would allow a communist takeover in Portugal. Such a disturbance would certainly spill over into the rest of the Iberian Peninsula, something unacceptable to Bonn. Moreover, by giving its support, West Germany believed it would be showing Salazar that he was not alone in the Western World, despite the difficulties created by some other European allies, as well as by the Kennedy administration. It is clear, therefore, that a Portuguese withdrawal from NATO was something to be avoided at all costs by the German government.[49]

On the other hand, the FRG was trying to enter Africa, with the objective of gaining some leverage over the Afro-Asian bloc. Besides economic interests (mainly related to the access to raw materials and to the exportation of German products), Bonn's objective was to avoid international recognition of the 'other Germany', the German Democratic Republic (GDR). In particular, it tried to

[47]   IAN/TT, AOS/CO/GR-10, 'Report of the conversations between the Defense Ministers of Portugal and the Federal Republic of Germany', 16 January 1960.
[48]   Ana Mónica Fonseca, *A força das armas*, pp. 43–53.
[49]   Ana Mónica Fonseca, 'Dez anos de relações luso-alemãs: 1958–1968', *Relações Internacionais*, 11 (2006), 47–60 (pp. 51–52).

gain the support of the new African states for its positions regarding Berlin (which became even more relevant after the construction of the Berlin Wall, in August 1961).[50] Bonn then developed a broad range of instruments to gain the attention of the developing countries in Asia and Africa, which were mainly applied through the so-called development aid. In the early 1960s it created the Ministry of Economic Cooperation,[51] with the main objective of managing the funds provided for this purpose by the federal government.[52] As we can see, Bonn's position regarding Portuguese colonial policy was always conditioned by the Cold War, either by the importance of political stability in the Iberian Peninsula, or by the competition with East German influence in the Third World.

Bearing this in mind, the solution was to follow an ambiguous policy: Bonn decided not to take any position that could challenge Portuguese colonial policy, whilst trying to avoid any action that could be understood by the Third World as supporting the maintenance of the Portuguese empire. The resulting policy was in practice extremely favourable towards Portugal. In terms of military cooperation, large quantities of aeroplanes, weapons and ammunition were given to Portugal, from the beginning of 1961 and throughout the rest of the decade. The most important aircraft were the *Dornier DO-27* (suited to transportation) and the *Harvard T-6* (used as a bomber). The *Dornier DO-27*s were later converted in Portugal for reconnaissance purposes, as well as for undertaking surveillance operations with armed support to ground forces.[53] Although the German authorities knew that these planes were to be sent to Africa, they trusted in the Portuguese declaration that 'os aviões pertenciam ao Ministério da Defesa Portuguesa e serão utilizados em defesa dos interesses da NATO' [the planes belonged to the Portuguese Defence Ministry and will be used in defence of NATO interests].[54] This declaration, requested by the German government as a guarantee, was clearly ambiguous and it could be understood in many senses, which favoured both the Portuguese and German interests. From the Portuguese point of view, it corresponded to the reality, because the ideology stated that the defence of Europe should begin in Africa, and Salazar believed that the Colonial Wars were also a way of preventing Soviet influence in the African territories. On the other hand, this declaration also suited the West German government, allowing it to say to the African states, who accused it of helping Portugal in the Colonial Wars, that Salazar's government had given assurances that it would use the equipment only inside the NATO region.[55]

[50]   Ibid.
[51]   *Bundesministerium für Wirtschaftliche Zusammenarbeit*, BMZ
[52]   Bastian Hein, *Die Westdeutschen und die Dritte Welt: Entwicklungspolitik und Entwicklungsdienst zwischen Reform und Revolte, 1959–1974* (Oldenburg: Institute für Zeitgeschichte, 2004), pp. 38–41.
[53]   John P. Cann, *Contra-insurreição em África, 1961–1974: o modo português de fazer a guerra* (Lisbon: Edições Atena, 1998), p. 177; *Politisches Archiv von Auswaertiges Amt*, B 26, 113, 'Note of the Auswaertiges Amt', 6 October 1961.
[54]   *AHD-MNE*, PEA, M. 486, 'Telegram 132 from the Portuguese Embassy in Bonn', 18 October 1963.
[55]   Ana Mónica Fonseca, *A força das armas*, p. 165.

A good example of the advantageous cooperation between Portugal and the FRG are the agreements of 4 November 1963, in which the FRG sold to the Portuguese Air Force a total of forty-six *Dornier DO-27*s and seventy *Harvard T-6*s. They were sold at a low price, and were paid for by the maintenance of German planes in the *Oficinas Gerais de Manutenção Aeronáutica* (OGMA). As we can see, the Portuguese government would not have to give any money for the aeroplanes; it was a direct exchange of services, and of much greater value to Portugal than to West Germany.[56]

With the changing international context and with the German persistence in penetrating the African continent, Portuguese–German relations deteriorated in the second half of the 1960s. The pressures of the African states and the economic crisis of the period, as well as the coming to power of the SPD (in coalition with the CDU/CSU) in December 1966, caused the reduction of the Beja Base project, with consequences for military relations as a whole. Mainly because of its economic difficulties, the German government decided to reduce the Beja Airfield project, handing Portugal, nonetheless, a final reward. As compensation for abandoning the base, the German Defence Ministry sold Portugal thirty *Dornier DO-27*s — again at a very favourable price — and allowed relations between Lisbon and the *Dornier* company to be established so that the aeroplanes could be manufactured in Portugal. In May 1969, with Marcello Caetano now head of government, Portugal and the FRG agreed that the Beja Air Base would become a training base for civil aviation companies, specifically TAP and Lufthansa. All the other projects, including the residential area, hospitals and the ammunitions storehouse, were either abandoned or dramatically reduced.

The German Social Democrats' arrival in power in Bonn thus coincided with a decline in Portuguese–German military cooperation. While in opposition, the SPD had gone as far as to develop some contacts with the liberation movements of the Portuguese colonies.[57] However, once in government, and despite having their party leader, Willy Brandt, in the Foreign Affairs Ministry, the Social Democrats did not have the political space or, indeed, the political will, to dramatically change their relations with Portugal. In fact, the West German government's strategy towards Portugal was changing: relations with Portugal should be kept up, but with the general objective of favouring the liberalization of the regime, and of drawing Lisbon into the EEC. Thus, the arrival of the SPD in power would not mean a radical interruption of the relationship between Portugal and the FRG.[58]

---

[56] AHFA, EMFA, Proc. nº 551,13 — Agreement between the Federal Ministry of Defence and Portuguese National Defence Ministry, 4 November 1963.

[57] Rui Lopes, 'Between Cold War and the Colonial Wars: The Making of West German Policy towards the Portuguese Dictatorship, 1968–1974' (unpublished doctoral thesis, London School of Economics and Political Science, 2011), pp. 185–220.

[58] Antonio Muñoz Sánchez, 'La Socialdemocracia alemana y el Estado Novo (1961–1974)', *Portuguese Studies Review*, 13.1/2 (2005), 477–503 (p. 484).

This was even more obvious after 1969, when the SPD become the majority party in Bonn (in coalition with the Liberals). Despite actively pursuing an understanding with the Eastern bloc and the Soviet Union (which was obtained in the mid-1970s), Bonn continued with its ambiguous position regarding Portuguese colonial policy. In fact, the division inside the government was even greater now. The Foreign Affairs Minister, the Liberal Walter Scheel, asserted that military cooperation should be preserved, as it was 'the only realistic and adequate alternative for the Western Alliance strategic objectives *and* the West German economic interests'.[59] On the other hand, the Minister for Economic Cooperation, Erhard Eppler (from the left wing of the SPD), argued that it was time to end military cooperation with Portugal, and that Bonn should begin supporting the African liberation movements — an ambition that was eventually achieved through the Friedrich Ebert Foundation.[60] However, once again, this division had no direct results on Portuguese–West German relations. There was in fact a decrease in military cooperation, but at the economic level Portuguese–West German relations grew stronger. The participation of West German corporations in the construction of the Cabora Bassa Dam, for which Bonn gave important credit guarantees, was an important signal of continuity.[61]

Only in September 1973, when both West and East Germany were admitted to the United Nations, did the Federal Republic publicly criticize Portuguese colonial policy. Willy Brandt was aware that the Democratic Republic would most certainly support any type of radical resolution against Portugal in the UN General Assembly, thus supporting African ambitions and reinforcing East Germany's leverage in the Third World. He therefore had to decide whether to maintain the ambiguous, and increasingly difficult, policy of cooperation with Portugal, thus facing criticism in the international arena, and even within his own Party, or to radically change the Federal Government's position. The increasing criticism from the SPD and of the Social Democrat youth, on the one hand, and publication in July 1973 of an article in *The Times* denouncing the Wiriyamu massacre, in Mozambique, left Chancellor Willy Brandt with no option: in September 1973, he declared in the UN General Assembly the FRG's support for 'the liquidation by the United Nations of the remaining colonialism, especially in Africa'.[62]

---

[59] 'Memorando do Ministério Federal dos Negócios Estrangeiros sobre a Cooperação militar luso-alemã', 16 de Novembro de 1970, Akten der Aussenpolitik der Bundesrepublik Deutschland (AAPBRD), 1970, pp. 2069–70.
[60] The Friedrich Ebert Stiftung (FES) is a political foundation associated with the SPD, which developed intense international activity. During this period in particular, the FES represented the left wing of the Social-Democratic Party. One of the most obvious examples of this is the fact that it became public knowledge that the Foundation was giving moral and financial support to the nationalist movements of Angola, Mozambique and Guinea. See Patrick von zur Mühlen, *Die internationale Arbeit der Friedrich-Ebert-Stiftung: Von den Anfängen bis zum Ende des Ost-West-Konflikts* (Bonn: Dietz Verlag, 2007).
[61] Rui Lopes, 'Between Cold War and the Colonial Wars', pp. 128–34.
[62] By referring directly to *the* remaining colonialism, there was no doubt that this was a reference to Portugal. Thomas Kreyssig, *Die Portugal-Politik der SPD von 1969–1976 auf transnationaler und*

As can be seen, the relations between Portugal and the Federal Republic of Germany during the 1960s were based essentially on the military rather than political aspects. These were of great importance to the Portuguese regime's colonial policy, mainly because they were fundamental for the maintenance of the wars in Africa. Despite West Germany's constant dilemma between supporting Portugal and penetrating Africa, we can say that the cooperation with Portugal was favoured. Contrary to expectations, the arrival of the SPD in power (first, in the Grand Coalition, then as the majority party) did not greatly affect the economic and military cooperation between Bonn and Lisbon, as the West German participation on the Cabora Bassa Dam attested. Only when it was forced to take a public position regarding Portuguese colonialism did the FRG opt to criticize its ally, always keeping in mind the constraints of the Cold War and in particularly the competition with East Germany.

Final Remarks: The Cold War and Diversification of Portuguese Alliances in Order to Resist Decolonization

Decolonization and the Cold War were two parallel processes that characterized the second half of the twentieth century. Even though decolonization was a social and political process that pre-dated the start of the Cold War, the ideological competition between the superpowers in the early 1950s quickly affected the struggle for independence of the colonial territories. For a small country such as Portugal, which attached major importance to its colonial possessions, the decolonization movement that emerged at the end of World War II caused great apprehension. Fearing that the end of the empire would lead to both the end of the *Estado Novo* and the loss of Portugal's importance in Europe, the regime took advantage of its authoritarian nature, resisting the granting of any kind of self-determination to its colonies.

This was facilitated by Portugal's position in the Western bloc. Being a founding member of NATO, mainly because of the geostrategic position of the Azores, Portugal was led by Cold War constraints to establish close relations with the main Atlantic power, the United States, despite Salazar's deep distrust of Washington's traditional anti-colonial position. However, as developments in the Third World increased pressure on the European colonial powers, Portugal clearly understood that it would have to find alternative sources of support for the maintenance of its colonial policy. Taking advantage of the close relationship with France and the FRG, within NATO, Portugal gradually shifted its foreign policy towards the continental European countries. But why choose France and West Germany?

Both Paris and Lisbon decided to keep their colonial territories for as long as possible. France eventually abandoned its empire, at the beginning of the 1960s,

internationaler *Ebene*, Masters Seminar Work for the Luwig-Maximilians-Universität in Munich, 1990, p. 35.

but this did not mean that these two countries would follow separate paths regarding the decolonization issue. In fact, there were two distinct reasons behind French support for Portugal in its international struggle against the anticolonial movement. First, because France continued to see Africa as one of its strategic areas of interest and as such would not abstain from taking a position in this region. Second, and more importantly, de Gaulle's France opted to manifest a high degree of autonomy in relation to the United States. When the Atlantic superpower demonstrated its unwillingness to support Portugal, even voting against its ally in the UN, France immediately accused Washington of abandoning Portugal. France, by contrast, would assume its responsibility in supporting Portugal, both politically and military.

West Germany, in turn, supported Portugal for reasons mainly related to the stability of the Western bloc. Indeed, West German–Portuguese cooperation derived directly from the participation of both countries in NATO. However, after the beginning of the colonial wars, the FRG decided to maintain the close relationship it already had with the *Estado Novo*. In making this decision, Bonn had faced a typical Cold War dilemma, divided between supporting a Western ally and penetrating Africa, a region increasingly important, not only for economic reasons, but particularly for reasons related to the competition with the German Democratic Republic. Only at the beginning of the 1970s did West German support for the Portuguese regime's colonial policy diminish in its importance, once again due to the evolution of the Cold War and the admission of both East and West Germany to the UN.

Therefore, the Cold War constraints were the main motives which led to France's and West Germany's support for Portuguese colonial policy, and that, conversely, allowed the survival of the *Estado Novo* until 1974.

South Africa and the Aftermath of Portugal's 'Exemplary' Decolonization: The Security Dimension

FILIPE RIBEIRO DE MENESES AND ROBERT MCNAMARA

UNI-Maynooth

Allister Sparks, in his seminal study of Apartheid, *The Mind of South Africa*, writes: 'though it occurred five thousand miles away among another people in another continent, in South Africa the Portuguese Revolution was an event of catalytic importance that changed the whole directional flow of public affairs'. 25 April 1974 was, for Sparks, a 'simultaneous turning point at which the Afrikaner revolution created and entered a phase of crisis and decline, and at which the black revolution began its rise.'[1] The end of the Salazar/Caetano New State, and the hurried decolonization that followed, would indeed alter dramatically the balance of power in southern Africa, but it took the decision-makers in Pretoria time to realize this — time that they did not, in fact, possess. The purpose of this article is to examine the reaction of those decision-makers to the events in Lisbon and, of course, in Mozambique and Angola, and to show that there was no coordinated, over-arching response: like other regional powers, and even the superpowers, South Africa was caught off guard by the 'Carnation Revolution', and struggled, as the pace of developments increased, to identify precisely where its national interests lay, being hampered in its attempts by too great a confidence in its ability to survive the ongoing transformation of the region, and by internal power struggles.

Before the Revolution

By the late 1960s, South Africa had become firmly convinced of the necessity of preserving Portugal's rule in the latter's African territories. Isolationist premier Henrik Verwoerd had been replaced by John Vorster, who encouraged increasing cooperation between both the South African Defence Forces (SADF) and the powerful intelligence services under the direction of Henrik van den Bergh and their Portuguese and Rhodesian counterparts.[2] Military cooperation

---

[1]   Allister Sparks, *The Mind of South Africa* (Johannesburg: Jonathan Ball, 2003), p. 303.
[2]   See for instance P. Correia, and G. Verhoef, 'Portugal and South Africa: Close Allies or Unwilling Partners in Southern Africa during the Cold War?', *Scientia Militaria: South African Journal of Military Studies*, 37.1 (2009) <http://ajol.info/index.php/smsajms/article/view/48731>. A recent treatment

Portuguese Studies vol. 29 no. 2 (2013), 227–50
© Modern Humanities Research Association 2013

had culminated in October 1970 in Exercise ALCORA, which provided for increasingly close staff talks between the militaries of the three countries and the development of which accelerated considerably from the autumn of 1973 until April 1974.[3] In this period South Africa and Rhodesia sought ever closer military ties, and this desire sparked off a high-level disagreement within Portuguese military circles regarding Pretoria's proposed 'total strategy'.[4] Nonetheless, as Jamie Miller has recently observed, under 'Operation Cadiz', launched in September 1973, P. W. Botha, the South African Defence Minister, committed South Africa to bankrolling Portuguese counter-insurgency to the tune of R150 million over five years.[5] Thanks to these funds significant purchases — including of French-designed *Crotale* surface-to-air missiles — were made by the Portuguese in the months preceding the April 1974 revolution.[6]

Despite the coming into being of Exercise ALCORA, and the countless threat assessments it produced, there is only scant evidence that South Africa, and especially its intelligence services, anticipated the revolution of 25 April 1974, carried out by the mid-ranking officers of the Armed Forces Movement (MFA). In some respects this reflected the inadequacies of BOSS, headed by General H. J. van den Bergh, 'probably the strongest man in the country after Vorster',[7] which had increasingly colonized the intelligence field, much to the chagrin of the Directorate of Military Intelligence of the SADF. However, there is little evidence extant that the Defence Forces' military and naval attaché, their eyes and ears in Lisbon, was any better informed. On the Rhodesian side, Ken Flower, head of the Central Intelligence Organization (CIO), claimed to be sceptical about the long-term survival of the Portuguese empire in Africa,

---

of some of these issues can also be found in Jamie Miller 'Things Fall Apart: South Africa and the Collapse of the Portuguese Empire, 1973–74', *Cold War History*, 12.2 (2012), 183–204.

[3]   On Exercise ALCORA, see Filipe Ribeiro de Meneses and Robert McNamara, 'The Last Throw of the Dice: Portugal, Rhodesia and South Africa, 1970–1974', *Portuguese Studies*, 28.2 (2012), 201–15, as well as two forthcoming articles in *International History Review*: 'The Origins of Exercise ALCORA, 1960–1971', and 'Exercise ALCORA: Expansion and Demise, 1971–1974'. ALCORA is inserted into a wider Portuguese diplomatic strategy in Luís Barroso, *Salazar, Caetano e o Reduto Branco: a manobra político-diplomática de Portugal na África Austral (1951–1974)* (Lisbon: IESM/Fronteira do Caos, 2012).

[4]   The secret reservations of General Costa Gomes, Chief of Staff of the Armed Forces and second post-revolution President of the Republic, can be seen for instance in Paço de Arcos, Arquivo da Defesa Nacional, Secretariado Geral da Defesa Nacional, Caixa 7624, 'Constituição de Forças de Reserva e Estratégicas ALCORA', 25 October 1973. Given the importance of the commitments being entered into with South Africa and Rhodesia at the time, it is difficult not to link these commitments to the publication, by General António de Spínola (Costa Gomes' second-in-command and the first post-revolution President of the Republic), of his famous book *Portugal e o Futuro* (Lisbon: Arcádia, 1974), which argued that the war could not be brought to an end by military means.

[5]   Miller, 'Things Fall Apart', p. 190.

[6]   ADNPdeA, SGDN, Série 25, Caixa 57, 'Acordo do empréstimo de 150 milhões de rands firmado com a RAS', 18 September 1975. The deal was alluded to in very vague terms by Silva Cunha in his interview with José Freire Antunes (January 1995), and published in the latter's *A Guerra de África, 1961–1974*, 2 vols (Lisbon: Temas e Debates, 1996), I, 333–42.

[7]   *Foreign Relations of the United States, 1969–1976*, vol. XXVIII, *Southern Africa* (Washington, DC: Government Printing office, 2011), Doc. 10, Intelligence Note From the Director of the Bureau of Intelligence and Research (Hughes) to Secretary of State, Rogers, 24 June 1969.

and was despondent when he visited Portugal just before the coup — but this prescience was only made public in his memoirs, published long after the fact.[8]

February 1974: A Snapshot of the Threat to the 'White Redoubt'

ALCORA's Intelligence Sub-Committee issued a report on the threat to white-rule southern Africa dated 15 February 1974, which serves to demonstrate the dangers faced by the ALCORA territories in the short, medium and long term, as perceived by Portugal, Rhodesia and South Africa.[9] The report concentrated on the African liberation movements, invariably referred to as 'terrorists', the Organization of African Unity (OAU), the Communist Bloc and the West. Terrorism and subversion, backed by the OAU, was seen to have achieved 'significant successes' in Rhodesia and Mozambique during 1973.[10] The embargo imposed during the October war in the Middle East by the oil-producing Arab states, it was noted, had 'already had a restricting effect on the military capabilities of ALCORA'.[11] The terrorist threat to Rhodesia was likely to grow, and encompass three distinct fronts: across the Zambezi river from Zambia by ZAPU; from the Tete district of Mozambique, now partially controlled by FRELIMO, by ZANU; and from an increasingly hostile Botswana. Even South Africa, despite its *cordon sanitaire* of Rhodesia and the Portuguese territories, might be dragged into the firing line, due to the 'more militant attitude among the Bantu population', and the growing likelihood of Botswana becoming 'a relatively safe base for infiltrations to the RSA (Republic of South Africa) and SWA (South West Africa) in the medium term'. FRELIMO's progress could also lead to South African African National Congress (SAANC) terrorist activities in the Northern Transvaal. Angola was likely to see an extension of terrorism as well, and the possibility of armed intervention by neighbouring states, presumably Zaire, in the oil-rich Cabinda enclave could not be ruled out. Mozambique, however, was estimated to be the target selected by the OAU 'among the territories of ALCORA as its primary objective with the intention to deny the Portuguese control of the territory. For this purpose it is possible that the OAU will exert pressure on FRELIMO to intensify its action and on the hostile neighbour countries to grant great support to that movement.'[12] While there was no immediate threat of large-scale OAU military intervention, as it would be hampered by inter-state rivalries, conflicting

---

[8] Ken Flower, *Serving Secretly: An Intelligence Chief on Record. Rhodesia into Zimbabwe 1964 to 1981* (London: John Murray, 1987), p. 117.

[9] Pretoria, South African National Defence Archive, INT/2 ALCORA 13 'Exercise ALCORA: An Assessment of the Threat to the ALCORA Territories in the Short, Medium and Long Terms 15 February 1974'.

[10] Ibid, paragraph 5.

[11] Ibid, paragraph 7.

[12] Ibid, paragraph, 11.

interests, internal security demands, and cost, the completion of the Tanzania–Zambia (TANZAM) railway might 'make support of such force operating against the ALCORA Territories more feasible.'[13] The threat from the Soviet Union and China could also be expected to grow. All this would take place in a world where the Western Powers (among which more left-wing governments could be expected) were 'likely to act with indifference bordering on timidity so far as support for ALCORA is concerned, despite their apparent revulsion at the use of force for political purposes by some sections of the Western World'.[14] In other words, while the external situation was growing bleaker for ALCORA, there was no suggestion of imminent collapse from within, and it was surely ALCORA's greatest failing that, in spite of the growing resources put into institutional liaison between the militaries of the three countries, South Africa and Rhodesia had no advance warning of the military coup in Lisbon.

A Catastrophic Intelligence Failure

South African diplomats and intelligence officials certainly knew trouble was brewing in Portugal in early 1974. On 3 January Ambassador Montgomery reported rumours of a right-wing coup involving, among others, General Kaúlza da Arriaga, a former Commander-in-Chief in Mozambique.[15] The first concrete sign that the regime of Marcello Caetano was under threat came with the publication of General António de Spínola's book *Portugal e o Futuro*, which started from the premise that there was no military solution to Portugal's wars in Africa, and proposed a much looser, federal, relationship with the colonies. After some hesitation in government circles, Spínola and Costa Gomes, the two highest-ranking officers in the country's armed forces, were dismissed after refusing to pay homage to the government at a hastily improvised ceremony (Costa Gomes having authorized the publication of the work). BOSS sent the Ministry of Foreign Affairs an intelligence briefing on 20 March 1974 for comment. It concluded that *Portugal e o Futuro* was an attempt to propose an Algeria-style Gaullist solution to the colonial wars. However, Caetano's speech of 16 February had rejected Spínola's federal solution, since Portuguese settlers and economic interests would not be respected by the independence movements. The brief speculated that Caetano might have encouraged the publication as a kite-flying exercise, only to be forced, by the reaction of the right-wing ultras, to remove Spínola and Costa Gomes. In any case, the danger had passed.[16] This completely contradicts the later claim of Eschel Rhoodie, the Secretary of the

[13]   Ibid, paragraph 12.
[14]   Ibid, paragraph, 16.
[15]   South African Department of Foreign Affairs, Pretoria, 1-14-1 Vol. 9 Portugal Political Situation and Developments 4.10.72 to 21.5.74, Letter, South African Ambassador in Lisbon to the Secretary for Foreign Affairs, Lisbon, 3 January 1974..
[16]   SADFAP 1-14-1 Vol. 9 Portugal Political Situation and Developments 4.10.72 to 21.5.74, Die Sekretaris Van Buitelandse. Portugal: Magstryd In Politieke Kringe, 20 March 1974.

Department of Information, that Van den Bergh had predicted the coup a year before and had informed the CIA, which had sent him a letter of congratulation for being the only intelligence organization to anticipate it.[17] Moreover, it does not tally with the other BOSS documents that occasionally turn up in the files of the Department of Foreign Affairs. Immediately after the revolution, for example, BOSS issued a memorandum which reflected a relatively sanguine attitude to the revolution. Its key conclusion was that:

> Despite Spínola's strong commitment to a political solution, a continued Portuguese military presence in Africa seems inevitable for some time. If Lisbon does not move in a reasonable length of time, the rebels could attempt to step up their activities against the territories, which are not capable of maintaining their own defence without substantial help from Lisbon. [...] [Guinea] is an economic liability with no hope of producing the immediate and long term economic riches of Angola and Mozambique. Lisbon is unlikely to risk the loss of Angola and Mozambique, however, and the insurgents there are unlikely to accept the type of federation presently being considered by Spínola.[18]

Admittedly, there was a lot of Portuguese reassurance being given to the South Africans about the continued commitment to a presence in Africa in the aftermath of the coup. The Portuguese Ambassador in Washington informed his South African counterpart that, while a revolution was indeed taking place, the new regime was led by sober men. João Hall Themido explained, mistakenly, that General Spínola, now President of the Republic, was both the leader and the catalyst of the revolution (in fact, he turned out to be a relatively powerless figurehead, but few realized this at the time); and whilst he could give little information about Africa beyond what had been in the press, he believed that the regime was sincere when it spoke of a 'Lusitanian community'. Moreover, it was his impression 'that the chances of orderly devolution in Angola — and even in Mozambique — were "fair". He emphasized that it was not policy to capitulate precipitately in Africa.'[19] The South African Ambassador in Paris, in a despatch in June 1974, mentioned that the French government 'was like ourselves in South Africa, somewhat taken by surprise at the sudden change of government in Portugal in April. The conclusion was that the move had been well-planned and the coup d'état executed in great secrecy.'[20] In other words, the situation in Lisbon was nearly impossible to read. But this was not necessarily the case. A State Department official, Ellwood Rabenold Jr, presciently referred

---

[17]   Interview with Rhoodie cited in James Saunders, *Apartheid's Friends: The Rise and Fall of South Africa's Secret Service* (London: John Murray, 2006), pp. 50–51.

[18]   SADFAP, 1–14–1 Vol. 10, Portugal Political Situation 27.5.74 to 10.9.74, BOSS to Secretary for Foreign Affairs, 6 June 1974, enclosing memo 'Estimate of Portuguese Situation for Mike Glendenhuys', 1 May 1974.

[19]   SADFAP 1–14–1 Vol. 10, Ambassador Washington to Secretary for Foreign Affairs, Pretoria, 4 June 1974.

[20]   SADFAP 1–14–9 Vol. 5 Portugal Foreign Policy and Relations 9.11.72 to 30.6.75, Ambassador Paris to Secretary for Foreign Affairs, Pretoria, 14 June 1974.

to conflicting views between those such as Spínola, who favoured a federal plan, and others, such as the new Foreign Minister, Mário Soares, whose views seemed to align more with the liberation movements.[21]

South Africa was soon faced with a major new strategic dilemma on its northern frontiers as it gradually became clear that Spínola and the National Salvation Junta were not free to implement their African policies. Lisbon was coming under intense international pressure to move to a straightforward handing of power to the liberation movements, while radical elements in Portugal, within and without the MFA, saw this kind of 'exemplary' decolonization as intertwined with their domestic agenda of establishing an avowedly revolutionary state. Most importantly, however, the Portuguese army had lost the will to fight, thus destroying any possibility of a gradual handover of power. For some months, however, the messages emanating from Portugal remained confused. General Costa Gomes, restored by Spínola to the position of Chief of Staff of the Armed Forces, visited Africa in May, and rejected the idea of immediate independence. While offering an olive branch of partnership to the liberation movements, he also claimed that Portugal would fight on to safeguard Mozambique if the rebels rejected his offer of talks.[22] This turned out to be an empty boast. At roughly the same time, moreover, Jorge Jardim, the Portuguese settler leader in Mozambique and Salazar's one-time enforcer in Africa, was in Lisbon. The correspondence in the South African files suggests that he was attempting to forge links with Pretoria and that General de Toit, the head of Military Intelligence, showed some interest.[23] Jardim's activities and

[21]   A United States Bureau of Intelligence and Research memorandum speculated that South Africa might intervene militarily in southern Mozambique if the Portuguese withdrew precipitately. South Africa, it was felt, would tell Washington that white-rule southern Africa had to continue 'as an anti-Communist Bastion'. The memorandum rejected this argument in advance, pointing out that 'there is an underlying instability in southern Africa stemming from minority racial rule. The latest developments in Lisbon should make this more rather than less apparent as time goes on.' Department of State Central Files, 1973–76, Record Group 59, 040027Z, May 74, 'INR Assessment of African Repercussions of the Portuguese Coup', 30 April 1974.
[22]   South African Institute of Race Relations, A Survey of Race Relations in South Africa, 1974 (Johannesburg: South African Institute of Race Relations, 1975), p. 104.
[23]   SADFAP 1–113–3 Relations with Mozambique 20.3.65 to 26.5.82, Ambassador Lisbon to Secretary Foreign Affairs, 29 May 1974. Jorge Jardim, a former junior minister in the 1950s, and Salazar's special agent in Africa throughout the 1960s, was by now established as a major political and economic force in Mozambique. He also provided an important personal link to Malawi's President, Hastings Kamuzu Banda, who named him Malawi's Consul at Beira. Jardim was the most prominent member of a political current, to which his newspapers in the city of Beira gave great coverage, which argued that FRELIMO could be persuaded to share power with hastily assembled political parties and settler groups. Jardim had, even before the revolution, convinced President Kenneth Kaunda of Zambia of the merits of a similar programme, which he described as the 'taming' of FRELIMO. See his memoirs, Moçambique, terra queimada (Lisbon: Intervenção, 1976). An account of Jardim's action-packed life is provided by José Freire Antunes in Jorge Jardim: agente secreto (Venda Nova: Bertrand, 1996). It is believed that some white settlers from Mozambique with links to Jardim, including future RENAMO leader Orlando Cristina, supplied the Rhodesians with Portuguese police files from which they could begin to build up a picture of likely recruits for that opposition organization. On this see Tom Young, 'The MNR/Renamo: External and Internal Dynamics', African Affairs: The Journal of the Royal African Society, 89.357 (1990), 491–509 (p. 494).

his past fed Portuguese suspicions that he was a possible leader of a unilateral declaration of independence by settlers, something he denied.[24] This was causing the South African Ambassador in Lisbon some concern. When Jardim finally left Lisbon for Blantyre, Ambassador Montgomery gave a great sigh of relief.[25] Meanwhile, the South African Ambassador in Paris reported in early June 1974 that Mário Soares' first meeting with Samora Machel of FRELIMO had not gone well, as the liberation movement only wished 'to discuss the modalities of a transfer of power to a FRELIMO government.' According to the report, this 'was unacceptable to the Portuguese government as a whole, although some of the politicians in the government adopt a softer line on the matter.'[26]

South Africa's ability to read the situation clearly was further muddled by the fact that Exercise ALCORA continued into the autumn of 1974. An ALCORA Top Level Committee (ATLC) meeting was held at the end of June in Pretoria. Remarkably, the planning to give ALCORA greater solidity through the establishment of the Permanent ALCORA Planning Organization (PAPO) continued, and the meeting went through a considerable agenda, including weapons procurement, intelligence matters and future developments.[27] However, it was acknowledged in the report by Major General Clifton, Director General Special Plans of PAPO, that morale and productivity had suffered as a result of the Portuguese coup.[28] It was only in July that the political balance of power in Lisbon became clear to the naked eye. That month, the first post-revolution government fell, and its replacement, led by Colonel Vasco Gonçalves, represented a significant shift to the left, with the MFA clearly in the ascendancy and Spínola, correspondingly, in retreat. This, allied to the breakdown in the Portuguese army's discipline, meant that the liberation movements in Guinea and Mozambique could ignore Spínola's calls for referendums or pre-independence elections. The very speed of the ensuing Portuguese collapse at the negotiating table meant that one obvious alternative for South African and Rhodesian strategy, a settler-led counter coup, with or without Jardim, never had time to organize itself properly. On 7 September 1974, when the Lusaka Accord was announced, naming 25 June 1975 as Mozambique's independence day, white settlers in Lourenço Marques and Beira attempted to rise against it. They attacked black neighbourhoods, freed

[24] See SADFAP 1–14–3 Vol. 1, Portugal relations with SA 15.7.64–13.8.82, South African Embassy Lilongwe to Secretary Foreign Affairs, Pretoria, 5 Aug 1974.

[25] SADFAP 1–113–3 Relations with Mozambique 20 Mar 1965 to 26 May 1982, Ambassador Lisbon to Secretary Foreign Affairs, 11 June 1974.

[26] SADFAP 1–14–9 Vol. 5 Portugal Foreign Policy and Relations 9.11.72 to 30 .6.75, Ambassador Paris to Secretary for Foreign Affairs, Pretoria, 14 June 1974. Soares, of course, was one of those politicians, but for the time being he respected the wishes of President Spínola, whose instructions he was following. The same cannot be said for his fellow negotiator and future revolutionary pin-up Otelo Saraiva de Carvalho, who at one point in the talks sided openly with FRELIMO.

[27] SANDFAP, ALCORA 6, Minutes of 7th ATLC Meeting, Pretoria, 24–28 June 1974.

[28] Ibid, Annex 1, Report by Director General Special Plans.

imprisoned DGS (secret police) agents, seized the airport and radio stations, and appealed for help among all FRELIMO's opponents, in Mozambique and abroad, but with no success.[29] South Africa appears not to have played any role in the outbreak, although many of those who took part gathered around the South African consulate shouting 'Viva a África do Sul'. Unimpressed, the consul-general in Lourenço Marques suggested that South Africa could gain considerable advantage from FRELIMO's lack of support from different ethnic groups 'provided that we are seen to remain absolutely neutral so that we do not engender animosity from any quarter in the country.'[30] Vorster, in an interview with *Newsweek*, was dismissive of fears of a black government in Mozambique. He was equally dismissive of Portugal's colonial model:

> After all events in Mozambique, Angola and Guinea-Bissau have proved our policy of separate development right. The root of the trouble in all these territories was that the Portuguese policy was one of assimilation — which was a negation of the nationhood of their people [...] if relations were that good why did they fight each other so much? Why are they still fighting? Why are the whites running out of Mozambique and Angola?[31]

This arrogance, this sense of being somehow above the fray and impervious to the great currents that had just engulfed the Portuguese colonies, and would soon do the same for Rhodesia, was characteristic of South Africa's political masters. Nevertheless the thought of FRELIMO — a Marxist liberation movement — coming to power must have given them cause for concern. FRELIMO's leadership was on the record as saying that it would not cooperate with South Africa, even to the extent of denying it electricity from the soon-to-be-completed Cabora Bassa dam.[32] The ALCORA Intelligence documents referred to above demonstrate that the South African military feared that Mozambique might become a base for the SAANC from which to attack into Northern Transvaal.[33] However, South Africa showed itself willing, at least initially, to follow a conciliatory path; perhaps its leaders simply could not believe that a Mozambican government, whatever its political creed, would dare to act against Pretoria, given the enormous dependence of the Mozambican economy on South African goodwill. Indeed, in May 1974, just a month after the Lisbon revolution, Vorster stated, with regard to Mozambique, that he was not worried about 'the colour of the people concerned'; he pledged non-interference in Mozambican affairs, and said that South Africa was interested solely in stable government

---

[29]   Malyn Newitt, *A History of Mozambique* (London: Hurst & Company, 1995), pp. 538–40.
[30]   SADFAP 1–113–3 Mozambique Relations with SA 20.3.65 to 26.5.82, Consul Lourenço Marques to Secretary Foreign Affairs, 16 September 1974 and SADFAP 1–113–3 Vol. 6A Mozambique relations with S.A. 10.12.73 to 28.8.74, Consul, Lourenço Marques to Secretary Foreign Affairs, 19 October 1974.
[31]   *Newsweek*, 16 September 1974.
[32]   According to journalist Ray Vicker, Cabora Bassa represented a 450 million dollar investment, with most of the money being South African in origin. *Wall Street Journal*, 7 August 1972.
[33]   Mário Joaquim Azevedo, 'A Sober Commitment to Liberation? Mozambique and South Africa, 1974–1979', *African Affairs*, 79.317 (1980), 567–84 (p. 568). See also 'An Assessment of the Threat to the ALCORA Territories', 15 February 1974, para. 11.

there.[34] Ian Smith, the Prime Minister of Rhodesia, whose sanctions-busting strategy was deeply dependent on a friendly Mozambique, discovered that Vorster really meant these words when the two met in July. Smith explained to Vorster that he had contact with 'powerful forces in Mozambique' who had a plan to take over Mozambique south of the Zambezi and form a kind of Federation with South Africa and Rhodesia. This would allow Rhodesia to continue to use the port facilities at Beira. Vorster initially showed interest in the plan and said he would consider it and contact Smith on the matter, but proved slow to respond. Some months later, he rejected the idea outright, having 'come to the conclusion that there would be an unfavourable reaction from the rest of the world, and that therefore they could not support it.'[35] While Smith is imprecise on the date of the reply, it would appear to have been after 7 September 1974, the date of the abortive settler uprising in Mozambique which had cost some 115 lives.[36]

Ian Smith and other observers suggest that at this point South Africa had already committed itself to a policy of détente with Black Africa, which was only officially promulgated by Vorster in the South African parliament in October 1974. However, Vorster remained committed to keeping a South African Police unit in Rhodesia, arguing that it was there to prevent a terrorist threat to South Africa developing.[37] And there remain persistent rumours that Defence Minister P. W. Botha and the SADF were on the verge of intervening in Mozambique around this time, only to be thwarted by BOSS agents.[38] BOSS tended to provide the like-minded Department of Foreign Affairs with intelligence material that emphasized the reasonableness of FRELIMO and its leader, Samora Machel.[39] In any case, FRELIMO had rapidly cooled its anti-South Africa rhetoric. In September 1974, the newly installed Prime Minister, Joaquim Chissano, made it clear that FRELIMO would not interfere with Rhodesia or South Africa and would not be a 'saviour' or 'messiah' for either country's majority African populations, who would have to resolve their respective problems on their own.[40]

Early in September 1974, Ken Flower, General van den Bergh and Brand Fourie, Secretary of the Department of Foreign Affairs, were in Lisbon for meetings with the Portuguese. There, António de Almeida Santos, the Minister

---

[34]   Quoted in John Barratt, 'Detente in Southern Africa', *The World Today: Chatham House Review*, 31.3 (1975), 120–30 (p. 124). See also Vorster on 1 August 1974 in Parliament, Hansard 4 Cols, 1857–60.
[35]   Ian Smith, *Bitter Harvest: The Great Betrayal and the Dreadful Aftermath* (London: John Blake, 1997), pp. 160–61.
[36]   *A Survey of Race Relations in South Africa, 1974*, p. 111.
[37]   *Rand Daily Mail*, 6 October 1974.
[38]   Dan O'Meara, *Forty Lost Years: The Apartheid State and the Politics of the National Party* (Athens: Ohio University Press, 1996), p. 219.
[39]   See for instance SADFAP 1–113–3 Vol. 6B, Mozambique Relations with SA 3.9.74 to 24.10.74, BOSS Memo to Secretary Foreign Affairs, 24 October 1974, containing an astonishingly detailed report on a meeting of British Officials and Ministers.
[40]   Azevedo, 'A Sober Commitment to Liberation?', p. 580.

for Inter-Territorial Coordination, outlined the likely agreement between Portugal and FRELIMO that was to be the basis of the Lusaka Accords. General van den Bergh gave an absolute assurance that South Africa would not allow mercenary forces to be organized in South Africa against Angola or Mozambique and that Jorge Jardim had been warned not to engage in such activities.[41] Flower stayed longest in the Portuguese capital and looked up some of his old contacts. These, contrary to the assurances given earlier by Foreign Minister Mário Soares, suggested that FRELIMO's word was worth nothing. And while there was talk of a potential right-wing coup in Portugal, which might influence the course of events in Angola, it seemed as if the situation in Mozambique had developed to a point where there was no turning back.[42] Flower was rather more forthcoming in his memoirs about his knowledge of what was going on in Lisbon, referring to his direct participation in the plotting of a counter-coup which involved Spínola himself.[43] This, presumably, was Spínola's failed attempt to rally the 'silent majority' to his side, later that month, which ended not with a defeat for the left, but rather the President's resignation, and led to the strengthening of the MFA's hold over the institutions of the Portuguese state.

Picking up the Pieces after Mozambique

Exercise ALCORA ended at a meeting on 14 and 15 October 1974 in Lisbon. General J. A. Pinheiro, the assistant to the Chief of Staff of the Armed Forces (a position which General Costa Gomes held on to, despite his recent acceptance of the Presidency of the Republic), addressed the meeting and made clear that ALCORA was over, due to the recent Lusaka agreements with FRELIMO. Not even the 'hot-pursuit' operations so beloved of Rhodesian forces would be allowed any longer. The codename ALCORA was to be dropped and PAPO would cease to exist on 31 October 1974. Despite the ending of what had become to all intents and purposes a military alliance, the meeting concluded on a friendly note, without recrimination.[44] Whether as a direct or an indirect result of the end of the ALCORA strategy, which had subcontracted out the defence of South Africa to the Portuguese military, Vorster's government stepped up its moves towards détente with the rest of Africa. This seems to have informed Pretoria's policy on Mozambique and its decision from October 1974 to pursue a policy of pressurizing the Rhodesian government to come to terms with African nationalists. By the end of the year, South Africa had, with the cooperation of Zambia in particular, negotiated a very shaky ceasefire between the Rhodesian

[41]   SADFAP 1–14–3 Vol. 1 Portugal Relations with SA, 15.7.64 to 13.8.82, Meeting in Lisbon, 2 September 1974, between Dr Almeida Santos, B. G. Fourie and General van den Bergh.
[42]   SADFAP 1–14–1 Portugal Political situation 27.2.70 to 3.5.84, Representative Salisbury to Secretary for Foreign Affairs, 18 September 1974.
[43]   Flower, Serving Secretly, pp. 144–45.
[44]   SANDFAP, ALCORA 7, Minutes of the 8th ATLC Meeting, Lisbon 14–15 October 1974.

government and the liberation movements which opposed it. While various negotiations over the next two years — Victoria Falls (August 1975), the Kissinger Plan (September 1976), and the Geneva conference (December 1976)[45] — ended in failure, primarily on the rocks of the Rhodesian Prime Minister's intransigence and the serious splits in the liberation movements, they forestalled the drift to full-scale war in Rhodesia for nearly two years.

In Pretoria, however, not everyone was convinced of the merits of détente. Meeting in February and September 1975 under the auspices of a successor liaison group to ALCORA, Rhodesian military and SADF officers produced a document on the 'Military Threat to the Republic of South Africa and Rhodesia'.[46] Reiterating that the threat stemmed from 'black political aspirations' supported by the OAU, the Communist Bloc and certain Western countries, it concluded that the surrender of effective Portuguese control in Mozambique had added momentum to the dangers facing both countries and contributed to 'an aggressive and uncompromising attitude towards the Republic of South Africa (RSA) and Rhodesia [...] The white-controlled states of southern Africa face the present developing threat in an atmosphere of increasing hostility and isolation.' It was noted that the OAU, which had met in Dar es Salaam in April 1975, had as its 'ultimate aim the total elimination of white rule in southern Africa.' There was also concern about President Amin of Uganda, the then Chairman of the OAU, and his attempt to revive the concept of an all-Africa Army, though it was noted that certain elements in the OAU had reservations about Amin's 'reputation and unpredictability'. While President Kaunda of Zambia was in favour of détente with South Africa, he had made clear that any collapse in the negotiations between the African National Council and the Rhodesian government not attributable to intransigence on the part of the ANC would lead to Zambia supporting whatever course the ANC chose to use to attain majority rule.[47] Meanwhile, it was concluded that Mozambique's precarious economy precluded any 'drastic political or economic steps against Rhodesia or the RSA', although its support for ZANU was likely to continue and the SAANC was likely to be granted facilities in the near future, if only on a low-profile basis. The report concluded that the *Movimento Popular de Libertação de Angola* (MPLA) was best placed to succeed in taking power in Angola. The strategy of détente was useful in preventing revolutionary aims and had led to some new political thinking in some African states 'which had curbed the activities of terrorist organisations.' Conversely, however, it had

---

[45] See for instance, R. W. Johnson, *How long will South Africa survive?* (London: Macmillan, 1977), pp. 1–16; Sue Onslow, ' "We must gain time": South Africa, Rhodesia and the Kissinger Initiative of 1976', *South African Historical Journal*, 56 (2006), 123–53 and Ian Smith, *Bitter Harvest*, pp. 160–222. There is a huge volume of correspondence on these events in the Ian Smith Papers at Cory Historical Library, Rhodes University, Grahamstown, South Africa in Box 4–0006 M (Official Communications with South Africa, Volumes 1–7).

[46] SANDFAP, ALCORA 13, 'The Military Threat to the Republic of South Africa and Rhodesia', September 1975.

[47] 'The Military Threat to the Republic of South Africa and Rhodesia', 24 September 1975, paragraph 7.

'adversely affected the counter terrorist campaign in Rhodesia'.[48] The instability engendered by the collapse of Portuguese power, 'especially the instability in Angola and Mozambique', had 'resulted in Communist countries and Communist organizations intensifying their efforts to exploit and manipulate the conflict situation as whole, to gain initiative and influence.'[49]

On 21 October 1975, a Portuguese diplomat based at the Permanent Representation to the United Nations reported that Portugal had no intention of handing over power solely to the MPLA. This official also suggested that Mozambique had plans to initiate discussions with South Africa regarding the establishment of diplomatic relations with Pretoria, as it was feeling the economic pinch from the loss of tourist revenue.[50] At least in the immediate aftermath of Mozambique's independence, South Africa appeared to have reached a *modus vivendi* with its newly independent neighbour. However, this would change. FRELIMO's escalating support for ZANU in its war against Rhodesia, particularly after the failure of Vorster's détente initiative and the Kissinger Plan by the end of 1976, would see Mozambique become the major target of Rhodesian retaliation. This included a series of military assaults against ZANU-controlled guerrilla and refugee camps and the aiding and abetting of the Mozambique National Resistance (RENAMO), which waged a terrifyingly brutal war against FRELIMO and the civilian population of Mozambique. The end of Rhodesia in early 1980 would see South Africa take over the aiding of RENAMO from the Rhodesian CIO 'lock, stock and barrel' in order to pressure Mozambique not to back any of the South African liberation movements.[51] South African agents also carried out a series of raids and bombings on ANC activists. The Nkomati Accord (1984) forced FRELIMO to shut the ANC office in Mozambique in return for a South African pledge to stop support for RENAMO. However, relations remained strained and when President Samora Machel was killed in a plane crash in South Africa, in 1986, many believed it was the work of South African agents.[52] Still, South Africa had at least avoided being dragged into conflict in Mozambique in 1974–75. The same was not true of Portugal's other major colony in southern Africa, Angola.

The Intervention in Angola

The intervention in Angola was, according to Colin Legum, an exiled South African journalist, 'possibly the most traumatic event in South Africa's history since the Anglo-Boer war at the turn of the century.'[53] South African troops had

[48]   Ibid, paragraph 11.
[49]   Ibid, paragraph 12.
[50]   SADFAP 1–14–1 Vol. 12 Portugal Political Situation and Developments 6.5.75 to 31.10.1975, SA mission New York, 23 October 1975.
[51]   Flower, *Serving Secretly*, p. 262.
[52]   See Saunders, *Apartheid's Friends*, pp. 218–21.
[53]   Colin Legum and Tony Hodges, *After Angola: The War over Southern Africa* (London: Holmes & Meier, 1976), p. 35.

been committed to a conflict in southern Africa and some of its soldiers had been taken prisoner. However, South African strategy in Angola developed very slowly and with considerable reluctance. While, on the one hand, there was less of an economic imperative to reach an understanding with whoever emerged triumphant in Angola, on the other, the situation in Angola was very different to the one which had played itself out so quickly in Mozambique. Spínola had been able to retain a say in Angolan affairs until September 1974, trying to preserve, there at least, his vision of a Lusitanian community; the much larger white settler population seemed determined to stay in the territory, and capable of doing so; and the presence of three liberation movements, each with its own international connections, contributed massively to this incredibly complex situation, fraught with dangers but also with opportunities. The consul-general in Luanda, Emmett 'Mike' Malone, differentiated little between the three competing liberation movements in his reportage. He noted, for instance, that the *Frente Nacional de Libertação de Angola* (FNLA) Minister of the Interior in the transitional government that was established by the January 1975 Alvor accords had issued a bellicose statement claiming the SADF was in the process of seeking a pretext for invading Angola.[54] All three movements seemed to be responsible, he explained, for the chaos that engulfed Angola in general, and Luanda in particular, as Portuguese power disintegrated throughout 1975, undermined by domestic politics, the army's state of mind, and international pressure. This included shooting at South African Airways flights, which ended their service in Luanda, an important stopover on the way to Europe and the Americas.[55] As late as June 1975, the United States did not see any preparations for South African intervention.[56]

South Africa's invasion of Angola has generated a considerable literature.[57]

---

[54]   SADFAP 1-22-3 Vol. 5 Angola Relations with SA, 5.3.75. to 25.7.75, Consul-General Luanda to Secretary Foreign Affairs, 18 April 1975 and 23 April 1975. The Minister for the Interior (FNLA) repeated such accusations in July: see Secretary for Foreign Affairs to SA Legation Lisbon, 11 July 1975.

[55]   SADFAP 1-22-3 Vol. 5 Angola Relations with S.A., 5.3.75. to 25.7.75, Discussion with High Commissioner Cardoso, 16 April 1975.

[56]   See attachment to Doc. 113, Minutes of a National Security Council Meeting, 27 June 1975, in *Foreign Relations of the United States, 1969-1976*, vol. xxviii, *Southern Africa*.

[57]   On South Africa, in particular, Robin Hallett, 'The South African Intervention in Angola, 1976', *African Affairs*, 77.308 (July 1978), 347–86; Deon Geldenhuys, *The Diplomacy of Isolation: South African Foreign Policy Making* (New York: St. Martin's Press, 1984), pp. 75–84; Dan O'Meara, *Forty Lost Years*, pp. 209–29; James P. Barber and John Barratt, *South Africa's Foreign Policy: The Search for Status and Security, 1945-1988* (Cambridge: Cambridge University Press, 1990), pp. 186–96. See also John A. Marcum, 'Lessons of Angola', *Foreign Affairs*, 54.3 (1976), 407–25. More recent accounts of value include Edward George, *The Cuban Intervention in Angola, 1965-1991: From Che Guevara to Cuito Cuanavale* (London: Frank Cass, 2005), pp. 49–115 and P. Gleijeses, *Conflicting Missions: Havana, Washington, Pretoria* (Alberton, South Africa: Galago, 2002), pp. 230–347. On the role of the United States, Thomas J. Noer, 'International Credibility and Political Survival: The Ford Administration's Intervention in Angola', *Presidential Studies Quarterly*, 23.4 (1993), 771–85, provides a useful summation of the literature. Important memoirs include Henry Kissinger, *Years of Renewal* (New York: Simon & Schuster, 1999); John Stockwell, *In Search of Enemies: A CIA Story* (New York: Norton, 1978); and Magnus Malan, *My Life with the SADF* (Pretoria: Protea, 2006). Two works, sympathetic to the SADF, essential for the military aspects are S. du Preez, *Avontuur in Angola: Die Verhaal van Suid-Afrika*

The standard narrative is straightforward, but somewhat misleading. South Africa appears to have done little in Angola until August 1975, when workers involved in construction of the Calueque Dam complex on Cunene River, about 20km from the Namibian frontier, came under threat from some or all of the liberation movements, as Portuguese power in Angola drained away. This led to a small force of SADF troops occupying the complex. Then, in the middle of October, South African forces moved northwards, supposedly in hot pursuit of guerrillas, but in reality to prevent the Soviet and MFA-backed MPLA from coming to power. Considerable debate has raged over whether or not this was done with the blessing of the United States. Days before 11 November 1975, the date set at the Alvor talks for Angolan independence, the South Africans were close to Luanda but chose, puzzlingly, not to attempt to seize it, although they did aid, with air and artillery support, the disastrous FNLA offensive on Luanda from the north, which was broken up by a small force of Cuban and MPLA troops. Cuba, alarmed by the South African advance, soon went from deploying a relatively modest number of advisers to the MPLA to rushing tens of thousands of front-line soldiers into Angola. With the United States unwilling to provide much practical or moral cover after Congress had banned all financial aid to Angola, overt or covert, through the Clark Amendment of 19 December 1975, the SADF began a withdrawal southwards in mid-December 1975, shadowed all the way by the Cubans and the MPLA. By March 1976, the SADF had left Angola. Of its allies, the FNLA had been broken and the *União Nacional para a Independência Total de Angola* (UNITA) relegated to a guerrilla force. To its supporters, the SADF, betrayed by a decadent United States suffering from a Vietnam syndrome, remained undefeated. To its detractors, however, it had narrowly avoided a military catastrophe at the hands of a superior Cuban expeditionary force.

South African Decision-Making

How did it all go so wrong for Pretoria? According to one account, South Africa appears to have considered encouraging the development of irredentism among the major tribal grouping in southern Angola and Northern Namibia, perhaps creating a Great Ovambo state that would act as a buffer between it and the South West Africa People's Organization (SWAPO), which stepped up its activities in the face of the vacuum left behind by the Portuguese. Such a move was greatly feared by all three Angolan liberation movements.[58] Nevertheless, South African officials met with representatives of the three major liberation movements seeking concrete assurances that they would respect the border

---

se Soldate in Angola, 1975–1976 (Pretoria: Van Schaik, 1989) and F. J. du T. Spies, *Operasie Savannah: Angola 1975–1976* (Pretoria: SADF Directorate of Public Relations, 1989).
[58]   Hallett, 'The South African Intervention in Angola, 1976', pp. 351–52.

and by implication not support the developing SWAPO campaign.[59] The *Financial Times*, indeed, claimed that the MPLA had reportedly acquiesced in this demand. In July 1975, a South African general, D. R. Marais, was quoted as claiming that two to three thousand SWAPO cadres were being trained in southern Angola, although this claim was swiftly debunked by another senior officer. However, SWAPO attacks led to South African cross-border incursions into Angola, which apparently involved the SADF in clashes with SWAPO, MPLA and UNITA forces.[60] Meanwhile, in April 1975, the South African government had asked the Portuguese High Commissioner to Angola to take action to protect the workers involved in the construction of the abovementioned Calueque Dam on the Cunene River. In May 1975, an alarmist SADF report advocated increased support for the FNLA and UNITA to forestall the MPLA. After the failure of Portuguese authorities to take action, the SADF deployed a platoon which seized control of the complex.[61]

However, sometime in the autumn of 1975, Pretoria decided to become more deeply involved in the developing Angolan conflict. It is usually assumed that the Angolan intervention was primarily driven by P. W. Botha and the SADF, since it ran contrary to the détente strategy favoured by the Department of Foreign Affairs and General van den Bergh's BOSS, which appeared to have paid off in Mozambique. Crucially, then, the intervention in Angola fitted into a wider context of inter-departmental turf wars within the South African security and diplomatic establishment for control of foreign and defence policy. Escheel Rhoodie, Secretary of the Department of Information, later sacked in disgrace for his role in the Information Scandal ('Muldergate'), was in the 1970s a close ally of Van den Bergh. Rhoodie claims that in August 1975, without the approval of Vorster or the Cabinet, P. W. Botha sent South African troops to guard the Calueque hydro-electric plant and that this developed into a hot-pursuit operation against guerrilla groups that extended nearly to Luanda by November 1975. In this version, the invasion's 'pursue-to-Luanda' strategy became a fait accompli.[62] Somewhat in support of this, Deon Geldenhuys suggests that a lethargic John Vorster was consulted by Botha but had little input into the military campaign, which appears to have been ad hoc and opportunistic rather than working to any overarching strategy.[63] The Defence establishment was able to elbow the Department of Foreign Affairs aside over Angola under Vorster's rather 'unstructured decision-making'.[64] However, Jamie Miller, citing a range of South African sources and interviews, suggests a

[59] Spies, *Operasie Savannah*, pp. 60–65.
[60] Hallett, 'The South African Intervention in Angola, 1976', pp. 351–52.
[61] According to the account given by P. W. Botha to the House of Assembly, 26 January 1976, Hansard 1 Cols 44–52.
[62] See Eschel M. Rhoodie, *P. W. Botha: The Last Betrayal* (Melville: S. A. Politics, 1989), pp. 194–96. Apart from Rhoodie, the Muldergate scandal also claimed the careers of John Vorster (by then State President) and Connie Mulder, the Minister for Information (who was heir apparent to Vorster).
[63] Geldenhuys, *The Diplomacy of Isolation*, pp. 75–84; O'Meara, *Forty Lost Years*, pp. 220–21.
[64] Geldenhuys, *The Diplomacy of Isolation*, p. 82.

gradual escalation of South African involvement beginning with arms, border crossings, training and eventual intervention, with Botha and SADF leading the charge over the heads of BOSS and the Ministry of Foreign Affairs.[65]

The Portuguese initially complained about this Calueque occupation, although their inability to protect the facility meant that they were forced to tolerate it. Still, they requested that South Africa do everything possible 'to avoid any direct confrontations.'[66] It would appear that the SADF began to engage MPLA forces at this time and the Lisbon press, notably the communist-leaning *Diário de Notícias*, suggested that a full-scale South African invasion was underway, which the Embassy in Lisbon denied.[67] In September, Portuguese officials met a senior South African officer, General Armstrong, to discuss the situation in southern Angola. They were happy to allow the SADF to occupy the dam but believed that control should be ceded to the MPLA in due course. They brought with them a message that the MPLA wanted normal relations with South Africa and would honour the contract for the dam. The Portuguese emphasized that the MPLA was the only party that really counted and that it had more 'brains' than the others, as it commanded the allegiance of all the black professional class.[68] At this stage the scope of the South African intervention remained limited and arguably defensible. The country's military was protecting an important asset, into which South African resources had been poured, in the absence of the Portuguese, who were no longer capable of doing so. In truth, South Africa no longer cared about Portuguese sensibilities. In a contemptuous report, drafted in August 1975, the military attaché in Lisbon concluded,

> The importance of Portugal is over-estimated. If Angola is handed to the MPLA, which is expected shortly, the communist [*sic*] would be celebrating a big victory since such a move would be irrevocable. The communists in Portugal are at the moment holding on until the UDI for Angola is established, after which, Portugal may go either way, being of no real importance anyway. The goals of the Communists were Mozambique and Angola and not Portugal. Mozambique irrevocable [*sic*] an established communist state and Angola well on its way.[69]

At this stage, the Department of Foreign Affairs and BOSS remained firmly opposed to military intervention, as was notable from an inter-departmental

[65]   See Jamie Miller 'Yes, Minister: Reassessing South Africa's Intervention in the Angolan Civil War, 1975', *Journal of Cold War Studies*, forthcoming, *passim*. The authors are grateful to Jamie Miller for an advance copy.
[66]   SADFAP 1–122–3 Vol. 6 Angola Relations with SA, 26.7.75 to 13.11.75, Brand Fourie, Secretary Department of Foreign Affairs to Admiral Biermann, Chief of SADF, 21 August 1975.
[67]   SADFAP 1–122–3 Vol. 6 Angola Relations with SA, 26.7.75 to 13.11.75, Ambassador Lisbon to Secretary for Foreign Affairs, Pretoria, 3 September 1975.
[68]   SADFAP 1–122–3 Vol. 6 Angola Relations with SA, 26.7.75 to 13.11.75, Memo on Relations with Angola, 24 September 1975.
[69]   SANDFAP HSI AMI Groep 3 Houer 461, MI/LIA/1/ 1/4 Military Attaché Lisbon to Chief of Staff Intelligence, 'Portugal: Forecast with Reference to Angola', 18 August 1975.

meeting on 11 August 1975. Botha had received authorization from Vorster but remarkably neither Fourie nor Van den Berg was consulted for their view.[70] The occupation of the dam hardly constituted a major intervention but the very fact that the SADF were occupying a part of Angola brought Pretoria into the maelstrom of a post-colonial state in a process of disintegration. The Defence Forces' willingness to recruit ex-DGS agents and their private army, the fearsome *Flechas*, to bolster the anti-MPLA force being assembled in the south of Angola reflects this. It was also clear that the MPLA was going to win unless sufficient Western or South African aid could be brought to bear in support of its rival factions.

Sometime in the late autumn of 1975, the various competing blocs in the South African governmental apparatus began to coalesce around an interventionist strategy. Firstly, after initially not being especially discriminating about the liberation movements of Angola, South African officials had begun to make contact with both Jonas Savimbi's UNITA and Holden Roberto's FNLA. There are reports that General van den Bergh, the head of BOSS, had met the MPLA dissident leader, Daniel Chipenda, for three days of talks at Windhoek, in July 1975.[71] International circumstances certainly seemed to be pushing South Africa towards bolder action. The Mobutu regime in Kinshasa and President Kaunda in Lusaka, important partners in Vorster's proposed détente, were increasingly concerned about the MPLA coming to power. Moreover, US Secretary of State Henry Kissinger, alerted to the situation by Kaunda, had become increasingly committed to frustrating the MPLA's intentions. Convinced that this was a test of America's mettle after the recent fall of South Vietnam to the North Vietnamese, Kissinger rejected the advice to stay on the sidelines offered by both the State Department and the CIA, relatively sanguine about the possibility of the MPLA winning. However, the US decision to step up covert aid to the FNLA appears to have had a dual effect. On the one hand, it led to increased Soviet and Cuban support for the MPLA; on the other, it convinced South Africa that a successful intervention might rekindle relations with the United States. Again according to Rhoodie, General van den Bergh, after meeting with Holden Roberto, probably in October 1975 at Mobutu's palace in Kinshasa, told the South African cabinet that the CIA would support a pincer attack on Luanda by the FNLA from the north, and by South Africa and Jonas Savimbi's UNITA from the south.[72] This meeting tallies, chronologically at least, with the expansion of the South African military mission from defending Calueque to attempting to frustrate the MPLA's coming to power. It also suggests that

---

[70] SADFAP 1–22–3 Vol. 6 Angola Relations with SA, July to November 1975, Meeting on Calueque Dam, 11 August 1975.
[71] Hallett, 'The South African Intervention in Angola, 1976', p. 354.
[72] This is according to Eschel Rhoodie, quoted in Mervyn Rees and Chris Day, *Muldergate: The Story of the Info Scandal* (Johannesburg: Macmillan, 1980), p. 195. The CIA, as late as June 1975, according to DCI William Colby, was unwilling to get involved with the South Africans. See Doc 113, 'Minutes of a National Security Council Meeting', 27 June 1975, in *FRUS, 1969–1976*, vol. xxviii, *Southern Africa*.

the invasion, rather than being simply a Botha-directed solo run, in fact had wide support from among South Africa's most significant senior ministers. General Magnus Malan, the chief of the South African army, reports that a government order was given to launch 'Operation Savannah' on 15 October. The objectives were somewhat open to interpretation: to protect the interests of South Africa and SWA, to aid the FNLA and UNITA, and promote détente in southern Africa. There was no explicit 'march-on-Luanda' instruction given.[73] It would also appear that the intervention was to be highly secret, so as to spare the blushes of UNITA/FNLA and those African states which wished to see the MPLA stopped. There was also the problem that South Africa's laws banned the deployment of the SADF national servicemen outside the country's borders.[74] Soldiers were initially uniformed as mercenaries.

Declassified South African documents give no definitive rationale about the decision-making behind Pretoria's intervention. If, as seems likely, it was opportunistic, haphazardly organized, and had no clear grand strategy behind it, then maybe no documentary rationale is extant. The British Ambassador to South Africa nevertheless attempted to summarize, *post facto*, Vorster's aims:

> a) to prevent MPLA from acceding to power in Luanda or, conversely, of giving UNITA and FNLA a chance of taking a major share in government as successors to the Portuguese;
> b) to prevent any further supply of Russian weapons to MPLA by seizing the main entry port for these supplies in Luanda;
> c) if objective (a) failed, to help UNITA establish control over the Benguela Railway and so re-open it for use by Zaire and Zambia, two countries with which South Africa was trying to establish a position of influence as part of the détente policy;
> d) in the process to eliminate SWAPO bases in southern Angola.

This diplomat added, 'the South African Government must have hoped to achieve these results quickly, and secretly, in close collaboration with Dr Savimbi of UNITA and with some tacit, but for obvious reasons unacknowledged, support from Zaire and Zambia.'[75]

The American Link

South Africa was motivated by opportunism: its initial thrusts with relatively tiny forces brought great rewards as the MPLA's military wing, the FAPLA, was rapidly swept aside and the SADF was, at one stage, a mere hundred miles from Luanda. However, its Achilles heel was that it depended on the small and well-trained SADF force not running into anything more formidable than inexperienced FAPLA troops. Should the SADF encounter anything stronger,

---

[73]   Malan, *My Life with the SADF*, p. 118.
[74]   See Hilton Hamann, *Days of the Generals* (Cape Town: Zebra, 2001), pp. 32–33.
[75]   The National Archives UK, Kew, London (TNAUKKL), Foreign and Commonwealth Office, 51–425, Cape Town to James Callaghan, 9 February 1976, 'South Africa and Angola — The Penalties of Intervention'.

like Cuban or Soviet personnel, Pretoria hoped it might rely on the support of the United States. While Western and South African propaganda suggested that the Cuban intervention was merely a proxy for the Soviet Union, most recent writing on the event, based on Cuban archives and accounts, suggests that the massive deployment of Cuban forces after November 1975 was motivated by Cuba's own desire to save a sympathetic regime (MPLA) from total defeat. In reality, South Africa's intervention was catastrophic on every level. Militarily it failed to achieve its objective of capturing Luanda. Sufficient numbers of Cuban troops stiffened the MPLA, which allowed them to rout an FNLA offensive on 9 November.[76] The idea of a pincer movement on Luanda by the FNLA, UNITA and the SADF, which had so excited General van den Bergh in Kinshasa, was now a dead letter. The SADF contingent, which might have been sufficient to take care of the MPLA on its own, now faced the danger of a rapidly growing Cuban military force armed with heavy weapons, particularly artillery — the terrifying 'Stalin's Organs' rocket launchers — that outranged the World War II-vintage guns of the South Africans. In any case South Africa, according to Malan, had decided to stay in Angola either until 11 November (Independence Day) or the OAU meeting which was to decide the key question of which competing Angola government to recognize. However, it was not until the end of the year that a final decision to pull back was made and this was chiefly motivated by developments in the United States.

Washington turned out to be an unreliable ally. It was now paralysed as President Ford and Secretary Kissinger found that their ability to support South Africa was compromised by a general unwillingness to be too closely associated with Apartheid. However, they did not want South Africa to pull out of Angola, as a conversation between senior Administration officials on 21 November 1975 reveals:

> WILLIAM COLBY (Director, CIA): [South Africa would] like to get their troops out, and hire mercenaries. They say that they don't have the money to do this and have turned to us. I think that this is political dynamite. The press would be after us. They and Africans would say that the MPLA is supported by the big, brave Russians, while the others are backed by the bad South Africans and Americans. That would be unpleasant.
>
> JOSEPH SISCO (State Department): More than that. Your description is too mild. [...] I do not favor giving any support to the South Africans. [...] We would not want to discourage them, but leave them to their own devices.
>
> BRENT SCOWCROFT (National Security Council): We do not want to discourage them.[77]

[76]   South African artillery was airlifted especially for this purpose and took part in the battle, but could do little to stop the rout. This has been often described. An official South African perspective can be found in Malan, *My Life with the SADF*, pp. 124–26.
[77]   *FRUS, 1969–1976*, vol. XXVIII, *Southern Africa*, Doc. 139, 'Memorandum for the Record', Washington, November 21, 1975, 40 Committee Meeting.

The extent of the assurances the United States gave South Africa and how much they encouraged its intervention remains unclear and has not really been cleared up by the recent release of the relevant *Foreign Relations of the United States* volume on southern Africa between 1969 and 1976.[78] Donald Easum, the former Assistant Secretary of State for African Affairs, who was disliked and ignored (like much of the State Department) by Henry Kissinger for being overly sympathetic to black Africa, was of the view that the Secretary of State had used 'back-channel' business contacts to encourage P. W. Botha to intervene in Angola, probably in October.[79] This should be contrasted with Kissinger's own account — 'South Africa had opted for intervention without prior consultation with the United States' — a view surprisingly endorsed by John Stockwell, a dissident CIA officer, in his hostile account of the American intervention in Angola.[80]

The South African Ambassador in Washington, R. F. 'Pik' Botha, was well aware that the Ford administration was torn between wishing to stop the Soviets and Cubans winning while simultaneously wishing to remain distant from South Africa, in the face of a growing backlash in Congress. However, his understanding of events in Angola was mainly shaped by watching the fighting on the US networks, as he appears to have been given little information about what was going on from Pretoria. Domestically, South African intervention was blanketed in extraordinary secrecy, with no reports on radio or in the newspapers. Eventually Pik Botha was informed by Foreign Minister Hilgard Muller that the SADF mission had support at the highest levels in Washington. Pik Botha demurred, warning nevertheless that an imminent Senate vote would cut off funding.[81] When he informed Vorster of this, the Prime Minister refused to believe him. Muller told the US Ambassador on 15 December 1975 that the South African view, based on their information, was that, psychologically speaking, the ideal moment for the US and the Western Powers to

---

[78]   *FRUS, 1969–1976*, vol. xxviii, *Southern Africa, passim*.

[79]   *The Foreign Affairs Oral History Collection of the Association for Diplomatic Studies and Training*, interview with Donald B. Easum, Published 17 January 1990, Library of Congress, Manuscript Division, Washington, DC 20540 USA, Digital ID mfdip 2004eas01 <http://hdl.loc.gov/loc.mss/mfdip.2004eas01>: 'In fact, there's been a lot of suspicion all along the line that he had friends and connections, and that he permitted certain information to flow independently of official State Department channels to Vorster. I don't know this for a fact, but when the South Africans invaded Angola massively in what I think was called the Proteus invasion in October of 1975, there are many people who believe that he let — was it then Botha? He let Botha know through business contacts, or whatever, that Botha would be supported if he did that. And when Botha didn't get that kind of US military support, Botha was downcast, and said he'd been betrayed by the Americans. And many of us think that Kissinger, for whatever reason, couldn't follow through on pledges he had made.'

[80]   Henry Kissinger, *Years of Renewal*, p. 821, John Stockwell, *In Search of Enemies*, p. 186. However, Stockwell accused the CIA of cooperation with the South Africans, *passim*. Kissinger seemed to suggest the CIA as one of the major sources of leaks that holed the entire operation below the waterline. See Kissinger, *Years of Renewal*, p. 827.

[81]   See the extensive excerpts from an interview with R. F. Botha in South African Democracy Education Trust, *The Road to Democracy in South Africa, Volume 2 [1970–1980]* (Pretoria: Unisa Press, University of South Africa, 2007), pp. 65–68.

apply 'maximum pressure' had arrived.[82] A couple of days prior to this, Edward W. Mulcahy, the acting Assistant Secretary of State for African Affairs, had specifically claimed that the US administration had support in the Senate, and even the House of Representatives, to continue aid. Indeed Mulcahy informed the South Africans that he had gone out of his way to give a sympathetic rendering of South Africa's case over Namibia and Pretoria's other problems to Senator Dick Clark, who, according to the Embassy, had found it 'very interesting and even remarkable.'[83] However, Congress was opposed to any possibility of being sucked into the southern African conflict, particularly as it was clear that much of the administration — most notably CIA Director William Colby — saw little difference between the Angolan factions, and on 19 December 1975 the Clark Amendment stopped all US aid to FNLA and UNITA, so destroying the credibility of those in the South African government who had claimed to have US backing.[84] As an American official ruefully noted: 'The key to keeping our side in Angola from collapsing is So. Africa. As far as Africans are concerned they would agree to have So. Africa clean up Angola, but we couldn't pay the domestic price in this country.'[85]

When the Clark Amendment was passed, Pik Botha was recalled for consultations at Vorster's Eastern Cape holiday home, along with other senior ministers and advisers. They met on New Year's Eve 1975 to discuss strategy in the light of the new developments, which included the withdrawal of US support and the capture of a small number of SADF troops. No official account of this meeting has surfaced. Pik Botha, in any case, found that the Chief of the South African Army, Magnus Malan, was now the chief proponent of an orderly withdrawal as there was 'a danger of encirclements and major battles.' The consensus of the meeting was that withdrawal had to begin.[86] Politically, the intervention had failed, since its very occurrence had gravely discredited Pretoria's Angolan allies, the FNLA and UNITA. African countries that had sat on the fence regarding recognition of the MPLA, such as Nigeria, Algeria, Ethiopia, Tanzania, the Sudan and Ghana, all ended up recognizing the MPLA government when the extent of South African intervention became clear. The OAU condemned the intervention. Furthermore, the support of the United States proved transient as Congress cut off supplies and money to the FNLA and UNITA; Vorster, P. W. Botha, and Nationalist Party MPs all expressed

---

[82]   SADFAP 1–22–3 Vol. 7 Angola Relations with SA 24.10.75 to 31.12.75, Secretary for Foreign Affairs, Pretoria to SA Embassy Washington, 15 December 1975.
[83]   SADFA 1–22–3 Vol. 7 Angola Relations with SA 24.10.75 to 31.12.75, SA Embassy Washington to Secretary for Foreign Affairs, 12 December 1975.
[84]   Thomas J. Noer, 'International Credibility and Political Survival', p. 778.
[85]   FRUS, 1969–1976, vol. XXVIII, Southern Africa, Doc. 156, 'Memorandum of Conversation', Washington, 19 December 1975, note 5 for deputy Secretary of State, Ingersoll's note.
[86]   See Malan, My Life with the SADF, pp. 130–31, whose account tallies with Pik Botha's in The Road to Democracy in South Africa, Volume 2, pp. 65–68.

great bitterness about this betrayal in the South African Parliament.[87] Lastly, it was made clear, as South Africa prepared to confront the Cubans, that the United States could not openly support the apartheid regime. Faced with international isolation and potential military disaster, the South Africans retreated before a major confrontation with the Cuban expeditionary force could develop. In the early weeks of 1976, with the SADF in full retreat, the Cubans and the MPLA captured all the major towns of central and southern Angola, though they behaved with circumspection and did not attempt to engage the South Africans.[88] Neither did they attempt to push into South West Africa. In early March, through the mediation efforts of the British, the Soviets and the Nigerians, the South Africans received assurances that the Calueque dam would be respected.[89] In the end, South Africa's withdrawal was only temporary and it found itself dragged into a border war that would rage until the end of the 1980s on the Namibian–South African frontier.[90] More importantly, however, the perception of the defeat of the invincible South African military machine contributed to an uprising in the townships, beginning with Soweto in 1976, that would rage until the end of Apartheid in the 1990s.

Conclusion

Portugal's hurried (and, in the Angolan case, opaque) decolonization in 1974–75, and South Africa's inept response, represented an existential threat to the Apartheid regime, but its leaders did not yet realize this. The nearest thing to a post-mortem we have on the Angolan debacle is a report for the liaison committee of senior South African and Rhodesian military officers, which appears to have replicated at least some of the old functions of Exercise ALCORA.[91] The aim of the report was to reassess the threat to the two remaining white regimes in the aftermath of the new reality of 'direct intervention by a foreign power which had now been established'.[92] With regard to Soviet objectives in southern Africa, it noted: 'There can be little doubt that the USSR would not have escalated the war in Angola had the USA and the Western World shown any determination to counter Soviet involvement.' Soviet objectives included the neutralization of South Africa's détente policy, 'which was proving an embarrassment to them', and gaining a foothold in Angola, to offset Western and Chinese influence in Africa, securing riches and

---

[87]   Hallett, 'The South African Intervention in Angola, 1976', p. 383.
[88]   Ibid.
[89]   Botha in *The Road to Democracy in South Africa, Volume 2*, p. 68.
[90]   See George, *The Cuban Intervention in Angola, 1965–1991*, and Gleijeses, *Conflicting Missions: Havana, Washington, Pretoria*.
[91]   SANDFAP, HIS AMI Groep 3 Houer 404, 'Minutes of discussions between delegations from Rhodesian Security Forces and SADF held in Pretoria during the period 26–27 February 1976'.
[92]   SANDFA, HIS AMI Groep 3 Houer 404, 'The Effect of the Developments in Angola on the Security Situations of Rhodesia and the RSA', paragraph 2.

strategic raw materials in Angola, and expanding its maritime influence in the southern oceans.[93] The USSR had virtually achieved its main objective in Angola and a period of consolidation could be expected. An escalation beyond the borders would put a strain on Soviet resources. The continued technical responsibility of Britain for Rhodesia and South Africa's control of South West Africa made a Soviet-backed conventional attack on either unlikely. The risk of a more conventional attack would be influenced by 'actions and reactions' of Rhodesian and South African forces and whether the Soviet objectives 'could be attained by merely continuing to support the revolutionary onslaught, which can be gradually stepped up should the situation become more favourable.'[94]

The OAU remained committed to the Lusaka declaration and the 'total elimination of White Rule in southern Africa, the order of priority being Rhodesia, South-West Africa and finally the Republic of South Africa.'[95] It was noted that the Defence Sub-Committee of the OAU Liberation Committee had adopted a report rejecting peaceful solutions to the Rhodesian crisis. Other rhetoric suggested an intensification of the armed struggle in 'Zimbabwe and Namibia'. The more militant members of the OAU had been 'buoyed up' by the successes in Mozambique and Angola. 'They', it was noted, 'have seen how "liberation" can be hastened by support from foreign external sources using heavy weapons.'[96] However, the report was of the view that 'at the moment there is no likelihood of a conventional war threat emanating from the OAU, or any of its components.' This did not mean it could not be reviewed should the 'terrorist' campaign fail or should Mozambique, for instance, claim that its territorial integrity was threatened: 'In this case the lesson of the Angolan civil war (the effectiveness of heavy weapons against lightly armed troops) may be applied and result in OAU countries sending military aid, or external forces (e.g. Cuban) may be 'invited to assist in the attainment of OAU aims.' Rhodesia would be most vulnerable to such an escalation.[97] It was a grim prognosis, and one echoed in the minute of a British Foreign Office official, Peter Young:

> Détente [in Southern Africa] is in ruins and, arguably, the threat to Namibia is now greater than it would have been if the MPLA had won sooner and South Africa had adopted the same attitude to them as they have done to FRELIMO. Certainly, there are now many more Cubans and a stronger Russian presence and influence which could threaten Namibia. But the important question is how all this will affect the Government's internal policies and life within the Republic. I agree [...] that the present government are unlikely now to act logically and adopt more liberal policies towards the majority. The Nationalists are much more likely to

[93]   Ibid, paragraph 5.
[94]   Ibid, paragraph 6.
[95]   Ibid, paragraph 8.
[96]   Ibid, paragraph 10.
[97]   Ibid, paragraphs 11–12.

react the other way. But if Rhodesia fell violently and Mozambique became uncooperative, demands for change from the opposition may well compel Mr Vorster to alter course. Whatever happens, I think the historians will mark South Africa's Angolan venture as a significant turning point away from peaceful evolution.[98]

Research for this article was made possible by grants from the Instituto Camões, the British Academy, and the Irish Research Council for the Humanities and Social Sciences.

[98]   TNAUKKL, FCO, 51–425 P. M. H. Young Central and Southern African Department (FCO) to Mr Reid (FCO), 4 March 1976.

Portugal and the UN:
A Rogue State Resisting the Norm of
Decolonization (1956–1974)

BRUNO CARDOSO REIS

ICS-UL

This article looks at the Portuguese reaction to an increasingly numerous and hostile anti-colonial majority in the United Nations (UN), the central international norm-setting organization after 1945. More specifically I will focus on the persistence of a Portuguese policy of denying colonialism, that is, of formally declaring that Portugal was not a colonial empire but rather a unitary state with territories in different continents. Why would Portugal stick to this position for almost two decades, in the face of widespread scepticism and hostility from within a UN increasingly dominated by an anti-colonial stance — formally in the shape of General Assembly resolution 1542, of 1960 — that accused Portugal of being a colonial empire while refusing to accept this reality, and given the inevitable consequences of an emerging international norm of decolonization?[1] Belgium also endured growing hostility at the UN for a long period. It faced a rising tide of anti-colonialism from 1946, as a founding member of the UN. In fact, even a speedy but messy decolonization of the Belgian Congo in 1960 did not put an end to criticism by the anti-colonial bloc at the UN of the neo-colonial relationship between Belgium and the Congo in general, and Katanga in particular, which presented a new target for criticism by the Afro-Asian bloc. This seems to indicate that confrontation of a state with the UN could be expected when there was a clash between normative change at the global level and core guidelines, 'constitutive' norms at the national level.[2] This was the case regardless of regime type, authoritarian in the case of Portugal, parliamentary democracy in the case of Belgium. It also shows that a number of facilitating conditions were necessary in allowing prolonged resistance to international norms, of which two stand out:

---

[1] The question of whether or not Portugal was a colonial empire is still a matter of some political controversy in Portugal. I follow a mainstream academic definition by Michael Doyle, *Empires* (Ithaca, NY: Cornell University Press, 1986): an empire exists whenever 'the *effective* sovereignty' of dependent peripheral territories is exercised by 'the dominant metropole' that 'exerts political control over the internal and external policy' of the former (p. 12).

[2] Theo Farrell, *Norms of War: Cultural Beliefs and Modern Conflict* (Boulder, CO: Lynne Riener, 2005), pp. 8–9.

Portuguese Studies vol. 29 no. 2 (2013), 251–76
© Modern Humanities Research Association 2013

(1) Minimal support to the rogue state by one or more of the five permanent members of the UN Security Council, ensuring that more damaging resolutions with mandatory sanctions were halted, softened or vetoed;

(2) Strongly nationalist domestic politics, so that losing votes at the UN would not weaken but, on the contrary, reinforce a preference for resistance to international norms.

But to pursue this analysis to its conclusions it is important, first, to look into the existing literature on the subject.

The question of the fight against the growing tide of anti-colonialism in the UN inevitably arises whenever the colonial policy of the *Estado Novo* is placed in an international context.[3] It has been the main topic of a number of unpublished dissertations and articles, both in Portuguese and in English, that provide us with the basic outline of what happened during this period in terms of the confrontation of Portuguese diplomacy at the UN with the anti-colonial bloc.[4] It makes no sense therefore to treat the subject as new ground and engage in a purely descriptive analysis. Even so, I will try to show that the earlier period, pre-entry and late 1950s are not as well known as the 1960s and 1970s, and there are some missing pieces that need to be fitted into the jigsaw.

It would be hard, moreover, to identify in the existing literature explicit debates or historical controversies. There seems to be a consensus that the UN became a major source of public attacks against the Portuguese regime and its policy of denying colonialism, and that this was reciprocated by the hostility towards, and disparaging views of, the UN on the part of the *Estado Novo* leadership. But what is not quite clear is the reason for the persistence of the Portuguese regime in its confrontation with the UN, or how to evaluate its results in comparative terms.

This topic deserves attention because decolonization changed global politics and the global balance of power — a point repeatedly made during these years

---

[3]   e.g. Pedro A. Oliveira, *Os despojos da Aliança* (Lisbon: Tinta da China, 2007); Fernando Martins, 'A questão colonial na política externa portuguesa: 1926-1975', in *O império africano (séculos XIX e XX)*, ed. by Valentim Alexandre (Lisbon: Edições Colibri, 2000), pp. 137-65; António C. Pinto, 'Portugal e a resistência à descolonização', in *História da expansão portuguesa*, vol. v, ed. by F. Bethencourt and K. Chaudhuri (n.p.: Temas & Debates, 2000), pp. 51-64; Norrie MacQueen, *The Decolonization of Portuguese Africa: Metropolitan Revolution and the Dissolution of Empire* (London: Longman, 1997), pp. 52-58 *passim*.

[4]   More specifically focused on the UN see e.g. A. E. Duarte Silva, 'O litígio entre Portugal e a ONU (1960-1974)', *Análise Social*, 30.130 (1995), 5-50; Fernando Martins, 'Portugal e a ONU: uma história da política externa e ultramarina portuguesa no pós-guerra, 1941-1968' (unpublished MA dissertation, Lisbon, FCSH, 1996) and the article derived from the same, Idem, 'A política externa do Estado Novo, o Ultramar e a ONU, uma doutrina histórico-jurídica 1955-1968', *Penélope*, 18 (1996), 189-205. See also Denis C. Beller, 'The Portuguese Territories Issue in the UN: An Analysis of the Debates' (unpublished PhD dissertation, UCLA, 1970); Leah Fine, *Colour-blind Colonialism? Lusotropicalismo and Portugal's 20th Century Empire in Africa* (unpublished MA dissertation, Barnard College, 2007); Norrie MacQueen, 'Belated Decolonization and UN Politics against the Backdrop of the Cold War: Portugal, Britain, and Guinea-Bissau's Proclamation of Independence, 1973-1974', *Journal of Cold War Studies*, 8.4 (2006), 29-56.

by the Portuguese governing elite, which regretted the end of a Eurocentric international system. Decolonization ended the legitimacy of formal empires that had been an important feature of world politics for millennia. Yet decolonization as a world-historical event was incomplete while Portugal still held large territories overseas, resisting until 1974 this new UN-centred norm. It is worth analysing further why, for more than a decade, a small power like Portugal actively resisted the normative change leading to speedy decolonization, as supported by the two Cold War superpowers and many other countries.

In this article, my main aim is to deal with some key questions, namely:

• Why did Portugal apply for UN membership in 1945, and accept it in 1955?

• Why did Portugal remain in the UN, while increasingly facing pariah status as a result of resistance to the emerging anti-colonial norm, instead of either conforming or abandoning the organization?

• Were there different stages in this Portuguese diplomatic approach?

• How should we evaluate the success or failure of Portuguese diplomacy in the UN, particularly in comparison with a similarly small state like Belgium?

• What defines success for an authoritarian and nationalist regime like the *Estado Novo* in its dealings with the UN?

• What are the implications of this case for wider debates about the dynamics of the UN?

In addressing these questions the two initial sections of this article are more descriptive and are divided chronologically: first, an initial period of relative Portuguese success that was somewhat overshadowed by the problems that followed; second, a longer period of increasing crystallization of opposing views despite some occasional periods of détente as a result, for instance, of negotiations in the early 1960s between Portugal and African states facilitated by the UN, or of expectations of change when Marcello Caetano replaced Salazar in 1968. A comparison of Portuguese and Belgian policy at the UN will follow. A final section will then try to say what drove Portugal to resist the emerging norm of rapid decolonization, as well as the wider significance of this in relation to ongoing debates about decolonization and about clashes over international normative change at the UN.

UN Membership: Accession and Resistance (1945–1960)

Why did Portugal become a member of the UN at all? (Switzerland refused this possibility until the end of the Cold War.) Why did the Portuguese regime choose to remain at the UN despite mounting criticism at that forum? This is all the more surprising given the often dismissive attitude of the leaders of the *Estado Novo* towards international organizations.

Salazar, however — and this is an important point that seems to have been ignored by the existing historiography — did not always show contempt towards the UN. In a speech in May 1945, he signalled publicly his interest in the new international organization then being created. He stated that whilst 'Portugal is not among those that are now undertaking the delicate task of rebuilding the community of nations', it was 'a normal member of the international community' and, unlike Switzerland or the Vatican, its 'neutral status had ceased with the end of the war'. Salazar then went further and praised the efforts to design a new international organization. He did so, most significantly, not despite but precisely because of reports of a planned division of labour between a democratic General Assembly, in which the 'basis is the Nation' and member states were all 'sovereign and equal', and a Security Council, reserved only for a few great powers. To the founder of the authoritarian *Estado Novo* this seemed not only a necessary 'concession to the reality of international politics', but also, and more importantly, a recognition of 'an aristocratic principle in the effective direction of society'. Salazar's core belief in *Realpolitik* as well as in 'hierarchy' as the basis of politics, both foreign and domestic, is therefore made explicit. This is an important indicator of what would be Salazar's future approach towards the UN: a mixture of pragmatism in search of some great-power support and an elitist distancing from the will of the emerging non-Western majority.[5] To persuade key countries to use, or at least threaten, a veto became the only realistic possibility for Portuguese diplomacy in the 1960s to contain the impact of the anti-colonial majority at the UN General Assembly. But this was also an appropriate response according to the elitist Western-centric beliefs central to the political culture of the *Estado Novo*.

This positive perception of the UN by Salazar seemed out of character and soon proved so mistaken that it was forgotten by both his critics and his admirers alike. The power given to the permanent members of the Security Council meant that the USSR was able to veto Portuguese admittance for a decade. Also, starting as early as 1946, the General Assembly became a major forum for anti-colonialism. Salazar was not alone in failing to predict how quickly the UN — boosted by the strategic and ideological disputes of an emerging Cold War — would take on this role.

The main colonial powers, Britain in particular, had managed to guarantee that the only practical obligation of administering powers regarding their colonial territories under the charter of the UN was — according to Article 73 — to provide 'statistical and other information of a technical nature relating to economic, social, and educational conditions in the territories'. This was explicitly to be for 'information purposes' only, and any reporting would be 'subject to such limitation as security and constitutional considerations may require'. These tight formal guarantees seemed more than enough to justify the

---

[5] A. Oliveira Salazar, speech 18 May 1945 in *Salazar: pensamento e doutrina política. Textos seleccionados*, ed. by M. C. Henriques et al. (Lisbon: Verbo, 2007), p. 106.

initial confidence of all colonial powers that they would have nothing to fear from the UN. The preeminent role of colonial statesmen in helping to shape this new organization — in particular from Britain and its dominions, men like General Smuts — could only have reinforced this.[6] Therefore getting Portugal into the UN, without the UN interfering in national colonial policies, seemed a reasonable expectation in 1945.

In 1946–47 anti-colonialism gained a growing influence in the General Assembly, where, by definition, colonial powers were a minority. Crucially, after 1945, this minority no longer included the leading global powers. Colonialism did not have the support of either of the two Cold War superpowers, which were instead interested in winning over to their side a majority of states — not least newly independent states — by all means possible. Portugal was aware of the problems created by this growing hostility from an increasing majority of states at the UN, not least because there was a tradition of diplomatic exchanges with other colonial powers, first and foremost with Britain, but also with Belgium and France. New post-1945 multilateral institutions, while increasingly creating difficulties for colonial powers, also provided new opportunities to exchange views, if only informally.

With regard to Portugal's membership of NATO, colonial powers sometimes converged to some extent, from 1949 onwards, in stressing the strategic importance of her overseas territories for Western security. There were also other less regular official discussions devoted specifically to colonial issues, including defence.[7] The most regular and public of these meetings, regarding cooperation on technical issues in Africa, eventually led to the creation of the Combined Commission for Technical Co-operation in Africa south of the Sahara (CCTA) in 1950, officially as an organization devoted to the promotion of African development. In fact it had also been created by the colonial powers to try to ensure that the UN and its specialized agencies were kept out of development efforts in colonial Africa.[8] All of this could not have failed to impress the Portuguese elite. It contributed to what turned out to be a misplaced confidence in the existence of a solid agreement among colonial powers to resist rapid decolonization in sub-Saharan Africa.

Furthermore, domestic politics made Portuguese admission to the UN desirable for the *Estado Novo*. Failure to get into the UN was being used by its political opponents as evidence that Salazar's authoritarianism had led to international isolation after 1945. Portuguese admittance to NATO had already made

[6] Cf. Mark Mazower, *No Enchanted Palace: The End of Empire and the Ideological Origins of the UN* (Princeton, NJ: Princeton University Press, 2009), *maxime* p. 17.
[7] See Christopher Coker, *NATO, the Warsaw Pact, and Africa* (Basingstoke: Macmillan, 1985); G. R. Berridge, *South Africa, the Colonial Powers and African Defence: The Rise and Fall of the White Entente, 1948–60* (London: Macmillan, 1992).
[8] References in Belgian documents are very clear in this regard, cf. e.g. AMAE, AF II, DG Politique, Section Aff. Coloniales, Note 1549 pour DGP 'Sur l'activité de l'OIT en Afrique' (6 March 1956); or Note Grojean for DGP on meeting Chargé Affaires Portugal Aragão (13 April 1956).

that argument harder to sustain. But the fact that Portugal was finally admitted to the UN, on 14 December 1955, and its continued membership after that date, meant that the Portuguese state — regardless of the nature of the regime or the international criticism that it might attract — was recognized as a full member of the post-1945 international system. Admission to the UN could be and was portrayed by the Portuguese regime as a victory. True, Portugal was admitted as part of a 'package deal' with sixteen other new member states. But what mattered politically for Salazar and his regime was that this could be presented as proof that the US, which led the Western powers in supporting Portuguese membership, valued Portugal as an ally.[9] Moreover, the linkage involved in the deal made it difficult for Portugal to refuse entry, because this might have jeopardized the whole deal and put the Western bloc at a disadvantage.[10]

A point that needs to be underlined, however, is that behind this wish to gain admittance to the UN there seems to have been another dimension, now forgotten, linked to the fight of the *Estado Novo* against decolonization. A member state of the UN had the automatic right to appeal to the International Court of Justice in a dispute with another member state. Portugal did this just one day after becoming a member of the UN — on 15 December 1955 — asking the Court to rule against India and its policy of annexation of Goa and the other Portuguese enclaves in the Indian subcontinent. Dominated by law professors like Salazar, the Portuguese ruling elite was convinced that it could win the legal argument, and it did. This success could only have confirmed their already strong conviction of the appropriateness of a legalistic approach to the challenge of anti-colonialism. When this proved increasingly ineffective, the Portuguese elite attributed these set-backs to abusive re-interpretations or changes to existing international law. Portuguese entry into the UN system, ironically ended up being favourable to a reactionary retrenchment by the Portuguese regime into its core legalist argumentation for being an empire in denial.[11]

What do I mean by Portuguese colonialism in denial? In 1952 the Portuguese Constitution was amended to state that Portugal no longer had colonies; the territories concerned were now to be designated *províncias ultramarinas* [overseas provinces] and to be regarded as integral parts of a unitary pluri-continental state. This Portuguese constitutional amendment was, paradoxically or not, a revealing formal recognition of international normative change, particularly at the UN. This point was made by hard-line critics from within the regime, who saw even a purely formal concession to foreign pressure as

---

[9] Cf. authorized biography of Salazar by his last foreign minister A. Franco Nogueira, *Salazar. IV. O ataque (1945–1958)* (Porto: Civilização, 1986), pp. 330, 389–90, 400.

[10] Cf. Resolution 109 UN SC 14 December 1955 at <http://www.un.org/ga/search/view_doc. asp?symbol=S/RES/109 (1955)> [accessed 14 March 2013]. Of the sixteen, only Portugal and Spain were firmly aligned with the West, the others were either neutral, like Austria or Finland, or more or less recently independent moderate countries like Jordan, Nepal, Cambodia, Laos or Libya.

[11] Nogueira, *Salazar. IV*, pp. 400–01.

unacceptable.[12] Portuguese colonialism did not dare face this global normative change head-on; it had to deny its true nature. At the same time, of course (even if it is not possible to develop the theme here), the defenders of this change from colonies to overseas provinces could and did claim for it a Portuguese historical lineage.[13]

Based upon this constitutional change and using legal arguments, Salazar and his diplomats simply refused to conform to a norm that recent experience had shown to be the beginning of many difficulties for other colonial powers in the UN. In response to the usual letter from the Secretary General, in February 1956, asking Portugal for information about any dependent territories under Article 73 of the Charter, the Lisbon government simply answered that it had no non-self-governing territories. Constitutionally, Portugal was a single unitary state, albeit one spread across different continents. Should this interpretation be accepted, the regime was convinced that 'seria o colapso de toda a política de cerco do Ocidente' [it would put an end to the encirclement of the West] by the countries of the Afro-Asian Bloc which were 'desnorteados' [disorientated] and reacting with 'exaltação emotiva' [heightened emotions]. This was not, evidently, what then happened. Even discounting the rhetorical exaggeration of Franco Nogueira's language, he was right that what was at stake in this issue was ultimately how far the internationalization of the colonial question would go and whether Western states could put an end to the UN majority pressure on colonial issues or not.[14]

In the short term, for a few initial years, this strategy did seem to result in a measure of diplomatic success for Portugal. Her diplomats were also able to make a tactically clever use of UN procedural rules, for example regarding the requirement for a two-thirds majority for votes on important issues — and the anti-colonial bloc had conceded this was such an issue by making repeated claims about the vital threat to global order that Portuguese denial of colonialism represented. This guaranteed a delay in any decision against Portugal because of lack of a sufficient anti-colonial majority in the General Assembly before 1960.

Portuguese diplomacy realized it could not hope to get any significant support at the UN by fighting its case by an open advocacy of colonialism, nor were purely procedural tactics sufficient. Wisely, therefore, it supplemented its case by arguing the need to respect the norm of non-intervention in internal affairs in refusing any discussion of Portuguese constitutional matters, including its change of the status of overseas territories. Most states at the UN held this principle as an important normative shield against abusive foreign interventions by powerful states, and were careful not to erode it. In the initial

---

[12]   Armindo Monteiro former Minister of Colonies in the 1930s; cf. Pedro A. Oliveira, *Armindo Monteiro: uma biografia política* (Lisbon: Bertrand Editora, 2000).
[13]   See Cláudia Castelo, '*O Modo Português de Estar no Mundo*': *o luso-tropicalismo e a ideologia colonial portuguesa (1933–1961)* (Porto: Afrontamento, 1998).
[14]   Nogueira, *Salazar. IV*, p. 424.

vote on the matter, in 1957, Portuguese diplomats achieved a draw — thirty-five countries for the Portuguese position, with thirty-five countries against; five countries abstained and five were absent. These relatively positive results at the UN in the late 1950s were also a result of the Portuguese government being able to use its remaining soft power to gather votes or abstentions from more conservative Latin American governments, in particular Brazil, as well as from NATO allies, using arguments of cultural identity and political solidarity. Only in 1959–60 did the growing anti-colonial majority in the UN manage to seriously challenge the Portuguese interpretation. But this was the high point of Portuguese diplomacy at the UN.

The tables were turned on Portugal in what was to be a defining moment in the normative history of decolonization. On the same day — 14 December 1960 — Resolution 1514 condemning colonialism in general was approved, alongside Resolution 1542 which explicitly rejected the Portuguese position as being one of colonialism in denial and in disguise.[15]

The formulation of the Portuguese answer to these new international challenges, and its persistent defence, was led by able professional diplomats like Franco Nogueira, with the help of other bright young legal minds including Adriano Moreira, a future overseas minister. Nogueira came more quickly and more enduringly into pre-eminence as a direct result of his leading role in the Portuguese delegations sent to the General Assembly after 1956, primarily with the mission of fighting anti-colonialism. He was appointed in rapid succession to increasingly important roles at the Portuguese Foreign Ministry: first, deputy director of political affairs in 1958, and full director in 1959; then director-general in 1960. Eventually, in 1961, he became Foreign Minister, a position he retained until 1969.[16]

As regards the legal argument for the Portuguese case, it was published in book format in English as well as other foreign languages, in 1963, as part of a national and international campaign of public diplomacy led by Nogueira. The key point in the Portuguese argument was that, in re-interpreting Article 73, the UN General Assembly was violating the Charter and therefore resolutions such as 1542 had no legal value. Article 73 explicitly excluded constitutional matters. Portuguese delegates also argued that, more generically, Chapter XI was — unlike others — not titled 'international' by the Charter and this was why the General Assembly was not given explicit powers over colonial affairs, and was now illegally usurping them. But the main objection was, as pointed out, that Portuguese jurists strongly believed that the UN could not question or interpret the Portuguese Constitution as it stood when Portugal was accepted as a member of the UN — if the UN had any reservations about it, then it should

---

[15]   Belgium and France voted against this motion in support of Portugal, but Britain and the US abstained.
[16]   Manuel de Lucena, 'A. M. G. Franco Nogueira', in *Dicionário de História de Portugal. Suplemento*, ed. by A. Barreto e M. F. Mónica (Porto: Figueirinhas, 1999), vol. VIII, pp. 605–17.

have made them at the time of accession, in December 1955. The anti-colonial offensive against the Portuguese regime was portrayed as a violation of key norms of the UN Charter, namely Article 2, regarding sovereign equality and non-intervention. The case presented by the Portuguese representatives went even further, accusing the General Assembly of violating the very universality of the rights and norms it claimed it was defending in arguing for the end of colonialism, by applying ethnicity and territorial discontinuity as a criterion for determining the absence of self-determination. Moreover, it disregarded the principle of equality, because not only Portugal but also other countries — like the US in the case of Hawaii or Alaska — should be subject to it. This was presented by Portuguese decision-makers and diplomats as a form of 'racism in reverse', proof of an anti-White and an anti-Western prejudice held by a majority of the General Assembly.[17]

So why did Portugal not leave the UN at some point in the 1960s? True, there was only one precedent for withdrawal, Indonesia in 1965, but that was only for a matter of months, and had not been a diplomatic success. The reasons are not difficult to deduce from what has previously been said about the Portuguese government wanting Portugal to become a member. Once Portugal had been admitted to the organization, the Portuguese regime could not easily leave without political loss of face, given the mounting international and internal criticism. Moreover, relinquishing any rights that they believed Portugal had was anathema to the highly nationalistic and authoritarian *Estado Novo*. Portugal had a right to be at the UN and, as far as the regime's elite was concerned, it had right on its side. Abandoning the organization would be to confess to a lack of either courage or strong arguments in defence of the cause of a Greater Portugal. This was unthinkable for the proudly nationalistic legal scholars that led the Portuguese regime.

After 1960: The Struggle for Support in the UN

The year 1960 was an important turning point in terms of decolonization, as no less than sixteen countries became independent in the African continent, the biggest and most sudden change in membership in UN history. It was a trend that was reinforced as more African countries gained independence during the years that followed.[18]

As regards the preferences of the *Estado Novo*'s political culture, if it was acceptable to lose the support of the non-Western majority of the UN, it was very important to retain the support of at least some big Western powers, not only for pragmatic reasons, but also for normative reasons: after all, Portugal claimed it was defending Western civilization in Africa against Communism.

---

[17]   A. Franco Nogueira, *The United Nations and Portugal: A Study in Anti-Colonialism* (London: Sidgwick and Jackson, 1963).

[18]   UN, 'Growth in UN Membership', in <http://www.un.org/en/members/growth.shtml> [accessed 16 February 2012].

The sudden shift, in 1960, in the balance of power in the UN General Assembly and its committees was all the more disappointing for the Portuguese governing elite, because it was in large part due to a sudden and unexpected shift in policy of the other major colonial powers resisting decolonization, France and Belgium. Indeed, until 1959 governments in Paris and Brussels as well as in Lisbon had converged in a determination to resist decolonization in the name of a shared belief in a necessarily slow pace for real overseas development, and a cultural and strategic preference for some kind of integration into a unitary state over full independence. As far as these three European powers were concerned, with the emergence of two superpowers, the US and the USSR, controlling vast territories and resources, the Cold War only made some kind of *Eurafrica*, i.e. a close association between European knowledge and African resources, all the more necessary. This may have been a product of the French 'official mind', but was eagerly adopted by Belgian and Portuguese officials also.[19] The sudden change of direction towards rapid decolonization by France and Belgium was all the more unexpected because Portugal had been engaged, since 1957, in regular diplomatic quadripartite consultations with Belgium, Britain and France, with a strong focus on the UN. In fact, the Belgian elite was initially thinking more in terms of decades than years — much less one year — when it publicly announced it had started considering devolution of power, in early 1959. Also the end-state was believed to be some kind of close association between Belgium and its Congo.[20]

In France, Michael Debré — who, as de Gaulle's Prime Minister, presided over the sudden acceleration of French decolonization, from a French Union, to a French Community, to Francophone independence — confessed this was the result of a number of improvisations, in particular in response to the frustration of pro-French African leaders at a status lower than full independence, making UN membership a prized outcome.[21] The fact that Belgian and French decolonization suddenly and radically escaped the timetables and end-states established made the Portuguese ruling elite even more determined in its denial of colonialism and, therefore, its refusal to decolonize. It is facile but wrong to blame the Portuguese elite for being unable to foresee and anticipate what was in fact a sudden transformation, unexpected even for top Belgian and French decision-makers.

The end-result was, in any case, a very negative change for Portuguese policy at the UN. It was obvious then, even for the traditionally more accommodating British diplomacy, that this change would make the enlarged UN Committee on Decolonization 'an infernal nuisance' for colonial powers.[22] Britain and

---

[19]   Guy Martin, 'Africa and the Ideology of Eurafrica: Neo-Colonialism or Pan-Africanism?', *Journal of Modern African Studies*, 20.2 (1982), 221–38.

[20]   Cf. Jean Stengers, *Congo: mythes et réalités* (Brussels: Éds. Racine, 2007), *maxime* p. 271 ff.

[21]   Michael Debré, *Gouverner. 3. Mémoires 1958–1962* (Paris: Albin Michel, 1988), pp. 326–29.

[22]   Senior Colonial Office official Christopher Eastwood cit. in Wm. Roger Louis, 'Public Enemy Number One: Britain and the United Nations', in *Ends of British Imperialism: The Scramble for Empire, Suez and Decolonization* (London: I. B. Tauris, 2006), p. 702.

Portugal were now the major remaining colonial powers. While British officials sometimes seriously considered abandoning the UN Committee on Decolonization, and eventually did so in 1971, the British government never seriously contemplated resisting the trend towards relatively rapid decolonization. Yet this was exactly what Portugal, a much smaller state, did: it retained all its overseas territories, making no gestures towards independence, while remaining in the UN. In doing so, Portugal became increasingly a rogue state, not only because of tensions with the Afro-Asian or Non-Aligned Bloc but also with some of its Western allies, particularly the US, the Nordic countries, and even Britain and the Netherlands.

The Portuguese Foreign Minister, on attending the first UN General Assembly in this new situation, in New York in October 1961, reported back to Salazar that 'os afro-asiáticos dominam inteiramente as N.U. [...] apoiados no grupo comunista. Dispondo de maioria automática de 60 votos em qualquer assunto' [the Afro-Asian [bloc] is entirely dominant at the UN [...] supported by the communist bloc, enjoying an automatic majority of 60 votes on any issue]. But to the Portuguese 'official mind' this was no reason to compromise with it. On the contrary, the feeling was of the need to resist what Nogueira perceived as 'o maior desplante' [the absolute contempt] of the new majority at the General Assembly for existing norms, 'declarando aberta e oficialmente que a Carta e o Regimento estão antiquados e não têm o menor interesse; a lei é a vontade da maioria; e assim respondem quando se lhes pergunta em que texto ou textos se baseia um qualquer proposta ou resolução' [declaring openly and formally that the Charter and the rules of procedure are out-dated and do not have the least importance; the law is the will of the majority; and this is their answer when they are asked on what text or texts any proposal or resolution is based].[23] For the conservative legalism that was a cornerstone of the political culture of the *Estado Novo* it was evident that traditional precedents and set procedure should prevail, not majority voting or progressive ideals. Therefore this great change at the UN invited more resistance, not appeasement by the Portuguese regime.[24]

Portugal became the prime target of anti-colonialism as the only state not willing to grant independence to overseas territories, with only openly racist Rhodesia and South Africa competing for attention. What mattered was that, regardless of their legal status in the Portuguese Constitution, these distant dependent territories were perceived as colonies by most other states, including traditional allies of Portugal. Not only that, but Portugal was willing to fight wars against decolonization in three of these territories, Angola from 1961, Guinea from 1963, and Mozambique in 1964.

The signs of this normative change, however, predated these armed conflicts and may have helped to spark them — in particular, General Assembly Reso-

[23]   ANTT — AOS/CD 8 Letter from Foreign Sec. Franco Nogueira to PM Salazar (New York, October 1961 [read 3 November 1961]).
[24]   'Resistance' was pointedly the title of the pertinent volume of the authorized biography of Salazar by Franco Nogueira, *Salazar. V. A resistência (1958–1964)* (Porto: Civilização, 1984).

lution 1467 of December 1959 by which the Afro-Asian bloc finally managed to appoint a commission to interpret Portugal's position under Article 73. This in itself was a significant defeat of the procedural arguments being used by Portuguese diplomacy to block any such discussion. This was then followed by Resolution 1542, on 15 December 1960, that formally interpreted Article 73 of the Charter, specifically rejecting the 'Portuguese thesis' by stating that it was 'applicable to territories which were then' — i.e. at the time of the approval of the Charter in 1945 — 'known to be of the colonial type', making the 1952 Portuguese constitutional amendment irrelevant. It further stated that 'prima facie' it should be applied to any 'territory that is geographically separate and culturally and/or ethnically distinct from the country administering it'.

The increasing marginalization of Portugal at the UN culminated in a Security Council debate in November 1963, after Foreign Minister Franco Nogueira had gone through the motions of talking with a group of African countries, a move that had momentarily created great excitement and curiosity and even a more positive atmosphere in the General Assembly. But this was clearly not enough to change the Portuguese official mind. These were not true negotiations but more a typical diversionary measure by a rogue state, meant to deflect pressure from friendly governments. Nogueira made this more or less clear in informal consultations with the Brazilian and US representatives who had pressed for talks, and asked what Portugal had to offer: 'não faria nada' [would do nothing] or 'não sabia' [didn't know] were the answers.[25] The US would later complain that 'Portugal does not negotiate, it does not talk'. Or as the US representative Adlai Stevenson put it, Portugal was 'diverting attention from more important matters' at the UN. Nogueira was not disarmed by this, simply asking whey they didn't change the subject.[26] Of course, African states were equally unwilling to compromise their demands for total and rapid independence.[27] The episode ended with the Security Council urging Portugal to conform to the General Assembly resolutions, and the Portuguese delegation reaffirming that it considered these new norms of decolonization illegal and void.

Was this merely talk? In my view this growing international attention at the UN was, in fact, an important factor in spurring the violent anti-colonial uprisings in Angola, in February and March 1961, which marked the beginning of the protracted guerrilla campaigns against Portuguese colonialism. Evidently the UN did not create the anti-colonial insurgency single-handedly or *ab initio*, but it did provide an important initial spark. For these initially very weak insurgent movements, facing the full military and political might of the colonial state, it was very important to know that they had external support.

[25] ANTT-AOS/CD 7 Letter Franco Nogueira to Salazar from New York (19 October 1963).
[26] ANTT-AOS/CD 7 Letter Franco Nogueira to Salazar from New York (October 1963 [read 27 October 1963]).
[27] ANTT-AOS/CD 7 Letter Franco Nogueira to Salazar from New York (October 1963 [read 27 October 1963]).

Conversely, an armed uprising would evidently strengthen the hand of the countries arguing in the UN that Portugal ruled its African territories by force and not consent. A meeting of the Security Council was scheduled for 15 March 1961, the same day the UPA uprising started in northern Angola.[28] Moreover, the founding leader of the UPA, Holden Roberto, who led the 1961 March uprising that started the war for the independence of Angola, had been invited to a public session of the General Assembly. In a key meeting, on 14 January 1961, in which the decision to begin the armed struggle was made, he claimed support from the 'soldados internacionais que nos ajudarão' [international forces who will help us] — an exaggerated claim, to say the least, but one made credible because of the on-going intervention, since July 1960, of 'blue helmets' in the former Belgian Congo where the meeting was taking place. According to Holden Roberto, Tunisian blue helmets in the Congo did provide some weapons to the insurgents.

Portuguese troubles at the UN were also not unconnected with the unprecedented pressure by the Kennedy Administration on Portugal to decolonize, to the point of supporting UPA insurgents in Angola as well as a failed Portuguese military *pronunciamento* against Salazar, in April 1961. The new US Administration was, initially at least, eager to use the UN to project the US as a leading progressive role-model for the post-colonial world. This is why, in the March 1961 meeting of the Security Council, the US voted in favour of the resolution put forward by Liberia, a close ally of Washington in Africa. It was only defeated because Portugal at that time could still secure six abstentions at the Security Council (Formosa, Chile, Ecuador, Britain, France, Turkey), depriving the US of the required majority.[29]

The year 1961 would end with a military intervention by India resulting in the forceful annexation of the Portuguese enclaves in the Indian sub-continent. True, this violence, like that in Angola, signalled, if not the failure, then certainly the limitations of what the Afro-Asian bloc, even a significant power like India, could achieve diplomatically at the UN in order to change the behaviour of the Portuguese regime. But the Indian military intervention, like the armed uprising in Angola, was also an indication that Portugal paid a price in other than diplomatic terms for its resistance to the norm of decolonization and its increasingly marginalized status on the international stage. Portugal could not find strong support even from its most powerful allies, like the US and Britain, who, while critical of the use of force by India, would do nothing to seriously damage their relations with New Delhi. It was, furthermore, the

---

[28]   Cit. in Dalila C. Mateus and A. Mateus, *Angola 1961, Guerra colonial: causas e consequências. O 4 de Fevereiro e o 15 de Março* (Alfragide: Texto, 2011), pp. 20, 140.

[29]   For the US position and the complex internal debates around it cf. José F. Antunes, *Kennedy e Salazar: o leão e a raposa* (Lisbon: Difusão Cultural, 1992); Witney W. Schneidman. *Engaging Africa: Washington and the Fall of Portugal's Colonial Empire* (New York: University Press of America, 2004); Luís N. Rodrigues, *Kennedy–Salazar: a crise de uma aliança. As relações luso-americanas entre 1961 e 1963* (Lisbon: Ed. Notícias, 2002).

conviction of Portuguese intelligence and decision-makers that international pressure from the Afro-Asian Bloc had been decisive in persuading Nehru to approve a military option against the Portuguese in India. Still, Portuguese intransigence was credited by decision-makers in Lisbon with having caused some embarrassment to the credibility of both India and the UN, the former as an exemplary normative power, the latter as a normative shield against armed aggression.[30]

Thereafter, even while denying its prestige, the notion that the UN was responsible for violence from abroad in Portuguese overseas territories became important in Portuguese official discourse. On 30 June 1961, Salazar chose to make the UN the key target of his first major speech reacting to the beginning of the anti-colonial uprising in Angola, significantly titled 'O ultramar portu-guês e a O.N.U.' [The Portuguese Overseas Territories and the UN]. He restated some key themes of the Portuguese position in the UN, including the fact that the organization should not 'be taken too seriously'. Salazar labelled the new Afro-Asian majority in the General Assembly a 'multidão tumultuária' i.e. a 'riotous mob', acting illegally against Portugal and inciting violence. What was really serious, however, was that the US, the main Western power, since March 1961 'resolvem apoiar ostensivamente o grupo afro-asiático, com o fim confessado de congregar votos fiéis em deliberações que interessem à América contra a Rússia [are resolved to support openly the Afro-Asian bloc, with the avowed aim of gathering loyal votes in [future] deliberations of interest to America against Russia] in the Cold War. This was all the more scandalous for Salazar, because he made a point of publicly stating that he had only sought admission to the UN 'at the request of Britain and the US arguing for the need to reinforce the Western bloc in case of any crisis.' Therefore, he denounced the Kennedy administration for shattering the unity of the West — something Salazar acknowledged with 'profunda mágoa' [deep sorrow] that he was also doing by this speech, but only because he had no alternative except to denounce a mistaken policy that was undermining Western security and values. US policy for Africa was now 'paralela à da Rússia' [parallel to that of Russia] and 'revela-se inconciliável' [is exposed as irreconcilable] with the Atlantic Alliance, because it ignored the fact that the USSR was engaged in a 'trabalho de subversão' [promotion of subversion] in the African continent in order to weaken Europe by breaking this vital strategic linkage in the context of the Cold War.[31]

These points, and in particular the linkage between African insurgencies and global 'communist threats' trying to 'infiltrar o Hemisfério Sul' [infiltrate the southern hemisphere] so as to outflank NATO, were to become a recurrent theme in Portuguese statements in NATO meetings, from the 1950s until the

[30] Cf. Maria J. Stocker, *Xeque-Mate a Goa: o princípio do fim do império português*, 2nd rev. edn (Alfragide: Texto, 2011), pp. 271 ff.
[31] A. Oliveira Salazar, *O ultramar português e a O.N.U. Discurso proferido por Sua Excelência o Presidente do Conselho [...] na sessão extraordinária da Assembléia Nacional em 30 de junho de 1961* (Lisbon: SNI, 1961).

very end of the regime, including the NATO summit held in 1971 in Lisbon, despite widespread international pressure for a boycott.[32]

Until 1963 Portugal maintained a relatively high profile in the UN; after that date the Portuguese Foreign Minister adopted a lower profile. For instance during a 'stormy' session in the Security Council, Nogueira opted to follow proceedings from the Portuguese delegation's office, in order to 'signal the little importance we attached to this noise', even as it was growing 'ever louder'. He was content to meet Secretary-General U Thant in private afterwards, 'and repudiate *in toto* the accusations of the Afro-Asians'. This became the usual pattern: a strict reaffirmation of the Portuguese case, and a denial of any facts allegedly showing that Portugal was provoking an inter-state conflict in Africa that might justify more forceful intervention or sanctions. Above all, Nogueira was now engaged in an exercise in diplomatic damage control through back-door negotiations, using Western solidarity to 'chain-gang' allies and avoid a truly dangerous isolation.[33]

Particularly important in this context, evidently, was the position of the three Western permanent members of the Security Council — France, Britain and the US — not least because they could and did threaten to veto any resolutions that would increase the pressure on Portugal to a damaging extent. In the UN as well as NATO Portugal could usually count on support from France and Belgium, and more conditionally from Britain and the US from 1962 onwards, as well as from a few others. This is why we see Nogueira consulting with the French permanent representative in the UN and carefully reporting back to Salazar that France 'wished' to vote against any resolution targeting Portugal but that 'não pode ficar isolada' [it could not stand alone]. After all, Paris had given up its formal empire precisely to avoid isolation and maximize influence in Francophone Africa and the Third World, with great success, so the French diplomat claimed. He warned Portugal that it had to be careful with Britain and US. Nogueira concluded logically that this was 'uma notificação formal de que a França não usará do veto em nosso favor e nem sequer se absterá se os EU e a Inglaterra [*sic*] não se abstiverem também [a formal notification that France would not use its veto or even abstain if the US and England did not do the same].[34]

The official Portuguese perception of this period at the UN is made characteristically clear by Franco Nogueira in summarizing the state of affairs in 1966: 'não se eximem as Nações Unidas à aprovação das resoluções habituais

---

[32]   Quotation from last Foreign Minister of the regime, Rui Patrício (see note 53) [with Leonor Xavier], pp. 179–87. For the long-term view cf. António Telo, *Portugal e a NATO: o reencontro da tradição atlântica* (Lisbon: Cosmos, 1996), *maxime* pp. 290 ff.

[33]   A. Franco Nogueira, *Um político confessa-se* (Porto: Civilização, 1987), pp. 265–66. The concept of chain-ganging has become current in international relations to describe how a smaller power can use an alliance with a greater power to gain support from the latter. See Kenneth Waltz, *Theory of International Politics* (New York: McGraw-Hill, 1979), p. 167.

[34]   ANTT — AOS/CD 7, Letter Franco Nogueira to Salazar October 1963 [read 27 October 1963], heavily underlined.

contra Portugal. Mas o facto de salientar é outro' [the UN does not refrain from approving the customary resolutions against Portugal. But that is not the important point]. The important point was that the US and a number of Western countries, including Brazil, voted against, and 'nenhum país da NATO ou latino-americano votou contra Portugal' [no NATO or Latin American country voted against Portugal].[35]

When Salazar was replaced in September 1968 by Marcello Caetano, little changed, despite internal and international expectations. An explicit condition of Caetano's appointment by the very conservative President of the Republic, Admiral Tomás, was an unconditional assurance by the former not to make any major changes in Portugal's position of retaining its overseas territories.[36] To signal this internationally, Tomás also demanded that Salazar's last Foreign Minister, Nogueira, should remain in post for some time in the new government.[37] When the latter left, after a year, Caetano made clear in his speech at the official appointment ceremony of the new Foreign Minister, Rui Patrício, that 'a prioridade número um' [his first priority] would be to 'zelar, explicar, defender a nossa política ultramarina' [take care of, explain, and defend our overseas policies]. Patrício states that he never received any other mandate during his four years in charge of Portuguese diplomacy: 'A orientação fundamental da nossa politica externa era a de não aceitar e evitar a internacionalização do problema ultramarino' [the fundamental guiding principle of our foreign policy was that of not accepting and of stopping the internationalization of the overseas problem]; it should be treated as an internal affair. He therefore had to resist UN attempts at intervention, and avoid 'o desmoronar de toda a construção política e jurídica em que assentava a politica externa portuguesa' [the collapse of the whole political-juridical doctrine upon which Portuguese foreign policy rested].[38] This is a revealing formulation of the legalistic normative dogma dominating the Portuguese position at the UN.

The main novelty brought by Patrício, apart from his youth, was, he himself claims, that 'era menos arrogante e agressivo' [I was less arrogant, less aggressive] than his predecessor. Paradigmatic of this option was his decision to attend in person and speak publicly at the annual meeting of the UN General Assembly in 1972. This was clearly meant as an international test of the impact of the 1971 Constitutional Revision that gave Angola and Mozambique the official designation of states instead of overseas provinces, as part of a commitment to 'autonomia progressiva e participada' [progressive and participatory autonomy]. The UN majority saw this as too much legal formality and too little difference on the ground, especially because no clear signal of an acceptance of independence was forthcoming. Patrício's speech at the UN was

[35] A. Franco Nogueira, *Salazar. VI*, p. 239.
[36] Marcelo Caetano, *Depoimento* (Rio de Janeiro: Record, 1974), pp. 14–15.
[37] Américo Thomaz, *Últimas décadas de Portugal* (Lisbon: Eds. FP, n.d.), p. 296 ff.
[38] Cit. Rui Patrício, pp. 215–18.

largely ignored, visibly so by many delegates who simply left the chamber when he started speaking, in a perfect illustration of Portugal's pariah status.[39] In fact, 1972 would see more aggressive UN resolutions against Portuguese colonialism, with the General Assembly declaring the anti-colonial insurgencies legitimate and recognizing the armed movements as sole representatives of the local populations. This extension of recognition and legitimacy 'until now only accorded to sovereign states' by the vast majority of the UN, excepting only a 'handful of international pariahs', part of the same club as Portugal, represents another important marker in a reversal of traditional international politics — in which anti-colonial insurgents had been the pariahs, not the colonial states fighting them. The Algerian FLN had been probably the earliest example of this trend.[40] Even more important, the Security Council approved unanimously an appeal for a negotiated solution to the war that not even the US Nixon Administration felt it could vote against.

In 1973, there was further evidence that Portugal was increasingly a pariah for the majority of the UN. In September, the PAIGC had made a unilateral declaration of the independence of Guinea-Bissau. This was a major break from precedent in decolonization, and yet it was recognized by a majority of states. Its call for UN membership caused major embarrassment to Portugal, because even Western Cold War allies like Britain and the Netherlands were reluctant to appear too close to Portugal and its colonialism in denial. Still, as any pariah state must, Portugal did secure the support of at least one permanent member of the Security Council. The Nixon Administration guaranteed it would veto any decisive move of the UN in this respect.[41]

Patrício's final evaluation of this policy is predictably positive but in a significantly defensive and minimalist way: 'nenhum exército ameaçava [...] de invasão' [no army was threatening [the overseas territories] with invasion]. He also states that 'as deliberações da ONU, certamente cada vez mais ruidosas, continuavam tão ineficazes como dantes' [UN resolutions, though becoming ever more aggressive, were still as ineffective as before].[42] It was indeed the case that Portugal could still guarantee that at least one of the three Western powers with a veto in the UN Security Council 'frustrated the attempts of the [General] Assembly to engineer meaningful measures against' Portugal not only 'during the 1960s' but even in the 'early 1970s'.[43] In this crucial respect Portuguese diplomacy in the UN was a Cold War success story, pushing for a minimal but vital support in defending the *Estado Novo* policy of colonialism in denial. In that sense, Cold War politics did trump UN politics. The strategic importance of Portugal in the Cold War — particularly of the US base in the Azores —

---

[39]   Rui Patrício, p. 150.
[40]   Matthew Connelly, *A Diplomatic Revolution: Algeria's Fight for Independence and the Origins of the Post-Cold War Era* (Oxford: Oxford University Press, 2002), p. 279.
[41]   Norrie MacQueen, 'Belated Decolonization'.
[42]   Rui Patrício, p. 220.
[43]   Norrie MacQueen, 'Belated Decolonization', p. 56.

could not make it any less of a pariah in terms of international society and its new standard norms of no colonial empires. But this global geopolitical dispute did give it the necessary room for manoeuvre in resisting UN pressure.

The 'Portuguese thesis' and the 'Belgian thesis' in the UN

Belgium, like Portugal, was a small power with a large overseas territory. Also, despite being a parliamentary democracy and not an authoritarian regime, Belgium like Portugal resisted for a long time the UN norm of speedy decolonization. This makes Belgium a good benchmark for evaluating the relative success of Portuguese diplomacy at the UN, especially if we take into account that because of a *décalage* in the timing of its admission Belgium went through many of the same problems of Portugal and faced similar pressures, but earlier. Since Belgium was a founding member of the UN and was much more deeply integrated into the new multilateral institutions it felt anti-colonial international pressure from 1946 onwards. Like Portugal, it took Belgium more than a decade of continued pressure at the UN for this to produce results; and arguably mainly not because of outside pressure per se, but also because of very rapid change in the dynamics among Congolese elites and a risk of violent confrontation on the ground.

It seems clear that the often mentioned Belgian–Congolese 'union' seemed more necessary than ever for Belgium immediately after 1945, for its economic recovery after the Second World War and as a source of strategic depth and strategic resources like uranium during the initial stages of the Cold War. But the importance of political culture should not be underestimated, with the Constitution revised, as in the case of Portugal, in 1952, to affirm this union, and King Baudouin of Belgium in a heavily publicized official visit to the Congo, in 1955, giving voice to this national consensus in talking of Congo and Belgium as 'one nation'.[44] It should also be underlined that when rapid decolonization was accepted in 1959–60, this was not just because of international pressure or even fear of violence, but also because there was a strong, if quickly disproven, idea that a close association between Congo and Belgium could be preserved.[45]

It is crucial to note, therefore, how closely the Belgian official mind and its colonial discourse were aligned with those of Portuguese officials until the early 1960s. Despite the differences in regime type there were clearly significant parallels in political culture in this close linkage between nationalism and colonialism that made decolonization a political taboo for a long time in both countries, despite growing international criticism. The response to pressure by the UN was also very similar, even if with the aforementioned *décalage* in timing. Belgium was subjected to the international pressure of anti-colonialism earlier. But it is very revealing that the complaints written in the late 1940s by

---

[44] Cit. and commented in Jean Stengers, *Congo*, pp. 245–46.
[45] Jean Stengers, *Congo*, pp. 280–81 *passim*.

the Belgian Permanent Representative for Colonial Affairs at the UN could have been written by Portuguese diplomats a decade later. He denounced a 'generalized hostility to the colonial idea' leading to 'hasty voting of radical texts, clearly contrary to the Charter, sometimes even absurd'; he also complains that 'any negotiating is a fraud. What we accept as a maximum is definitively lost [...] but the adversary never gives up', and keeps demanding more concessions. The problem was that 'modest' demands in 1946 had already grown by 1947 to include 'information that was very clearly political', in violation of Article 73, and this trend was continued in 1948 and in 1949 and 'taken even further' in an unacceptable violation of the principle of non-interference in internal matters that 'constrains *all* organs of the UN'. [46] These would be precisely some of the key arguments used by Portugal a decade later.

The official response by Belgium to this hostile internationalization of colonial issues at the UN came to be known as the 'Belgian thesis'. Again in parallel with Portugal, this was essentially a conservative legalistic response to a progressive political challenge. Belgian diplomats at the UN argued that many states in the world had native or minority populations that were not given full citizenship. Belgium therefore demanded that the UN should request and analyse information on all non-autonomous native populations, not just those who happened to live in colonies. The Belgian argument — again in close parallel with Portuguese arguments — tried to turn to its advantage the universalistic non-discriminatory normative outlook advocated by the majority of member states of the UN.[47]

The 'Belgian thesis' evidently contained important flaws and omissions — e.g. no reference was made to racial inequality in terms of job opportunities, salaries, education, or political rights in the Congo.[48] Yet it was based in arguments that were not entirely groundless, not necessarily because the native Congolese were living very well — that was certainly not the case compared with the Belgian settlers — but because they were living as well as, or often better than, many native populations in other parts of world, in situations that have come to be called internal colonialism.

The key aspect from the point of view of our analysis, however, is that the 'Belgian thesis' was a major diplomatic failure from the very beginning, in contrast with the 'Portuguese thesis' of 1956, of simply refusing any UN scrutiny. It met with total opposition by many member states whose support it needed — starting with major Western powers like the US, Australia and

[46] Jacques Vanderlinden, *Pierre Ryckmans 1891-1959: coloniser dans l'honneur* (Brussels: De Boeck, 1994), p. 640. See also AMAE, Dossier XVIII 18875/ XXI, Statement by Belgium representative (M. de Bruyne) in UN GA (15 November 1949); and Letter from Belgium Perm. Rep. UN Langenhove to MAE Spaak (27 December 1949).

[47] The official 'long version' intended as tool of public diplomacy was *La Mission sacrée de Civilisation: à quelles populations faut-il en étendre le bénéfice? La Thèse Belge* (New York: Belgian Government Information Center, 1953).

[48] Stengers, *Congo*, p. 204 ff.

many in central and south America that did not want to see their policies for their native populations or other minorities subject to international scrutiny. The 'Belgian thesis' was right on the facts — many native populations were living in terrible conditions in independent states — but inept in its diplomatic tactics. This disconnect was probably related to the fact that this 'Belgian thesis' was, nonetheless, widely praised internally in Belgium, since it allowed foreign criticisms of the Belgian model of colonialism to be presented as dishonest.

In contrast, the 'Portuguese thesis' of colonialism in denial was born, if not of a legal fiction, then certainly of a legal *fiat*, that is, the constitutional amendment of 1952. But fiction or not, this 'Portuguese thesis' did allow Portugal, unlike Belgium, to win enough votes, initially, to achieve positive diplomatic results. This was recognized by other colonial powers, including officials in Belgium and Britain. British officials in particular had been very sceptical about Portugal's diplomatic strategy of colonialism in denial, as well as about the ability of Portuguese diplomats to cope with the new challenges of conducting diplomacy in multilateral institutions. It is therefore significant that the British Colonial Office had to admit that the 'behaviour of the Portuguese [in the UN] so far has been eminently satisfactory'; and the Foreign Office agreed to admit Portugal into its annual consultations with Belgium and France about colonial affairs before the UN General Assembly, precisely because Portugal had 'shown up particularly well during their first session at the UN' in 1956. This contrasts with a deeply sceptical British view of the diplomatic usefulness for Belgium of the 'Belgian thesis', even if might be useful for Britain to have someone else raise this awkward subject of internal colonialism.[49]

Particularly significant for its colonial partners was the Portuguese ability to attract Latin American votes. The region had been a focus of interest and concern by other colonial powers, particularly Belgium, but without much success.[50] Ironically, of course, it meant that this initial diplomatic victory for Portuguese colonialism in denial was rewarded by admittance to a closed diplomatic club of colonial powers, joining Britain, France and Belgium.

Success for the Portuguese regime at the UN, as with Belgium, does seem to have had some importance in domestic politics. In this context Portugal anticipated some of the strategies that have now become familiar of pariah regimes acting as spoilers of UN mainstream norms. Salazar, and his even more media-aware successor Marcello Caetano, ensured that *Estado Novo* propaganda took advantage of this hostile environment in the UN to spur nationalist sentiment and promote a rallying around the flag. This allowed the regime to denounce as treason any internal alignment with anti-colonial views.

It was in this context that Salazar coined the slogan 'combatemos [...] sem alianças, orgulhosamente sós' [we fight [...] without alliances, proudly alone].

[49] TNA, CO 936/541 Letter from FO (JAH Watson] to CO (JE Marnham) (12 March 1957); and Letter IRD CO (JE Marnham) to FO (Robert Swann) (12 February 1956)
[50] AMAE, AP I.I., Note DG Politique-Aff.Col. (16 October 1953) 'La Propagande Coloniale dans les Pays Anticolonialistes', pp. 13–17.

It was a useful propaganda slogan for public consumption as Foreign Minister Franco Nogueira himself recognized.[51] Rui Patrício too states that only twice did he feel genuinely popular, once being when a speech of his in the UN General Assembly, in 1972, was met with such hostility that it provoked a nationalist response in Portugal, albeit orchestrated, especially in the sections of the press most closely controlled by the regime.[52] But evidently Portuguese diplomacy continued to work hard, often behind the scenes, to retain or regain foreign support from key Western powers, which supplied credit and vital military equipment, as well as some measure of support at the UN by vetoing resolutions, or more often using the threat of veto to moderate them, thereby shielding Portuguese colonialism in denial from tougher international action.[53]

In following this path the Portuguese regime was drawing on a perception deeply rooted in Portuguese political culture, of Portugal as a small state, a brave pioneer of overseas expansion for the benefit of all, and of Western civilization in particular, that was being unfairly challenged by other states which deployed a variety of high-minded principles — freedom of the seas, freedom from slavery and forced labour, self-determination — as pretexts for depriving Portugal of its overseas territories. This was precisely the public position of Salazar, but it was also shared by his successor Marcello Caetano, who despite the fact that he was seen as the liberal face of the regime was in this crucial aspect representative of a wide consensus among the elites of the regime and even beyond, amongst more traditionalist leaders of the opposition.[54]

Influence and Significance of the UN in Portuguese Decolonization

What then is the significance of all this for the wider history of the UN and Portuguese decolonization during the period of the Cold War? I will emphasize five main points:

(1) The very existence of a Portuguese colonialism that was forced into denial of its true nature in official documents from 1952 onwards shows that the UN did have some influence, even if not in the most obvious way, since it was conditioned by Portuguese political culture and the perception of the national interest derived from it. Yet even when Portugal was still *not* a member of the organization, UN anti-colonialism was already driving the *Estado Novo* regime to adapt by redefining its colonies as overseas provinces the better to resist

---

[51]   A. Franco Nogueira, *Salazar. VI. O último combate (1964–1970)* (Porto: Civilização: 1985).

[52]   Rui Patrício [with Leonor Xavier], *Rui Patrício: a vida conta-se inteira* (n.p.: Temas & Debates, 2010), p. 187. For a vivid testimony of how much attention was given to media management and public opinion, both foreign and domestic, in the final stage of the Portuguese dictatorship see the memoirs of another trusted former student of Caetano and his Director of National Information, Pedro Feyor Pinto, *Na sombra do poder* (Lisbon: D. Quixote, 2011), pp. 224 ff. *passim*.

[53]   Cf. e.g. Ana M. Fonseca, *A força das armas: o apoio da República Federal da Alemanha ao Estado Novo (1958–1968)* (Lisbon: Instituto Diplomático, 2007); Daniel S. C. Marcos, *Salazar e de Gaulle: a França e a questão colonial portuguesa (1958–1968)* (Lisbon: Instituto Diplomático, 2007).

[54]   Marcello Caetano, *Portugal e a internacionalização dos problemas africanos (da liberdade dos mares à ONU)* (Lisbon: Ática, 1962).

the emerging international norm of speedy decolonization. The Portuguese regime did not clash head-on with the new norm, but tried to use a legalist way around it.

The less than obvious UN influence on Portugal did not end here. Perhaps the most effective and determined diplomatic enemy of the UN pro-decolonization majority, Franco Nogueira, pointed (somewhat paradoxically) to his performance there: 'os grandes debates realizados no Conselho de Segurança da ONU representaram talvez do ponto de vista profissional, o momento mais alto da minha carreira' [the great debates that took place in the UN Security Council perhaps represented, in professional terms, the high point of my career].[55] More importantly even, he recognized that while the UN did not succeed during the *Estado Novo* in changing the content of a Portuguese foreign policy of colonialism in denial, it did change its style. The UN was an important school for Portuguese diplomats resulting in significant changes in skills required, making them adept not just at traditional 'entendimentos bilaterais' [bilateral agreements] but also at multilateral 'diplomacia da praça pública [public square diplomacy].[56] The skills developed in this losing battle to keep Portuguese overseas territories would eventually become important, ironically, after 1976, in the negotiations leading Portugal into accession to the EEC/EU or even, later, to prolonged multilateral diplomatic effort to free East Timor from Indonesian occupation.

(2) Portugal during these years illustrates some of the dynamics of so-called pariah or rogue states going against mainstream global norms, providing material for an objective analysis of this type of important phenomenon, then still very much in its infancy.[57] But Portugal also shows the limitations of trying to ensure the prolonged and effective isolation of states which resist mainstream international norms. Resilient pariah states are successful in getting some support from key great powers, even within the UN system, for instance by their vetoing damaging sanctions, or threatening to do so. It is difficult to find a total pariah, in the sense of a truly isolated state. Even North Korea survives with support from at least one major power, namely China. Portugal was increasingly isolated in the UN — it was a pariah in that sense — but it could still rely on some vital support from within the Western bloc, particularly in the context of the global Cold War.

After some initial positive comments, quickly forgotten, Salazar repeatedly

---

[55]   Franco Nogueira with Maria J. Avillez 'Olhar para trás', *Entre palavras 1974/1984* (Lisbon: Difel, 1984), p. 215.

[56]   A. Franco Nogueira, *Salazar. IV. O Ataque (1945–1958)*, pp. 424–25.

[57]   Two pioneering works are Pascal Boniface, *Guide du savoir nuire à l'usage des dictateurs* (Paris: Éds. Michalon, 2000), who contrasts traditional *puissance* to *nuisance*; and Bruce Bueno de Mesquita and Alistair Johnson, *The Dictator's Handbook: Why bad behavior is almost always good politics* (New York: Public Affairs, 2011). I do not necessarily subscribe to their conclusions, but in different ways they try novel approaches to an issue that has not been sufficiently studied — rogue, marginal behaviour, trying to identify its logic.

made clear that he believed the UN was worse than useless; it was positively dangerous. The case of the Indian invasion of Goa in 1961 was presented by him as proof that his scepticism was justified: the UN was unable and unwilling to stop military aggression. In this, Salazar was merely reflecting a common criticism of international organizations in the name of *Realpolitik*. Yet in dealing with an allegedly irrelevant institution the Portuguese government did spend a lot of political capital pressing other countries, especially key allies like the US, Britain and France, for support. For Salazar, the UN 'tem poder apenas mítico' [has only a mythical power], except for the one 'consentido pelas grandes potências' [consented by the great powers]. As a realist, Salazar did not believe that he should sacrifice 'interesses portugueses a título permanente' [Portuguese interests of a permanent nature] to norms being promoted by the UN, but for this resistance to succeed it was essential to make sure some of those major powers sided with Portugal.[58]

(3) A global approach to the Cold War does help to explain some important features of this connection between the UN and Portuguese decolonization. Salazar perceived a national strategic need to keep vast overseas territories to maintain international relevance and independence. But he also saw this as convergent with Western strategic needs during the Cold War. True, American or British elites increasingly saw Portuguese colonialism in denial and the wars being fought to defend it from 1961 onwards as a problem for the Western bloc, not least in the UN. For Portuguese elites, however, Western Europe needed African strategic depth and resources to face a Soviet attack. To this was added, from 1967, with the closing of the Suez Canal by Nasser — a risk which Portuguese diplomacy had pointed up since 1956 — the argument of the strategic importance of Africa for trade and energy security in the Indian Ocean and the South Atlantic.

Portugal also insisted upon the importance of political solidarity as a public signal of the solidity of the Alliance, linking it with the credibility of the military deterrent of the Alliance, thereby constraining the full public expression of criticism, by the US and other key NATO allies, of Portuguese colonialism in denial. A further Cold War factor, not strategic but normative, limiting Western criticism of Portugal was that serious violations of human rights were also taking place in the Soviet Bloc, in Third World dictatorships, or even in the very intensive US counterinsurgency campaign in Vietnam. Finally, there was the strategic importance for the US military of their base in the Portuguese archipelago of the Azores for control of the North Atlantic and for effective projection of US military power into Europe and the Middle East.

As it had become clear to the US and other Western allies that Portugal would stick to its policy of colonialism in denial, these factors significantly limited

[58] Cit. in A. Franco Nogueira, pp. 419–20; for a Realist sceptical vision of international organisations cf. J. Mearsheimer, 'The False Promise of International Institutions', *International Security*, 19.3 (1994–95), 5–49.

how far the rest of the West would go in pressuring Portugal or in allowing the UN to do so. Furthermore, I argue for the need to pursue further a more global approach to the Cold War than one excessively centred on Washington and Moscow or even on a narrow understanding of Western Europe. The way the Portuguese empire ended had important implications in the following decade (1975–85), in undermining détente and exhausting the Soviet bloc in an overstretching of its economic and military resources in military aid to the periphery.[59] But regardless of that more obvious impact, this article also shows that the perception of the Cold War by the Portuguese *Estado Novo* and other European governments was not necessarily coincident with that of the US; that is, they might give greater importance to the Third World than did the decision-makers in Washington.

These Cold War factors made Portugal sufficiently effective for most of this period at 'chain-ganging' the majority of its key Western allies, including the US, to at least some form of minimal support or limiting of criticism within the UN. This was made easier because of limited Portuguese exposure to US aid, loans or investment, when compared with other small European colonial powers; as well as by the Portuguese ability to secure alternative partners with similar views of the Cold War, in terms of financing, investment and economics, as well as acquisition of war material — France and Western Germany from the early 1960s, and then later South Africa.

(4) In terms of the wider debates on the history of the UN, the comparison of the Portuguese and Belgian cases seem to vindicate Mark Mazower's key argument that the creation of the UN represented a triumph of the norm of sovereignty over minorities' rights that had been much more present in the League of Nations.[60] Indeed, when Belgian officials tried to exploit the question of 'minorities' framed in terms of equal attention and scrutiny to the rights of native minorities by the UN in all states, and not just to natives in colonies, they got no diplomatic support for that position. By contrast, Portuguese diplomats had some initial success in exploiting diplomatically the question of non-interference in internal matters, playing on the fear of many states that the UN would erode their sovereign immunity. It is relevant to note that this rogue strategy has since become typical of pariah or spoiler states resisting mainstream UN norms.

That this worked for Portugal only for a limited period of time, however, also shows that between 1945 and 1960 sovereignty was being reshaped and re-used by the anti-colonial bloc against the existence of colonial dependencies in the name of the right to self-determination of sovereign peoples outside the West.

---

[59]   Cf. e.g. Tony Smith, 'New Bottles for New Wine: A Pericentric Framework for the Study of the Cold War', *Diplomatic History*, 24.4 (2000), 567–91; Odd Westad, *The Global Cold War: Third World Interventions and the Making of Our Time* (Cambridge: Cambridge University Press, 2005); Vladimir Shubin, *The Hot 'Cold War': The USSR in Southern Africa* (London: Pluto Press, 2008).

[60]   Mark Mazower, *No Enchanted Palace*, pp. 113, 195 *passim*.

Before 1945, that is to say in the League of Nations, the limits of sovereignty were largely determined by Western imperial powers. Now, in the UN, this was being done against them.[61] More specifically, the role of India as a norm-setting entrepreneur challenging the doctrine of the European right to rule is confirmed by the Portuguese case. In fact, Portuguese sources explicitly validate it with the Portuguese Foreign Minister, for instance, expressing some interest that 'existem divergências graves' [there are serious disagreements] between Africans and Asians 'por cansaço da "tutela" indiana' [because of weariness at the Indian 'tutelage'].[62]

Portugal, on the other hand, and for two decades after entering the UN, in 1956, decided to stick to one of the original versions or visions of the UN that was by then looking increasingly outdated as the creation of Western sovereign states based on non-intervention in internal affairs. A very conservative and legalistic Portuguese political culture continued to perceive the West as intrinsically superior to the Rest, refusing to let go of the standard of civilization in its relations with other states or dependent territories. Defeats in votes at the UN could therefore be perceived as irrelevant because they were seen as the expression of the erroneous views or the prejudices of a growing but irrelevant number of non-Western countries. This was perceived not as an alarming sign of Portuguese isolation, but as an indication of the decadence of the UN, regarded as the vehicle of choice for inappropriate and even illegal expressions of anti-Western prejudices and interests, not as the promoter of new norms of political legitimacy.

(5) Lastly, political culture was a powerful foundation in building up resistance to foreign pressure, but it also proved to be a very serious if not insurmountable obstacle to any major change in policy to adapt to international normative change regarding colonialism. Empire was central to Portuguese nationalism and was therefore seen as a core element of Portuguese identity, formally expressed in the constitutional law of the regime, but also informally in the mass media and even in statements by significant opponents to Salazar and his regime.[63] The strategy derived from this political culture in dealing with the UN made it, in turn, very difficult for Portugal to give ground, or to adopt a more flexible approach to decolonization, for instance by trying to negotiate different solutions for different territories. Why did Marcello Caetano inform

---

[61]   For this wider debate cf. Thomas Maddux et al. 'Mark Mazower. No Enchanted Palace...', H-Diplo Roundtable Reviews, 11.47 (2010), at <http://www.h-net.org/~diplo/roundtables/PDF/Roundtable-XI-47.pdf> [accessed 11 October 2011].
[62]   Mazower, No Enchanted Palace, p. 153; ANTT — AOS/CD 8 Letter from Foreign Sec. Franco Nogueira to PM Salazar (New York, October 1961 [read 3 November 1961]).
[63]   Cf. on the traditional attachment to the colonies of the mainstream opposition to the regime of one of the key figures in decolonization in 1975, A. de Almeida Santos Quase memórias do colonialismo e descolonização (Cruz Quebrada: Casa das Letras, 2006), vol. I, p. 16; A. Costa Pinto, 'Nacionalismo', in Dicionário de História de Portugal. Suplemento, ed. by A. Barreto e M. F. Mónica (Porto: Figueirinhas, 1999), vol. VIII, pp. 589–93.

General Spínola that it was preferable to lose the war in Guinea than for Portugal to negotiate a way out in 1973? When he did so, he initiated the chain of events that led to the downfall of the authoritarian regime, because to do otherwise would mean violating the norm so vocally defended internationally, not least at the UN, that Portugal was a unitary *pluri-continental* state, and no parcel of it could be negotiated.

UN norms and political pressure in its institutions for speedy decolonization were neither immediately decisive nor irrelevant in Portuguese decolonization. Portuguese colonialism in denial in defiance of the new international norm of decolonization had political costs, but it also had significant human and material costs for Portugal, particularly in the form of protracted anti-colonial insurgencies. This was all the more significant because the conflict was made more prolonged and deadly by continued foreign support for the armed nationalist movements in Angola, Guinea and Mozambique, legitimized by the majority of the UN. Indirectly and in the medium term, therefore, the UN did play an important role in forcing major change that went against core beliefs in Portuguese political culture. Eventually, however, this would require a coup by the Portuguese military, exhausted by more than a decade of fighting. The state of internal flux in Portugal after regime change from April 1974 onwards made the UN norm of speedy decolonization much more difficult to resist at that moment. All of this provided a powerful boost to the coup leaders of the MFA Committee thanks to the impact of international pressure acting against the last-ditch attempts by General Spínola to achieve a controlled and relatively slow transfer of power, possibly ending in some form of close association with Portugal, at least in the case of Angola. Still, even in 1974–75, decolonization had to be made as acceptable as possible in terms of Portuguese political culture. The Portuguese military under the MFA was transformed into a 'fourth liberation movement'; a myth of decolonization transfigured what was arguably a Portuguese strategic defeat into a willing mutual liberation of the Portuguese-speaking world, which was presented by the new leftist governing elite in Lisbon as a liberated brotherhood.[64]

It was not just UN-led decolonization that showed the power of norms in international politics and security, however: it was also Portuguese resistance to it. It was not just the UN recurrent denunciation of Portuguese colonialism in denial that significantly conditioned the response of Portugal to decolonization. The Portuguese regime and its colonialism in denial also conditioned in an important way the calendar and the dynamics of UN formulation of norms for the final stage of decolonization.

---

[64]   A point first raised by Norrie MacQueen, *The Decolonization of Portuguese Africa*, pp. 80–84.

Lusophone Studies:
A Cumulative Area Bibliography, 2011–13

EMILCE REES

King's College, London

The following pages list publications and theses relating to the Portuguese-speaking world which were published from 2011 to early to mid 2013 in English. **Some items previously omitted have been included here.** Relevant online academic search resources have been used, namely the Copac® library catalogue, WorldCat® and the ProQuest Dissertations and Theses Database and for consultation, the British Library EThOS, for *all* theses produced by UK Higher Education. The Copac® library catalogue contains the merged online catalogues of major University, Specialist, and National Libraries in the UK and Ireland, including the British Library. ABIL (Association of British and Irish Lusitanists) list members are also thanked for their contribution. WorldCat® is a global catalogue of library collections of more than 72,000 libraries, with over 290,500,000 bibliographic records.

I. PUBLICATIONS

II. THESES

Portuguese Studies vol. 29 no. 2 (2013), 277–95
© Modern Humanities Research Association 2013

I. Publications

1.1 Anthropology and Folklore

ADAMS, Cristina, Rui S. S. MURRIETA, Walter A. NEVES and Mark HARRIS (eds), *Amazon Peasant Societies in a Changing Environment: Political Ecology, Invisibility and Modernity in the Rainforest*. New York: Springer, 2010. 382 pp.

SAPIEZINSKAS, Aline, and Rebecca HUDSON (transl.), *Cultural Heritage in Brazil: An Anthropological Perspective and Local Points of View*. Dartford: Xlibris. 144 pp.

UZENDOSKI, Michael, and Edith Felicia CALAPUCHA-TAPUY, *The Ecology of the Spoken Word: Amazonian Storytelling and Shamanism among the Napo Runa*. Urbana: University of Illinois Press, 2012. 245 pp.

VIRTANEN, Pirjo Kristiina, *Indigenous Youth in Brazilian Amazonia: Changing Lived Worlds*. Basingstoke: Palgrave Macmillan, 2012. 238 pp.

1.2 Arts, Architecture and Music

AVELAR, Idelber, and Christopher DUNN (eds), *Brazilian Popular Music and Citizenship*. Durham, NC: Duke University Press, 2011. 364 pp.

BRITO, Ronaldo, Guilherme BUENO and Sonia SALCEDO (eds), *Art in Brazil 1950-2011*. Catalog of an exhibition held October 12, 2011 — January 15, 2012, Centre for Fine Arts, Brussels. Brussels: Europalia International & Ludion, 2011. 197 pp.

BLAUFUKS, Daniel, *Works On Memory: Selected Writings and Images*. Cardiff: Ffotogallery, 2012. 147 pp.

BROWN, Lisa Beljuli, *Body Parts on Planet Slum: Women and Telenovelas in Brazil*. New York: Anthem Press, 2011. 156 pp.

BUENO, Eva Paulino, *Amácio Mazzaropi in the Film and Culture of Brazil: After Cinema Novo*. New York: Palgrave Macmillan, 2012. 196 pp.

BURRI René, Arthur RÜEGG and Clarice LISPECTOR (eds), *Rene Burri. Brasilia: Photographs, 1960-1993*. Zürich: Scheidegger und Spiess AG, Verlag, 2011. 224 pp.

CASIMIRO, Tânia Manuel, *Portuguese Faience in England and Ireland*. Oxford: Archaeopress, 2011. 200 pp.

CONDE, Maite, *Consuming Visions: Cinema, Writing, and Modernity in Rio de Janeiro*. Charlottesville: University of Virginia Press, 2012. 227 pp.

DISERENS, Corinne, Joanna LEHAN and Maria SCHINDELEGGER, *Appropriated Landscapes: Contemporary African Photography from the Walther Collection*. Göttingen: Steidl, 2011. 406 pp.

DIX, Steffen, and Jerónimo PIZARRO (eds), *Portuguese Modernisms: Multiple Perspectives on Literature and the Visual Arts*. London: Legenda, 2011. 388 pp.

GARRAMUÑO, Florencia, and Anna Kazumi STAHL (transl.), *Primitive Modernities: Tango, Samba, and Nation*. Stanford, CA: Stanford University Press, 2011. 232 pp.

HOLTEN, Bo, *Cantigas D'amigo: 5 Love Lyrics of Medieval Portugal Set For Equal Voices A Cappella 2010*. Copenhagen: Wilhelm Hansen, 2011. 1 score, 48 pp.

JODIDIO, Philip. *Niemeyer*. London: Taschen, 2012. 96 pp.

MILHAZES, Beatriz, *Catalogue exhibition held 20 Jan. — 15 May 2012, Fondation Beyeler, Riehen and Basel: 16 Feb. — 13 May 2012*; Fundação Calouste Gulbenkian, CAM Centre de Arte Moderna, Lisbon. Ostfildern: Hatje Cantz, 2012. German, English and Portuguese text. 69 pp.

MOEHN, Frederick, *Contemporary Carioca: Technologies of Mixing in a Brazilian Music Scene*. Durham, NC: Duke University Press, 2012. 289 pp.

O'BYRNE, Patricia, Gabrielle CARTY and Niamh THORNTON, *Transcultural Encounters amongst Women: Redrawing Boundaries in Hispanic and Lusophone Art, Literature and Film*. Newcastle: Cambridge Scholars, 2010. 225 pp.

O'CONNELL, John Morgan, and Salwa El-Shawan CASTELO-BRANCO (eds), *Music and Conflict*. Urbana: University of Illinois Press, 2010. 289 pp.

PODALSKY, Laura, *The Politics of Affect and Emotion in Contemporary Latin American Cinema: Argentina, Brazil, Cuba, and Mexico*. New York: Palgrave Macmillan, 2011, 218 pp.

POWE, Edward L., *ABC & 'Bay-ah-Bah' of Capoeira de Angola*. Madison, WI: Dan Aiki Publications, 2011. 211 pp.

RÊGO, Cacilda, and Carolina ROCHA (eds), *New Trends in Argentine and Brazilian Cinema*. Bristol: Intellect, 2011. 270 pp.

RODEIA, João Belo, *J. Carlos Loureiro: arquitecto = architect*. Casal de Cambra: Caleidoscópio, 2012. 318 pp.

ROSENTHAL, T. G., *Paula Rego: The Complete Graphic Work*. London: Thames & Hudson, 2012. 386 pp.

TILLIS, Antonio D. (ed.), *(Re) Considering Blackness in Contemporary Afro-Brazilian (Con) Texts*. New York: Peter Lang, 2011. 196 pp.

TREECE, David, *Brazilian Jive: From Samba to Bossa and Rap*. London: Reaktion Books, 2013. 224 pp.

YOUNG-SÁNCHEZ, Margaret, and Denise Pahl SCHAAN, *Marajó: Ancient Ceramics from the Mouth of the Amazon*. Denver, CO: Denver Art Museum. 2011. 88 pp.

1.3 Bibliographies, Directories and Guides

AARDE, Rudi, *Congo Basin and Angola*. New York: Marshall Cavendish Reference, 2011. 579 pp.

COCKS, Rodney, *Timor-Leste (East Timor)*, 3rd [updated] edn. London: Lonely Planet, 2011. 167 pp.

EUROPA PUBLICATIONS (ed.), *Africa South of the Sahara*. 42nd edn. London: Routledge (Europa regional surveys of the world), 2012. 1616 pp.

GARCÍA-DEL-REY, Eduardo, *Field Guide to the Birds of Macaronesia: Azores, Madeira, Canary Islands, Cape Verde*. Barcelona: Lynx, 2011. 341 pp.

GILBERT, Jonathan, and Rachel MILLS (eds), *Portugal, Madeira & the Azores*, 5th edn. London: Michelin Apa, 2011. 416 pp.

GREGG, Emma, and Richard TRILLO, *The Rough Guide to First-Time Africa*. London: Rough Guides, 2011. 432 pp.

HAMMICK, Anne, and Nicholas HEATH (eds), *Atlantic Islands: Azores, Madeira, Canary and Cape Verde Islands*, rev. 5th edn. St Ives, Cambs.: Imray Laurie Norie & Wilson, 2011. 412 pp.

HANCOCK, Matthew, *Lisbon*. London: Rough Guides, 2011. 159 pp.

HENSS, Rita, and Sara LIER, *Madeira, Porto Santo*. Basingstoke: Marco Polo, 2012. 140 pp.

HOPKINS, Dwight N., and Edward P. ANTONIO (eds), *The Cambridge Companion to Black Theology*. Cambridge: Cambridge University Press, 2012. 340 pp.

IRWIN, Aisling, Colum WILSON and Jacquie COZENS, *Cape Verde Islands*, 5th edn. Chalfont St Peter: Bradt Travel Guide, 2011. 336 pp.

MARTIN, James, W., *Historical Dictionary of Angola*, 2nd edn. Plymouth: Scarecrow Press, 2011. 346 pp.

OUP OXFORD, *Oxford Essential Portuguese Dictionary*, 2nd edn. Oxford: Oxford University Press, 2012. 484 pp.

PALIN, Michael, *Brazil*. London: Weidenfeld & Nicolson, 2012. 319 pp.

RECTOR, Monica, and Richard VERNON, *African Lusophone Writers: Dictionary of Literary Biography*, vol. 367. Detroit, MI: Gale Cengage Learning, 2012. 421 pp.

ROBERTSON, Ian C., and John HOSTE (line drawings), *A Traveller's History of Portugal*. London: Armchair Traveller, 2011. 228 pp.

ROGERS, Barbara Radcliffe, *Portugal. Thomas Cook Driving Guides*, 3rd edn. Peterborough: Thomas Cook, 2011. 288 pp.

1.4 Environment

JACKIEWICZ, Edward L., and Fernando J. BOSCO (eds), *Placing Latin America: Contemporary Themes in Geography*, 2nd edn. Lanham, MD: Rowman & Littlefield , 2012. 268 pp.

ROBINSON, Alex, *Brazilian Amazon*. Bath: Footprint, 2012. 127 pp.

SANTILLI, Juliana, *Agrobiodiversity and the Law: Regulating Genetic Resources, Food Security and Cultural Diversity*. Abingdon: Earthscan, 2012. 348 pp.

1.5 History, Politics and Social Science

Africa (general)

AARSÆTHER, Aslaug, *Chinese Colonialism or South–South Cooperation? The Case of Chinese Resources for Infrastructure Contracts in Angola*. Bergen: A. Aarsæther, 2011. 97 pp.

AGIER, Michel, *Managing the Undesirables: Refugee Camps and Humanitarian Government*. Cambridge: Polity, 2011. 300 pp.

ALMEIDA, Domingas, *As if living was like that*. Luanda: Angolan Writers Union, 2011. 187 pp.

AMOAH, Michael, *Nationalism, Globalization, and Africa*. New York, NY: Palgrave Macmillan, 2011. 286 pp.

ARENAS, Fernando, *Lusophone Africa: Beyond Independence*. Minneapolis: University of Minnesota Press, 2011. 368 pp.

BAUER, Gretchen, and Scott D. TAYLOR, *Politics in Southern Africa: Transition and Transformation*, 2nd edn. Boulder, CO: Lynne Rienner Publishers, 2011. 437 pp.

BEUTEL, Monika, with Purna Kumar SHRESTHA and Alex VERNON (eds), *Teachers Talking: Primary Teachers' Contributions to the Quality of Education in Mozambique*. London: VSO, 2011. 64 pp.

BLAKE, Cameron, *Troepie Snapshots: A Pictorial Recollection of the South African Border War*. Johannesburg: 30° South Pub, 2011. 384 pp.

BURROUGHS, Robert M., *Travel Writing and Atrocities: Eyewitness Accounts of Colonialism in the Congo, Angola, and the Putumayo*. New York: Routledge, 2011. 215 pp.

ECHENBERG, Myron J., *Africa in the Time of Cholera: A History of Pandemics from 1817 to the Present*. New York: Cambridge University Press, 2011. 208 pp.

GREEN, Toby (ed.), *Brokers of Change: Atlantic Commerce and Cultures in Pre-Colonial Western Africa*. Oxford: Oxford University Press for the British Academy, 2012. 320 pp.

JAMES, W. M., *A Political History of the Civil War in Angola, 1974–1990*. Somerset, NJ: Transaction, 2011. 327 pp.

KAMONGO, Sisingi, and Leon BEZUIDENHOUT, *Shadows in the Sand: A Koevoet Tracker's Story of an Insurgency War*. Pinetown, South Africa: 30° South Publishers, 2011. 320 pp.

LEAL, João, and Wendy GRAÇA (transl.), *Azorean Identity in Brazil and the United States: Arguments about History, Culture, and Transnational Connections*. North Dartmouth, MA: Tagus Press/University of Massachusetts Dartmouth, 2011. 184 pp.

MCWILLIAMS, Mike, *Battle for Cassinga: South Africa's Controversial Cross-Border Raid, Angola 1978*. Solihull: Helion, 2011. 80 pp.

MORIER-GENOUD, Éric, *Sure Road? Nationalisms in Angola, Guinea-Bissau and Mozambique*. Leiden: Brill, 2012. 270 pp.

ÖZERDEM, Alpaslan, and Sukanya PODDER, *Child Soldiers: From Recruitment to Reintegration*. Basingstoke: Palgrave Macmillan, 2011. 325 pp.

RENO, William, *Warfare in Independent Africa*. Cambridge: Cambridge University Press, 2011. 294 pp.

SESAY, Amadu, *Africa and Europe: From Partition to Interdependence or Dependence?* London: Routledge, 2010. 268 pp.

SHUBIN, Gennady, and Andrei TOKAREV (eds), *Bush War: The Road to Cuito Cuanavale: Soviet Soldiers' Accounts of the Angolan War*. Auckland Park, South Africa: Jacana Media, 2011. 200 pp.

SILVA, Sónia, *Along an African Border: Angolan Refugees and their Divination Baskets*. Philadelphia: University of Pennsylvania Press, 2011. 188 pp.

SOLOMON, Hussein (ed.), *Against All Odds: Opposition Political Parties in Southern Africa*. Johannesburg: KMM Review, 2011. 261 pp.

STASSEN, Nicol, *The Boers in Angola, 1928–1975*. Pretoria: Protea Book House, 2011. 656 pp.

STOKEL-WALKER, Chris, *African Lions: The Colonial Geopolitics of Africa's Gas & Oil*. Raleigh, NC: Lulu, 2011. 211 pp.

TE VELDE, Victoria, *The Commonwealth Brand: Global Voice, Local Action*. Farnham: Ashgate, 2011. 205 pp.

VAN DER WAALS, W. S., *Portugal's War in Angola, 1961–1974*, 2nd edn. Pretoria: Protea Book House, 2012. 320 pp.

WEIGERT, Stephen L., *Angola: A Modern Military History, 1961–2002*. New York: Palgrave Macmillan, 2011. 284 pp.

ZAYAS, Luis A., and Mary-Alice WATERS, *Soldier of the Cuban Revolution: From the Cane Fields of Oriente to General of the Revolutionary Armed Forces*. New York: Pathfinder, 2011. 224 pp.

Asia

BALA, Poonam (ed.), *Contesting Colonial Authority: Medicine and Indigenous Responses in Nineteenth- and Twentieth-Century India*. Plymouth: Lexington Books, 2012. 157 pp.

BORSCHBERG, Peter, *Hugo Grotius, the Portuguese and Free Trade in the East Indies*. Singapore: NUS Press, 2011. 482 pp.

CARTON, Adrian, *Mixed-Race and Modernity in Colonial India: Changing Concepts of Hybridity across Empires*. New York: Routledge, 2012. 140 pp.

CASTELO-BRANCO, Miguel, *The Portuguese–Siamese Treaty of 1820: Siam's First Attempt of Integration into the International Community*. Lisbon: Instituto do Oriente, 2011. 103 pp.

CORREIA, Luís de Assis (ed. and trans.), *Francisco Luis Gomes, 1829–1869: A Select Reader*. Goa: Goa 1556, 2011. 438 pp.

FERNANDES, Clinton, *The Independence of East Timor: Multi-Dimensional Perspectives — Occupation, Resistance, and International Political Activism*. Brighton: Sussex Academic Press, 2011. 261 pp.

GOLVERS, Noël, *Portuguese Books and their Readers in the Jesuit Mission of China (17th–18th Centuries)*. Lisbon: Centro Científico e Cultural de Macau, 2011. 309 pp.

GUNN, Geoffrey C., *Historical Dictionary of East Timor*. Lanham, MD: Scarecrow Press, 2011. 263 pp.

JARNAGIN, Laura (ed.), *Portuguese and Luso-Asian Legacies in Southeast Asia, 1511–2011*. Volume 1: The Making of the Luso-Asian World: Intricacies of Engagement. Singapore: Institute of Southeast Asian Studies, 2011. 323 pp.

JARNAGIN, Laura (ed.), *Portuguese and Luso-Asian Legacies in Southeast Asia, 1511–2011*. Volume 2: Culture and Identity in the Luso-Asian World — Tenacities & Plasticities. Singapore: Institute of Southeast Asian Studies, 2011. 368 pp.

LAU, Lisa, and Ana Cristina MENDES (eds), *Re-orientalism and South Asian Identity Politics: The Oriental Other Within*. London: Routledge, 2011. 162 pp.

MALEKANDATHIL, Pius, *Maritime India: Trade, Religion, and Polity in the Indian Ocean*. Delhi: Primus Books, 2010. 211 pp.

MOLNAR, Andrea Katalin, *Timor Leste: Politics, History, and Culture*. London: Routledge, 2010. 224 pp.

NEONBASU, Gregor, *We Seek Our Roots: Oral Tradition in Biboki, West Timor*. Fribourg, Switzerland: Academic Press, 2011. 386 pp.

NETO, Félix, Maria da Conceição PINTO and Etienne MULLET, *Forgiveness and Reconciliation in an Inter-Group Context: East Timor's Perspectives*. New York: Nova Science, 2011. 79 pp.

NIXON, Rod, *Justice and Conflict Resolution in East Timor: Integrating Indigenous Approaches into a 'New Subsistence State'*. London: Routledge, 2011. 288 pp.

RAMSDEN, Graeme, *Letters from Timor: A Chaplain's Tour of Duty*. Newport, NSW: Big Sky Publishing, 2011. 196 pp.

SIM, Yong Huei, *Portuguese Enterprise in the East: Survival in the Years 1707–1757*. Leiden: Brill, 2011. 212 pp.

SUBRAHMANYAM, Sanjay, *The Portuguese Empire in Asia, 1500–1700: A Political and Economic History*, 2nd edn. Chichester: Wiley-Blackwell, 2012. 340 pp.

VAN DER WOLFE, Willem, and Claudia TOFAN (eds), *The Truth and Reconciliation Commission in East Timor*. The Hague: International Courts Association, 2011. 502 pp.

VICENTE, Filipa Lowndes, and Stewart LLOYD-JONES (transl.), *Other Orientalisms: India between Florence and Bombay, 1860–1900*. New Delhi: Orient Blackswan, 2012. 346 pp.

ZHIDONG, Hao, *Macau History and Society*. Hong Kong: Hong Kong University Press, 2011. 294 pp.

Brazil

ALBERTO, Paulina L., *Terms of Inclusion: Black Intellectuals in Twentieth-Century Brazil*. Chapel Hill: University of North Carolina Press, 2011. 396 pp.

ARASHIRO, Zuleika, *Negotiating the Free Trade Area of the Americas*. New York: Palgrave Macmillan, 2011. 284 pp.

BAER, Werner, David V. FLEISCHER and Lawrence DE GEEST, *The Economies of Argentina and Brazil: A Comparative Perspective*. Cheltenham: Edward Elgar, 2011. 487 pp.

BAIOCCHI, Gianpaolo, Patrick HELLER and Marcelo K. SILVA, *Bootstrapping Democracy: Transforming Local Governance and Civil Society in Brazil*. Stanford, CA: Stanford University Press, 2011. 204 pp.

BLAKE, Stanley E., *The Vigorous Core of our Nationality: Race and Regional Identity in Northeastern Brazil*. Pittsburgh, PA: University of Pittsburgh Press, 2011. 315 pp.

BRUNO-JOFRÉ, Rosa, and Jürgen SCHRIEWER (eds), *The Global Reception of John Dewey's Thought: Multiple Refractions through Time and Space*. New York: Routledge, 2012. 272 pp.

BRUNS, Barbara, David EVANS and Javier Luque BRUNS, *Achieving World-Class Education in Brazil: The Next Agenda*. Washington, DC: The World Bank, 2012. 156 pp.

CHAUÍ, Marilena de Souza, and Maite CONDE (transl. and ed.), *Between Conformity and Resistance: Essays on Politics, Culture, and the State*. New York: Palgrave Macmillan, 2011. 256 pp.

CHAZKEL, Amy, *Laws of Chance: Brazil's Clandestine Lottery and the Making of Urban Public Life*. Durham, NC: Duke University Press, 2011. 346 pp.

CICALO, André, *Urban Encounters: Affirmative Action and Black Identities in Brazil*. Basingstoke: Palgrave Macmillan, 2012. 242 pp.

COOPER, Martin, *Brazilian Railway Culture*. Newcastle upon Tyne: Cambridge Scholars, 2011. 332 pp.

CRANE, Robert, and Carlos RIZOWY (eds), *Latin American Business Cultures.* Basingstoke: Palgrave Macmillan, 2011. 276 pp.

DAVIDSON, James Dale, *Brazil is the New America: How Brazil offers upward mobility in a collapsing world.* Chichester: Wiley, 2011. 331 pp.

ESFAHANI, Hadi Salehi, Giovanni FACCHINI and Geoffrey J. D. HEWINGS, *Economic Development in Latin America: Essays in Honor of Werner Baer.* Basingstoke: Palgrave Macmillan, 2010. 336 pp.

ETCHEMENDY, Sebastián, *Models of Economic Liberalization: Business, Workers, and Compensation in Latin America, Spain, and Portugal.* New York: Cambridge University Press, 2011. 374 pp.

FAUSTO, Carlos, *Warfare and Shamanism in Amazonia.* Cambridge: Cambridge University Press, 2012. 347 pp.

FISHLOW, Albert, *Starting Over: Brazil since 1985.* Washington, DC: Brookings Institution, 2011. 236 pp.

FLEURY, Afonso, and Maria Tereza FLEURY, *Brazilian Multinationals: Competences for Internationalization.* Cambridge: Cambridge University Press, 2012. 440 pp.

FOSTER, David William, *São Paulo: Perspectives on the City and Cultural Production.* Gainesville: University Press of Florida, 2011. 197 pp.

GABAN, Eduardo Molan, and Juliana Oliveira DOMINGUES, *Antitrust Law in Brazil: Fighting Cartels.* Alphen aan den Rijn: Wolters Kluwer, 2012. 413 pp.

GATES, Henry Louis, *Black in Latin America.* New York: New York University Press, 2011. 259 pp.

GIBBON, Sahra, Ricardo Ventura SANTOS and Mónica SANS, *Racial Identities, Genetic Ancestry, and Health in South America: Argentina, Brazil, Colombia, and Uruguay.* New York: Palgrave Macmillan, 2011. 256 pp.

GOERTZEL, Ted George, *Brazil's Lula: The Most Popular Politician on Earth.* Boca Raton, FL: BrownWalker Press, 2011. 216 pp.

HAYES, Kelly E., *Holy Harlots: Femininity, Sexuality, and Black Magic in Brazil.* Berkeley: University of California Press, 2011. 312 pp.

HODKINSON, Stephen, and Dick GEARY (eds), *Slaves and Religions in Graeco-Roman Antiquity and Modern Brazil.* Newcastle: Cambridge Scholars, 2012. 341 pp.

JONES, Gareth A., and Dennis RODGERS (eds), *Youth Violence in Latin America: Gangs and Juvenile Justice in Perspective.* New York: Palgrave Macmillan, 2010. 256 pp.

KIRKENDALL, Andrew J., *Paulo Freire and the Cold War Politics of Literacy.* Chapel Hill: University of North Carolina Press, 2010. 264 pp.

LÉVI-STRAUSS, Claude, John WEIGHTMAN and Doreen WEIGHTMAN (transl.), *Tristes Tropiques.* London: Penguin, 2011. 425 pp.

LINDSAY, Claire (ed.), *Traslados/Translations: Essays on Latin America in Honour of Jason Wilson.* London: Institute for the Study of the Americas, 2012. 112 pp.

MARES, David R., *Latin America and the Illusion of Peace.* New York: Routledge for the International Institute for Strategic Studies, 2012. 203 pp.

MARQUES, Eduardo Cesar Leão, *Opportunities and Deprivation in the Urban South: Poverty, Segregation and Social Networks in São Paulo.* Burlington, VT: Ashgate, 2012. 186 pp.

MAYHEW, Douglas, *Inside the Favelas: Rio de Janeiro.* New York: Glitterati, 2012. 352 pp.

MÉLEGA, Marisa Pelella, Mariângela Mendes DE ALMEIDA and Mariza Leite DA COSTA (eds), *Looking and Listening: Work from the São Paulo Mother–Baby Relationship Study Centre.* London: Karnac, 2012. 236 pp.

MELO, Marcus André, Njuguna NG'ETHE and James MANOR, *Against the Odds: Politicians, Institutions and the Struggle against Poverty.* London: Hurst, 2012. 221 pp.

PINAR, William (ed.), *Curriculum Studies in Brazil: Intellectual Histories, Present Circumstances.* Basingstoke: Palgrave Macmillan, 2011. 239 pp.

PORTO, Mauro P., *Media Power and Democratization in Brazil: TV Globo and the Dilemmas of Political Accountability.* London: Routledge, 2012. 227 pp.

PREUSS, Ori, *Bridging the Island: Brazilians' Views of Spanish America and Themselves, 1865–1912.* Orlando, FL: Iberoamericana Vervuert, 2011. 237 pp.

ROETT, Riordan, *The New Brazil.* Washington, DC: Brookings Institution Press, 2011. 176 pp.

ROHTER, Larry, *Brazil on the Rise: The Story of a Country Transformed.* New York: Palgrave Macmillan, 2010. 289 pp.

SATTAMINI, Lina Penna, and James NAYLOR GREEN. *A Mother's Cry: A Memoir of Politics, Prison, and Torture under the Brazilian Military Dictatorship.* Durham, NC: Duke University Press, 2010. 208 pp.

SCHWARTZ, Stuart B., *Early Brazil: A Documentary Collection to 1700.* New York: Cambridge University Press, 2010. 336 pp.

SELWYN, Ben, *Workers, State and Development in Brazil: Powers of Labour, Chains of Value.* Manchester: Manchester University Press, 2012. 208 pp.

SKAAR, Elin, *Judicial Independence and Human Rights in Latin America: Violations, Politics, and Prosecution.* New York: Palgrave Macmillan, 2011. 316 pp.

STERLING, Cheryl, *African Roots, Brazilian Rites: Cultural and National Identity in Brazil.* New York: Palgrave Macmillan, 2012. 259 pp.

TAKHTEYEV, Yuri, *Coding Places: Software Practice in a South American City.* Cambridge, MA: MIT Press, 2012. 257 pp.

TEIXEIRA, Carlos Gustavo Poggio, *Brazil, the United States, and the South American Subsystem: Regional Politics and the Absent Empire.* Plymouth: Lexington Books, 2012. 169 pp.

VADJUNEC, Jacqueline M., and Marianne SCHMINK (eds), *Amazonian Geographies: Emerging Identities and Landscapes.* New York: Routledge, 2012. 232 pp.

VAN BAERLE, Caspar, Blanche VAN BERCKEL-EBELING KONING (transl.), *History of Brazil under the Governorship of Count Johan Maurits of Nassau, 1636–1644.* Gainesville: University Press of Florida, 2011. 448 pp.

VARELLA, Drauzio, *Lockdown: Inside Brazil's Most Dangerous Prison.* London: Simon & Schuster, 2012. 368 pp.

VILAÇA, Aparecida, and David RODGERS (transl.), *Strange Enemies: Indigenous Agency and Scenes of Encounters in Amazonia.* London: Duke University Press, 2010. 392 pp.

WIEBEL, Esther, *Peri-urban Development in Recife, Brazil: Lessons Learnt from a Geographic Field Study.* Saarbrücken: VDM Verlag Dr. Müller, 2011. 202 pp.

WILDING, Polly, *Negotiating Boundaries: Gender, Violence and Transformation in Brazil.* Basingstoke: Palgrave Macmillan, 2012. 184 pp.

Portugal

BENNETT, Jeffrey S., *When the Sun Danced: Myth, Miracles, and Modernity in Early Twentieth-Century Portugal*. Charlottesville: University of Virginia Press, 2012. 256 pp.

BENTO GONÇALVES, António José, and António Avelino Bastista VIEIRA (eds), *Portugal: Economic, Political and Social Issues*. New York: Nova Publishers, 2012. 214 pp.

BICHO, Nuno F., Jonathan A. HAWS, and Loren G. DAVIS (eds), *Trekking the Shore: Changing Coastlines and the Antiquity of Coastal Settlement*. New York: Springer, 2011. 496 pp.

CATROGA, Fernando, and Pedro Tavares DE ALMEIDA, *Res Publica 1820–1926: Citizenship and Political Representation in Portugal*. Lisbon: Assembleia da República, 2011. 335 pp.

CLARKE, Nicola, *The Muslim Conquest of Iberia: Medieval Arabic Narratives*. London: Routledge, 2012. 243 pp.

COROLEU, Alejandro, and Barry TAYLOR (eds), *Humanism and the Christian Letters in Early-Modern Iberia (1480 — 1630)*. Newcastle: Cambridge Scholars, 2010. 222 pp.

COSTA RIBEIRO, Nelson, *BBC Broadcasts to Portugal in World War II: How Radio Was Used as a Weapon of War*. Lewiston, NY: Edwin Mellen Press, 2011. 532 pp.

GARCÉS, María Antonia (ed.), and Diana de Armas WILSON (transl.), *An Early Modern Dialogue with Islam: Antonio de Sosa's Topography of Algiers (1612)*. Notre Dame, IN: University of Notre Dame Press, 2011. 400 pp.

GOMES, Bernardino, and Tiago MOREIRA DE SÁ, *Carlucci vs. Kissinger: The U.S. and the Portuguese Revolution*. Lanham, MD: Rowman & Littlefield, 2011. 263 pp.

HATTON, Barry, *The Portuguese: A Modern History*. Northampton: Interlink, 2011. 261 pp.

HERR, Richard, and António COSTA PINTO (eds), *The Portuguese Republic at One Hundred*. Berkeley: Institute of European Studies-UC Berkeley, 2012. 253 pp.

LOCHERY, Neill, *Lisbon: War in the Shadows of the City of Light, 1939–1945*. New York: PublicAffairs, 2011. 344 pp.

MACKAY, Ruth, *The Baker Who Pretended to be King of Portugal*. London: University of Chicago Press, 2012. 328 pp.

MAILER, Phil, *Portugal, the Impossible Revolution?* Oakland, CA: PM Press, 2012. 288 pp.

NEAVE, Guy, and Alberto AMARAL (eds), *Higher Education in Portugal, 1974–2009: A Nation, a Generation*. Heidelberg: Springer, 2012. 427 pp.

PINTO, António Costa, *Contemporary Portugal: Politics, Society and Culture*, 2nd edn. Boulder: Social Science Monographs, 2011. 340 pp.

RIBEIRO DE MENEZES, Alison, and Catherine O'LEARY, *Legacies of War and Dictatorship in Contemporary Portugal and Spain*. New York: Peter Lang, 2011. 270 pp.

SOYER, François, *Ambiguous Gender in Early Modern Spain and Portugal: Inquisitors, Doctors and the Transgression of Gender Norms*. Leiden: Brill, 2012. 320 pp.

TEIXEIRA, Nuno Severiano, and António COSTA PINTO (eds), *The Euro-peanization of Portuguese Democracy*. New York: SSM-Columbia University Press, 2012. 261 pp.

(Portuguese). Discoveries and Empire

BALDRIDGE, Cates, *Prisoners of Prester John: The Portuguese Mission to Ethiopia in Search of the Mythical King, 1520–1526*. Jefferson, NC: McFarland & Co., 2012. 295 pp.

BETHENCOURT, Francisco, and Adrian PEARCE (eds), *Racism and Ethnic Relations in the Portuguese-Speaking World*. London and Oxford: British Academy/Oxford University Press, 2012. 300 pp.

BETHENCOURT, Francisco, *Racisms: From the Crusades to the Twentieth Century*. Princeton, NJ: Princeton University Press, 2013. Forthcoming.

BLACKBURN, Robin, *The Making of New World Slavery: From the Baroque to the Modern, 1492–1800*. New York: Verso, 2010. 608 pp.

BURKHOLDER, Mark A., and Lyman L. JOHNSON, *Colonial Latin America*, 8th edn. Oxford: Oxford University Press, 2012. 436 pp.

BURNET, Ian, *Spice Islands*. Dural Delivery Centre, NSW: Rosenberg, 2011. 200 pp.

BURTON, Richard Francis, Sir, *Wanderings in West Africa from Liverpool to Fernando Po*. Cambridge: Cambridge University Press, Volume: 2: Richard Francis Burton. 2011. 322 pp. Reprint. Orig. publ.: London: Tinsley Bros., 1863.

BYRNE, Paula Jane (ed.), *Judge Advocate Ellis Bent: Letters and Diaries, 1809–1811*. Annandale, NSW: Desert Pea Press, 2012. 150 pp.

CLIFF, Nigel, *The Last Crusade: The Epic Voyages of Vasco Da Gama*. London: Atlantic, 2012. 547 pp.

FERREIRA, Roquinaldo Amaral, *Cross-Cultural Exchange in the Atlantic World: Angola and Brazil during the Era of the Slave Trade*. New York: Cambridge University Press, 2012. 262 pp.

GREEN, Tobias, *The Rise of the Trans-Atlantic Slave Trade in Western Africa, 1300–1589*. Cambridge: Cambridge University Press, 2011. 366 pp.

HAGERDAL, Hans, *Lords of the Land, Lords of the Sea: Conflict and Adaptation in Early Colonial Timor, 1600–1800*. Leiden: KITLV Press, 2012. 479 pp.

HOWSAM, Leslie, and James RAVEN (eds), *Books between Europe and the Americas: Connections and Communities, 1620–1860*. New York: Palgrave Macmillan, 2011. 352 pp.

KHAN, Sheila, Ana Margarida Dias MARTINS, Hilary OWEN and Carmen Ramos VILLAR (eds), *The Lusotropical Tempest: Postcolonial Debates in Portuguese*. Bristol: Bristol University HiPLA. Lusophone Voices Series, 2012. 208 pp.

MATTHEE, Rudolph P., and Jorge Manuel FLORES, *Portugal, the Persian Gulf and Safavid Persia*. Leuven: Peeters, 2011. 312 pp.

MEUWESE, Mark, *Brothers in Arms, Partners in Trade: Dutch–Indigenous Alliances in the Atlantic World, 1595–1674*. Leiden: Brill, 2012. 367 pp.

PARÉS, Luis N., and Roger SANSI-ROCA, *Sorcery in the Black Atlantic*. Chicago, IL: University of Chicago Press, 2011. 312 pp.

RACINE, Karen, and Beatriz G. MAMIGONIAN, *The Human Tradition in the Atlantic World, 1500–1850*. Lanham, MD: Rowman & Littlefield, 2010. 286 pp.

RAVENSTEIN, Ernst Georg, Gaspar CORRÊA and Alvaro VELHO, *Vasco da Gama*. Middlesex: Viartis, 2011. 409 pp.

ROBSON, Martin, *Britain, Portugal and South America in the Napoleonic Wars: Alliances and Diplomacy in Economic Maritime Conflict*. London: I. B. Tauris, 2011. 320 pp.

ROQUE, Ricardo, and Kim A. WAGNER (eds), *Engaging Colonial Knowledge: Reading European Archives in World History*. Basingstoke: Palgrave Macmillan, 2012. 306 pp.

SARMENTO, João, *Fortifications, Post-Colonialism and Power: Ruins and Imperial Legacies*. Burlington, VT: Ashgate, 2011. 158 pp.

SILVA, Filipa Ribeiro da, *Dutch and Portuguese in Western Africa: Empires, Merchants and the Atlantic System, 1580–1674*. Series Atlantic World: Europe, Africa and the Americas, 1500–1830; v. 22. Leiden: Brill, 2011. 384 pp.

SMITH, Stefan Halikowski, *Creolization and Diaspora in the Portuguese Indies: The Social World of Ayutthaya, 1640–1720*. Leiden: Brill, 2011. 456 pp.

ZIR, Alessandro, *Luso-Brazilian Encounters of the Sixteenth Century: A Styles of Thinking Approach*. Lanham, MD: Rowman & Littlefield Pub. Group, 2011. 119 pp.

Overseas Communities

BRYANT, Sherwin K., Rachel Sarah O'TOOLE and Ben VINSON, III (eds), *Africans to Spanish America: Expanding the Diaspora*. Urbana: University of Illinois Press, 2012. 279 pp.

FREYRE, Gilberto, and Christopher J. TRIBE (transl.), *The English in Brazil: Aspects of British Influence on the Life, Landscape and Culture of Brazil*. Oxford: Boulevard, 2011. 404 pp.

HALKIAS, Daphne, Paul THURMAN, Nicholas HARKIOLAKIS and Sylvia M. CARACATSANIS (eds), *Female Immigrant Entrepreneurs: The Economic and Social Impact of a Global Phenomenon*. Farnham: Gower, 2011. 297 pp.

MCILWAINE, Cathy (ed.), *Cross-Border Migration among Latin Americans: European Perspectives and Beyond*. New York: Palgrave Macmillan, 2011, 278 pp.

1.6 Language

ACKERLIND, Sheila R., and Rebecca JONES-KELLOGG, *Portuguese: A Reference Manual*. Austin: University of Texas Press, 2011. 340 pp.

ALLEN, Maria Fernanda, *The Routledge Portuguese Bilingual Dictionary*. London: Routledge, 2011. 784 pp.

ARAM, Dorit, and Ofra KORAT, *Literacy Development and Enhancement across Orthographies and Cultures*. New York: Springer, 2010. 230 pp.

ARREGI, Karlos, Zsuzsanna FAGYAL, Silvina A. MONTRUL and Annie TREMBLAY, *Romance Linguistics 2008: Interactions in Romance. Selected Papers from the 38th Linguistic Symposium on Romance Languages (LSRL), Urbana-Champaign, April 2008*. Amsterdam. John Benjamins, 2010. 266 pp.

BOECKX, Cedric, Norbert HORNSTEIN and Jairo NUNES, *Control as Movement*. Cambridge: Cambridge University Press, 2010. 274 pp.

BYRD, Steven, *The Lexicon of Calunga and a Lexical Comparison with Other Forms of Afro-Brazilian Speech from Minas Gerais, São Paulo and Bahia*. Albuquerque: Latin American & Iberian Institute, University of New Mexico, 2010. 38 pp.

CABREDO-HOFFHER, Patricia, and Brenda LACA, *Layers of Aspect*. Stanford, CA: CSLI Publications, Center for the Study of Language and Information, 2010. 190 pp.

DA SILVA PIRES, Cibélia Renata, *Formation and Expansion of the Culture and Caipira Dialect [in the Area of Piracicaba]: A Study of the Brazilian Portuguese*. Saarbrücken: VDM Verlag Dr. Müller, 2010. 313 pp.

GROLLA, Elaine, *Pronouns as Elsewhere Elements: Implications for Language Acquisition*. Newcastle upon Tyne: Cambridge Scholars, 2010. 175 pp.

GRUNEBERG, Michael M., and Gabriel C. JACOBS, *Instant Recall Portuguese including Brazilian Portuguese*. New York: McGraw-Hill, 2010. 1 audio-CD and booklet 7 pp.

KAPLAN, Robert B., and Richard B. BALDAUF, *Language Planning in the Asia Pacific, Hong Kong, Timor Leste and Sri Lanka*. New York: Routledge, 2011. 264 pp.

KOFFI, Ettien, *Paradigm Shift in Language Planning and Policy: Game-Theoretic Solutions*. Berlin: Walter de Gruyter, Inc., 2012. 328 pp.

MUÑOZ-BASOLS, Javier, with Catarina FOUTO, Laura SOLER-GONZÁLEZ and Tyler FISHER, *The Limits of Literary Translation: Expanding Frontiers in Iberian Languages*. Kassel: Reichenberger, 2012. 370 pp.

PANAGIOTIDIS, E. Phoevos, *The Complementizer Phase: Subjects and Operators*. Oxford: Oxford Scholarship Online, 2010. 285 pp.

REULAND, Eric J., *Anaphora and Language Design*. Cambridge, MA: MIT Press, 2011. 368 pp.

RINKE, Esther, and Tanja KUPISCH, *The Development of Grammar: Language Acquisition and Diachronic Change. In Honour of Jürgen M. Meisel*. Amsterdam: John Benjamins, 2011. 422 pp.

SLADE, Rejane de Oliveira, revised by Marta ALMEIDA and Elizabeth JACKSON, *Bom dia, Brasil. 3rd edition of Português básico para estrangeiros*. New Haven, CT: Yale University Press, 2012. 368 pp.

SPENCER, Andrew, and Ana R. LUIS, *Clitics: An Introduction*. Cambridge: Cambridge University Press, 2012. 388 pp.

TYSON-WARD, Sue, *Beginning Portuguese*. London: McGraw-Hill Professional, 2011. 60 pp. + 2 sound discs.

VESTERINEN, Rainer, *A Cognitive Approach to Adverbial Subordination in European Portuguese: The Infinitive, the Clitic Pronoun Se and Finite Verb Forms*. Newcastle upon Tyne: Cambridge Scholars, 2011. 189 pp.

WALKER, James A. (ed.), *Aspect in Grammatical Variation*. Amsterdam: John Benjamins, 2010. 150 pp.

WHITLAM, John, *Modern Brazilian Portuguese Grammar: A Practical Guide*. London: Routledge, 2011. 496 pp.

WHITLAM, John, *Modern Brazilian Portuguese Grammar Workbook*. London: Routledge, 2011. 188 pp.

ZWARTJES, Otto, *Portuguese Missionary Grammars in Asia, Africa and Brazil, 1550–1800*. Amsterdam: John Benjamins, 2011. 359 pp.

1.7 Literature

ANTUNES, António Lobo, and Rhett MCNEIL (transl.), *The Splendor of Portugal*. Champaign, IL: Dalkey Archive Press, 2011. 535 pp.

ANTUNES, António Lobo, and Margaret Jull COSTA (transl.), *The Land at the End of the World*. London: W. W. Norton, 2011. 224 pp.

BAK, John S., and Bill REYNOLDS (eds), *Literary Journalism across the Globe: Journalistic Traditions and Transnational Influences*. Amherst: University of Massachusetts Press, 2011. 320 pp.

BERBARA, Maria, and Karl A. E. ENENKEL (eds), *Portuguese Humanism and the Republic of Letters*. Leiden: Brill, 2012. 476 pp.

BOTTO, António, Fernando PESSOA (transl.), Josiah BLACKMORE (ed.), *The Songs of António Botto*. Minneapolis: University of Minnesota Press, 2010. 232 pp.

BUARQUE, Chico, and Alison ENTREKIN (transl.), *Spilt Milk*. London: Atlantic, 2012. 177 pp.

CHIAPPINI, Ligia, Marcel VEJMELKA and David TREECE (eds), *Studies in the Literary Achievement of João Guimarães Rosa, the Foremost Brazilian Writer of the Twentieth Century*. Lewiston, NY: Edwin Mellen, 2012. 456 pp.

COELHO, Paulo, and Margaret Jull COSTA (transl.), *Aleph*. London: Harper, 2012. 300 pp.

COUTO, Mia, and David BROOKSHAW (transl.), *The Blind Fisherman*. Johannesburg: Penguin Books (South Africa), 2010. 258 pp.

COUTO, Mia, and David Brookshaw (transl.), *The Tuner of Silences*. Windsor, ON: Biblioasis International Translation, 2012. 224 pp.

CURY, Augusto, *The Dreamseller: The Calling*. London: Simon & Schuster, 2011. 246 pp.

DE BARROS, Manoel, and Idra NOVEY (transl.), *Birds for a Demolition*. Pittsburgh, PA: Carnegie Mellon University Press, 2010. 96 pp.

EARLE, Peter J., *The Barros Pawns*. Leicester: Matador, 2011. 282 pp.

EMPAYTAZ DE CROOME, Dionisia, *Brief History of Portuguese Poetry up to Camoens*. [s.l.]: [s.n.], 2012. 6 pp.

FREEMAN, John (ed.), *Granta 121: Best of Young Brazilian Novelists*. London: Granta Books, 2012. 264 pp.

FRIER, David (ed.), *Fernando Pessoa in an Intertextual Web: Influences and Interpretations*. Oxford: Legenda, 2012. 200 pp.

KANE, Adrian Taylor, *The Natural World in Latin American Literatures: Ecocritical Essays on Twentieth Century Writings*. Jefferson, NC: McFarland & Co., 2010, 252 pp.

LINS, Osman, and Adria FRIZZI (transl.), *Nine, Novena*. Los Angeles: Green Integer, 2010. 305 pp.

LISBOA, Maria Manuel, *The End of the World: Apocalypse and its Aftermath in Western Culture*. Cambridge: Open Book Publishers, 2011. 222 pp.

MATEUS, Isabel, Maria FIDALGO and Patricia Anne ODBER DE BAUBETA (transl.), *Contos do Portugal rural = Tales of Rural Portugal*. Series: Portuguese Insights: Bilingual Text Collection. Coimbra: Gráfica de Coimbra, Lda., 2012. 136 pp.

MATTHEWS, Charlotte Hammond, *Gender, Race and Patriotism in the Works of Nísia Floresta*. Woodbridge: Támesis, 2012. 217 pp.

MOSER, Robert, and Antonio Luciano de Andrade TOSTA (eds), *Luso-American Literature: Writings by Portuguese-Speaking Authors in North America*. New Brunswick, NJ: Rutgers University Press, 2011. 416 pp.

NUNES, Ana, *African American Women Writers' Historical Fiction*. Basingstoke: Palgrave Macmillan, 2011. 248 pp.

PAZOS-ALONSO, Cláudia, and Stephen PARKINSON (eds), *Reading Literature in Portuguese*. Oxford: Legenda, November 2013. Forthcoming.

PEIXOTO, José Luís, and Daniel HAHN (transl.), *The Piano Cemetery*. London: Bloomsbury, 2011. 276 pp.

PESSOA, Fernando, Jorge URIBE (ed.), Pedro SEPÚLVEDA (transl.) and Jerónimo PIZARRO (rev.), *A demonstração do indemonstrável = Proving the Unprovable. English Text with Parallel Portuguese Transl.* Lisbon: Ática, 2011. 84 pp.

PODDAR, Prem, Rajeev PATKE and Lars JENSEN (eds), *A Historical Companion to Postcolonial Literatures: Continental Europe and its Empires*. Edinburgh: Edinburgh University Press, 2011, 633 pp.

PUGA, Rogério Miguel, *Chronology of Portuguese Literature, 1128–2000*. Newcastle upon Tyne: Cambridge Scholars, 2011. 238 pp.

QUEIRÓS, Eça de, Gregory RABASSA (transl.), *The Correspondence of Fradique Mendes: A Novel*. Darmouth: University of Massachusetts Dartmouth, 2011. 140 pp.

ROBBINS, Sarah, Ann E. PULLEN and Nellie J. A. DARLING, *Nellie Arnott's Writings on Angola, 1905–1913: Missionary Narratives Linking Africa and America*. Anderson, SC: Parlor Press, 2011. 337 pp.

SARAMAGO, José, and Margaret Jull COSTA (transl.), *Cain*. London: Vintage, 2012. 150 pp.

SARAMAGO, José, and Giovanni PONTIERO (transl.), *The Lives of Things: Short Stories*. London: Verso, 2012. 145 pp.

SARAMAGO, José, and Margaret Jull COSTA (transl.), *The Elephant's Journey*. London: Vintage, 2011. 197 pp.

SCLIAR, Moacyr, David William FOSTER (transl.), *The War in Bom Fim*. Lubbock: Texas Tech University Press, 2010. 127 pp.

SCLIAR, Moacyr, Margaret A. NEVES (transl.), *The Centaur in the Garden*. Lubbock: Texas Tech University Press, 2011. 216 pp.

SOUSA, José Baptista de, *Almeida Garrett (1799–1854), Founder of Portuguese Romanticism: A Study in Anglo-Portuguese Cultural Interaction*. Lewiston, NY: Edwin Mellen Press, 2011. 267 pp.

TAVARES, Gonçalo M., and Rhett MCNEIL (transl.), *Joseph Walser's Machine*. Champaign, IL: Dalkey Archive Press, 2012. 160 pp.

TAVARES, Gonçalo M., and Daniel HAHN (transl.), *Learning to Pray in the Age of Technique: Lenz Buchmann's Position in the World*. Champaign, IL: Dalkey Archive Press, 2011. 342 pp.

VERÍSSIMO, Luís Fernando, and Margaret Jull COSTA (transl.), *The Spies*, London: MacLehose, 2012. 168 pp.

VIEIRA, Patricia I., *Seeing Politics Otherwise: Vision in Latin American and Iberian Fiction*. Toronto: University of Toronto Press, 2011. 198 pp.

VILLARES, Lúcia, *Examining Whiteness: Reading Clarice Lispector through Bessie Head and Toni Morrison*. London: Legenda, 2011, 202 pp.

WALSH, Pat, *At the Scene of the Crime: Essays, Reflections and Poetry on East Timor, 1999– 2010.* Melbourne: Mosaic Press, 2011. 366 pp.

WILLIS, R. Clive, *Camões, Prince of Poets.* Bristol: HiPLAM, 2010. 322 pp.

1.8 Religion

BOAVIDA, Isabel, Hervé PENNEC and Manuel João RAMOS (eds), and Christopher J. TRIBE (transl.), *Pedro Páez's History of Ethiopia, 1622.* Burlington, VT: Ashgate, 2011. 2 vols., 966 pp.

BOWDEN, Caroline (ed.), *English Convents in Exile, 1600–1800.* London: Pickering & Chatto, 2012. Part I: 3 vol. set. 1408 pp.

BRIERLEY, John, *Camino Portugués: Maps — Mapas — Karten: Lisboa, Porto, Santiago.* Revised edn. Forres: Camino guides, 2012. 80 pp.

KLEIN, Misha, *Kosher Feijoada and Other Paradoxes of Jewish life in São Paulo.* Gainesville: University Press of Florida, 2012. 256 pp.

LEVIE BERNFELD, Tirtsah, *Poverty and Welfare among the Portuguese Jews in Early Modern Amsterdam.* Oxford: Littman Library of Jewish Civilization, 2012. 590 pp.

MILGRAM, Avraham, and Naftali GREENWOOD (transl.), *Portugal, Salazar, and the Jews.* Jerusalem: Yad Vashem, 2011. 324 pp.

II. Theses

2.1 African Topics

AKOSAH-DARTEH, Francis, *To examine the factors that affect the growth of small-agribusinesses in Ghana: a case study of poultry industry.* D.B.A. (University of Durham) 2012. 570 pp.

ALMEIDA, Joelma, *Parental investment in growth and development: Cape Verdean migrants in a Portuguese poor neighbourhood.* Ph.D. (Loughborough University) 2012. 220 pp.

BANDALI, Sarah, *At the crossroads: exploring intersections between gender norms and HIV/AIDS vulnerability in rural Mozambique.* Ph.D. (London School of Hygiene and Tropical Medicine, University of London) 2011. 179 pp.

CARNEIRO, Gonçalo, *The role of ocean policies in poverty reduction: insights from Cape Verde, Portugal and São Tomé and Príncipe.* Ph.D. (Cardiff University) 2011. 265 pp. + 1 CD-ROM.

DE OLIVEIRA, Augusto Cesar Ciuffo, *'Squaring' the Black Atlantic Triangle: locating diasporic sites and memories in Lusophone Black African and (Afro-) Brazilian postcolonial cinemas.* Ph.D. (University of Bristol) 2010. 275 pp.

FIGUEIRA, Carla Sofia Casaca, *Languages at war in Lusophone Africa: external language spread policies in Mozambique and Guinea-Bissau at the turn of the 21st century.* Ph.D. (London, City University) 2010, 340 pp.

STEPHENS, Carla R., *The people mobilized: the Mozambican liberation movement and American activism (1960–1975).* Ph.D. (Temple University) 2011. 298 pp.

TAVARES, Maria, *Women who give birth to new worlds: three feminine perspectives on Lusophone postcolonial Africa.* Ph.D. (University of Manchester) 2011. 278 pp.

2.2 Asian Topics

BAKSHI, Sandeep, *Back/side entry: queer/postcolonial representations of South Asia.* Ph.D. (University of Leicester) 2011. 262 pp.

CAGLE, Hubert Glenn, *Dead reckonings: disease and the study of nature in Portuguese Asia and the Atlantic, 1450–1650.* Ph.D. (Rutgers University) 2011. 244 pp.

2.3 Brazilian Topics

ALVES, Ana Cristina, *China's oil diplomacy: comparing Chinese economic statecraft in Angola and Brazil.* Ph.D. (London School of Economics and Political Science) 2011. 237 pp.

AMORIM, Lauro Maia, *Blackness, translation, and the (in)visible: Harryette Mullen's poetry in Brazilian Portuguese.* Ph.D. (State University of New York at Binghamton) 2010. 216 pp.

BASTOS-GEE, Ana Claudia, *Information structure within the traditional nominal phase: the case of Brazilian Portuguese.* Ph.D. (University of Connecticut) 2011. 272 pp.

BUCCIFERRO, Justin Robert, *The economic geography of race in post-conquest Brazil.* Ph.D. (University of Colorado at Boulder) 2011. 244 pp.

COLLINS, Jane-Marie, *Intimacy and inequality: manumission and miscegenation in nineteenth-century Bahia (1830–1888).* Ph.D. (University of Nottingham) 2010. 415 pp. + 1 CD-ROM.

FERNANDES, Alinne, *Translation and Dramaturgy: The Case of Marina Carr's Irish Midlands on the Brazilian Stage.* Ph.D. (Queen's University, Belfast) 2012. 387 pp.

GARCIA OZEMELA, Luana M., *Race and diversity effects on earnings and educational outcomes in Brazil.* Ph.D. (Aberdeen University) 2011. 279 pp.

GRIMALDO GIRALDO, Claudia, *Investigating the evolutionary history of maize in South America.* Ph.D. (University of Manchester) 2012. 199 pp.

HANSEN, Quinn McCoy, *Clause-final negation in Brazilian Portuguese.* Ph.D. (University of Florida) 2010. 238 pp.

HANSFORD, Frances, *Bias and discrimination in intra-household food allocation: case study of a rural labour population in northeast Brazil.* D.Phil. (University of Oxford) 2011. 298 pp.

HELLER-LOPES, André, *Brazil's Ópera Nacional (1857–1863): music, society and the birth of Brazilian opera in nineteenth-century Rio de Janeiro.* Ph.D. (King's College, London) 2010. 479 pp.

HONG, Miriam Lee, *Exploring literary negotiations of culture and identity from the journal, Cultura Tropical and how Korean Brazilians construct a hybrid cultural identity.* Ph.D. (University of California, Berkeley) 2011. 79 pp.

JUNQUEIRA, Luciana, *Narrative analysis of oral personal experience across two languages and cultures: Brazilian Portuguese and American English.* Ph.D. (University of Alabama) 2010. 126 pp.

LESSA, Ana Cláudia, *Brazil: 'Que país é este'? music and power in Legião Urbana.* Ph.D. (University of Nottingham) 2011. 263 pp.

LIMA, Laura, *Worlding Brazil: the theory of emotional action and the development of thinking about security in Brazil 1930–2010*. Ph.D. (Aberystwyth University) 2012. 80 pp.

SAKUMA, Tomoko, *Language, culture and ethnicity: interplay of ideologies within a Japanese community in Brazil*. Ph.D. (The University of Texas at Austin) 2011. 220 pp.

SCHNEIDER, Caroline Lefeber, *Narrative and (Meta)Physical Paradox in 'Grande Sertão: Veredas' and 'Pedro Paramo'*. Ph.D. (University of California, Berkeley) 2011. 475 pp.

SCHNEIDER, Nina, *This is a country that advances: the official propaganda of the military regime in Brazil, 1968–1979*. Ph.D. (University of Essex) 2011. 513 pp.

SHERINGHAM, Olivia, *Thanks to London and to God: living religion transnationally among Brazilian migrants in London and 'back home' in Brazil*. Ph.D. (Queen Mary, University of London) 2011. 293 pp.

SIMÕES, Armando Amorim, *The contribution of Bolsa Família to the educational achievement of economically disadvantaged children in Brazil*. Ph.D. (University of Sussex) 2012. 277 pp.

SORRENTINO, Marcello, *Development in the mountains of confusion: Guaribas under the Zero-Hunger Programme*. Ph.D. (London School of Economics and Political Science) 2011. 349 pp.

SOUZA, Saulo Santos de, *Land reform, regional planning and socioeconomic development in Brazil*. Ph.D. (University of Cambridge) 2011. 217 pp.

ST. CLAIR, George, *Staying humble in the city: traditional Pentecostalism in contemporary São Paulo*. Ph.D. (London School of Economics and Political Science) 2011. 323 pp.

STEIBEL, Fabro Boaz, *The problem of 'negative advertising': content-based regulation of political advertising in Brazil and the US*. Ph.D. (University of Leeds) 2011. 165 pp.

TÄHTINEN, Lauri Matti Oskar, *The ideological origins of the Portuguese empire in Brazil*. Ph.D. (University of Cambridge) 2012. 234 pp.

TURNER, James Thomas Michael, *'Aquela loirinha, baixinha, não sabe dançar...': an ethnographic account of the accommodation of whiteness within the discourse and practice of the Brazilian female sexual subject in Florianópolis, Brazil*. Ph.D. (University of Hull) 2011. 272 pp.

2.4 Portuguese Topics

ASCENSÃO, Eduardo, *The post-colonial slum: a geography of informal settlement in Quinta da Serra, Lisbon*. Ph.D. (King's College, London) 2011. 427 pp.

DE ANDRADE, Cristiana Viegas, *Population in 19th-century Vila do Conde: the demographic dynamics of a north-western Portuguese urban parish*. Ph.D. (University of Cambridge) 2010. 369 pp.

DIAZ GRANADO, Miriam, *L2 and L3 acquisition of the Portuguese stressed vowel inventory by native speakers of English*. Ph.D. (University of Arizona) 2011. 249 pp.

DOS SANTOS GASPAR CABETE, Dulce, *Autonomy and empowerment of hospitalised older people: a Portuguese case study*. Ph.D. (Northumbria University) 2011. 2 vols.

EDWARDS, John Huw, *A capabilities approach to local and regional development in Europe: evidence from Alentejo, Portugal*. Ph. D. (University of Newcastle upon Tyne) 2012. 206 pp.

FOUTO, Catarina, *Edition and study of Teive's Epithalamium: the Epodon libri tres (1565) and neo-Latin literature in Counter-Reformation Portugal*. D.Phil. (University of Oxford) 2012. 298 pp.

GRAY DE CASTRO, Mariana, *Fernando Pessoa's Shakespeare*. Ph.D. (King's College, London) 2010. 280 pp.

HORTA, José António Gonçalves, *Images and representations of Ireland in Portugal (1830–1925): geographical knowledge and geographical imagination*. Ph.D. (University College Cork) 2009. 405 pp.

JORGE, Ana, *Ceramic technology and social networks in Late Neolithic to Early Bronze Age Portugal*. Ph.D. (University of Sheffield) 2011. 538 pp.

LEITE, Naomi, *Global affinities: Portuguese Marranos (Anusim), traveling Jews, and cultural logics of kinship*. Ph.D. (University of California, Berkeley) 2011. 248 pp.

LOPES, Rui Miguel Ponte Vieira, *Between Cold War and colonial wars: the making of West German policy towards the Portuguese dictatorship, 1968–1974*. Ph.D. (London School of Economics and Political Science) 2011. 285 pp.

LUCE, Alexandra, *British intelligence in the Portuguese world, 1939–45: operations against German intelligence and relations with the Policia de Vigilancia e Defesa do Estado (P.V.D.E.)*. Ph.D. (University of Cambridge) 2010. 340 pp.

MATOS, Patrícia Ribeiro Mendes Alves de, *Precarious labour in Portuguese call centres: an anthropological study*. Ph.D. (University of London, Goldsmiths College) 2011. 279 pp.

MIRANDA, Paula Susana Ferreira, *Not ashamed or afraid: Portuguese immigrant women in Toronto's cleaning industry, 1950s–1995*. Ph.D. (York University, Canada) 2010. 440 pp.

MORAIS, João Mourato, *Europeanisation and territorial governance: an inquiry into power and institutional culture change in Portugal*. Ph.D. (University College London) 2011. 204 pp.

NEVES FONTES, Fernando Gabriel, *Social citizenship and collective action: the case of the Portuguese Disabled People's Movement*. Ph.D. (University of Leeds) 2011. 270 pp.

OBIANUJU CHINYELU, Anya, *Investments in communities of learners and speakers: how African American students of Portuguese negotiate ethno-racialized, gendered, and social-classed identities in second language learning*. Ph.D. (UCLA) 2011. 358 pp.

OLIVEIRA, Carlos A., *Water supply to Portuguese regional hospitals: a contribution for the knowledge of the water consumption patterns in Portuguese regional hospitals*. Ph.D. (Kingston University) 2010. 353 pp.

PEREIRA, Maria do Mar, *Pushing the boundaries of knowledge: an ethnography of negotiations of the epistemic status of women's, gender, feminist studies in Portugal*. Ph.D. (London School of Economics) 2011. 366 pp.

SILVA PEREIRA, Vanessa, *Negotiating the alternative in a postmodern theatre: O Bando, Kneehigh, Foursight And Escola De Mulheres*. Ph.D. (University of Manchester) 2012. 332 pp.

Abstracts

Internationalism and the 'Labours' of the Portuguese Colonial Empire (1945–1974)

MIGUEL BANDEIRA JERÓNIMO AND JOSÉ PEDRO MONTEIRO

ABSTRACT. This article aims to analyse the relationship between the Portuguese Empire and two international institutions (the United Nations and the International Labour Organization) as concerns the organization and regulation of colonial labour after World War II. Stressing the historical ballast of this relationship, particularly during the inter-war years, the article points to the instances of debate and conflict as well as of cooperation developed by the several actors after 1945, in a context marked by mounting anti-colonial pressures and bipolar competition dynamics. Contrary to traditional accounts of an 'isolated' empire, this article sheds light on the need to include international and transnational scales of analysis in order to assess the actual trajectory of Portuguese late colonial State, marked by moments of reform as well as resistance to change.

KEYWORDS. Colonialism, imperialism, internationalism, colonial labour, international organizations.

RESUMO. Este artigo analisa a relação entre o Estado-império Português e diferentes organizações internacionais (a Organização das Nações Unidas e a Organização Internacional do Trabalho) em torno do problema da organização e da regulação do trabalho colonial após a Segunda Guerra Mundial. Sublinhando o lastro histórico desta relação, nomeadamente no período entreguerras, o artigo chama a atenção para as instâncias de debate e conflito, mas também de cooperação, desenvolvidas entre os vários actores após 1945 num contexto marcado por crescente contestação anti-colonial e pelas dinâmicas de competição bipolar. Contrariando as tradicionais narrativas de um império isolado, este artigo demonstra como a articulação de dimensões de análise internacionais e transnacionais é essencial para compreender a trajectória, caracterizada pela coexistência de momentos de reforma e resistência à mudança, do Estado colonial tardio português.

PALAVRAS-CHAVE. Colonialismo, imperialismo, internacionalismo, trabalho colonial, organizações internacionais.

The United States and Portuguese Decolonization

LUÍS NUNO RODRIGUES

ABSTRACT. This article argues that US policy regarding Portuguese colonialism and decolonization followed the general patterns of US African policy during the Cold War. The narrative of US–Portuguese relations demonstrates that,

despite the growing interest in African affairs since the late 1950s, Europe continued to be the political centre of the Cold War throughout the decades. The fear of losing the strategically located Azores base in a period of several important Cold War episodes, such as the Berlin and Cuban crises, and the Vietnam and Yom Kippur wars, outweighed the concerns with African developments and the rhetoric of anti-colonialism that briefly emerged in the late 1950s and the early 1960s.
KEYWORDS. Colonialism, Portugal, Cold War, Africa, United States.

RESUMO. Este artigo considera que a política dos EUA relativamente ao colonialismo e à descolonização portugueses seguiu as linhas gerais da sua política para com o continente africano durante a Guerra Fria. Apesar do interesse crescente nos assuntos africanos, a Europa continuou a ser o centro da Guerra Fria. O medo de perder a base dos Açores, num período de episódios cruciais da Guerra Fria, como as crises de Berlim e de Cuba ou as guerras do Vietname e do Yom Kippur, revelou-se mais importante do que a preocupação com África e a retórica do anti-colonialismo que emergiu no final da década de 1950 e nos primeiros anos da década seguinte.
PALAVRAS-CHAVE. Colonialismo, Portugal, Guerra Fria, África, Estados Unidos.

Live and Let Live: Britain and Portugal's Imperial Endgame (1945–1975)
PEDRO AIRES OLIVEIRA

ABSTRACT. The aim of this article is to provide an assessment of the interplay between Britain and Portugal in the three decades that witnessed the dissolution of their respective colonial empires. Operating within an authoritarian framework, Portugal's decision-makers were largely exempt from the pressures that in other European democracies contributed to accelerate the pace of decolonization. They were therefore keen to forge a close (and, seen retrospectively, dangerous) connection between the fate of the dictatorship in the metropolis and the survival of Portugal's rule in the overseas provinces. The article examines the destabilizing impact of Britain's colonial retreat on Portugal's empire and tries to make sense of the factors that held back successive British governments from assuming a more critical posture towards the *Estado Novo*'s policies. The article shows that although strategic and tactical calculations may have been paramount in the formulation of Britain's policies towards Portugal, the Foreign Office's historically benign posture vis-à-vis the dictatorship in Lisbon was also a factor to be taken into account. A final section briefly considers how the simultaneous 'regime change' in London and Lisbon in 1974 allowed the UK to play a small but not insignificant role in the final states of Portugal's decolonization.
KEYWORDS. Anglo-Portuguese relations, empires, decolonization, British foreign policy.

RESUMO. O artigo pretende oferecer uma visão das interacções entre Portugal e a Grã-Bretanha nas três décadas que coincidiram com a dissolução dos respectivos impérios coloniais. Operando num quadro político autoritário, a elite governante portuguesa encontrou-se em larga medida isenta das pressões que noutras democracias europeias contribuíram para acelerar o ritmo da descolonização. Isso levou-a a estabelecer uma conexão próxima (e, vista retrospectivamente, perigosa) entre o destino da ditadura na metrópole e a sobrevivência do domínio português no ultramar. Este artigo examina o impacto desestabilizador da retirada colonial da Grã-Bretanha no espaço imperial português e procura esclarecer as razões que impediram sucessivos governos britânicos de assumir uma postura mais crítica em relação às políticas do Estado Novo. O artigo procura ainda demonstrar que muito embora considerações de ordem estratégica e táctica tenham sido determinantes na formulação das políticas britânicas, o processo decisório em Whitehall foi igualmente influenciado pela postura historicamente benigna da diplomacia britânica em relação à ditadura portuguesa. Uma última secção analisa brevemente a forma como a mudança simultânea nos governos em Londres e Lisboa em 1974 permitiu ao Reino Unido desempenhar um papel pequeno mas não irrelevante nos últimos lances da descolonização portuguesa.

PALAVRAS-CHAVE. Relações anglo-portuguesas, impérios, descolonização, política externa britânica.

Cold War Constraints: France, West Germany and Portuguese Decolonization

ANA MÓNICA FONSECA AND DANIEL MARCOS

ABSTRACT. This article analyses how the evolution of decolonization process during the Cold War constrained France and West Germany's support for Portuguese colonial policy. At a moment when the United States seemed unwilling to give any assistance, either political or military, to Portugal, Lisbon turned to its European NATO allies, with whom it deepened the political and military cooperation already developed within the Alliance's framework. France's General de Gaulle saw support for Portugal as a way to challenge the US leadership of the western alliance, while West Germany was mainly concerned with maintaining political stability in Portugal and the Western bloc. The article therefore contextualizes French and West German support for Portugal within major Cold War considerations.

KEYWORDS. Colonialism, France, West Germany, Portugal, Cold War.

RESUMO. Este artigo analisa o modo como a evolução do processo de descolonização durante a Guerra Fria condicionou o apoio da França e da República Federal da Alemanha à política colonial portuguesa. Num período em que os Estados Unidos pareciam estar indisponíveis para auxiliar, política ou militarmente, Portugal, Lisboa aproximou-se dos seus aliados europeus da NATO, com quem aprofundou a cooperação política e militar já iniciada no âmbito da Aliança. A França do General de Gaulle viu no apoio a Portugal uma oportunidade para afrontar a liderança norte-americana na Aliança ocidental, enquanto a Alemanha Federal tinha como principal objectivo a estabilidade política, em Portugal e no bloco ocidental. Assim, torna-se claro que por detrás do apoio franco-alemão a Portugal estavam considerações relacionadas com a Guerra Fria.

PALAVRAS-CHAVE. Colonialismo, França, República Federal da Alemanha, Portugal, Guerra Fria.

South Africa and the Aftermath of Portugal's 'Exemplary' Decolonization: The Security Dimension

FILIPE RIBEIRO DE MENESES AND ROBERT MCNAMARA

ABSTRACT. The Portuguese Revolution of 1974–75 had a profound impact on southern Africa, forcing the government of John Vorster to re-evaluate South Africa's diplomatic and strategic options. But because events in Lisbon — as well as in Mozambique and Angola — evolved slowly, an overconfident Pretoria found itself unable to read the situation clearly. In this it was hampered by inter-agency power struggles, as well as its relationship with Rhodesia. Generally cautious towards Mozambique, South Africa was rather more reckless in its involvement in Angola. This resulted in an embarrassing diplomatic defeat which revealed the emptiness of its proposed policy of détente, as well as of hopes of a new understanding with the United States.

KEYWORDS. Decolonization, South Africa, apartheid, Portugal, Angola, Mozambique.

RESUMO. A Revolução Portuguesa de 1974–75 teve um impacte enorme na África Austral, forçando o governo de John Vorster a reavaliar as opções estratégicas e diplomáticas da África do Sul. Porém, dada a lentidão da evolução dos acontecimentos em Lisboa — e em Moçambique e Angola — Pretória, excessivamente confiante, foi incapaz de fazer uma leitura correta da situação. Este esforço foi ainda dificultado por querelas intestinas e a relação com a Rodésia. Cautelosa em relação a Moçambique, a África do Sul reagiu de forma mais arrojada em Angola, através de uma intervenção militar que se saldou por uma derrota diplomática. Este revés demonstrou quão era vazia a política sul-africana de détente na região e vãs as esperanças de um novo entendimento com os Estados Unidos.

PALAVRAS-CHAVE. Descolonização, África do Sul, apartheid, Portugal, Angola, Moçambique.

Portugal and the UN: A Rogue State Resisting the Norm of Decolonization (1956–1974)

Bruno Cardoso Reis

ABSTRACT. This article places the resistance by the Portuguese government to the growing wave of anti-colonialism in the UN in the context of wider debates regarding the role of the latter in the international history of decolonization and the dynamics of state resistance to UN norm-setting. It compares Portuguese and Belgian diplomatic approaches to anti-colonialism at the UN with the aim of improving our understanding of how successful and how specific the Portuguese policy towards decolonization really was. More specifically this article aims to explain why the Portuguese State sought entry to and remained in a UN hostile to overseas empires, and why it persisted in 'a denial of colonialism', despite its failure as a conventional diplomatic strategy.

KEYWORDS. Belgium, decolonization, international history, United Nations.

RESUMO. Este artigo olha para a resistência do governo português à crescente vaga de anticolonialismo na ONU no contexto de debates mais amplos a respeito do papel desta última organização na história internacional da descolonização e das dinâmicas típicas de estados resistentes às normas emergentes da ONU. Compara a abordagem diplomática portuguesa e belga ao anticolonialismo na ONU, com o objetivo de entender melhor quão bem-sucedida e quão específica era a política portuguesa relativamente à descolonização. Mais especificamente o artigo procura explicar: Porque é que o Estado português procurou entrar e se manteve numa ONU hostil a impérios ultramarinos? Por que é que persistiu num 'colonialismo em negação' apesar do seu fracasso como estratégia diplomática?

PALAVRAS-CHAVE. Bélgica, descolonização, história das relações internacionais, Organização das Nações Unidas.